THE U.S. OPEN

[1895–1965]

The Complete Story of the United States
Championship of Golf

THE U.S. OPEN
[1895–1965]

TOM FLAHERTY

E. P. DUTTON & CO., INC.

NEW YORK   1966

The author and publisher wish to thank Time, Inc., for permission to use the photograph of Ralph Guldahl, the one facing page 97, and those following pages 128 and 160, © Time, Inc.

IN MEMORY OF MY FATHER

Acknowledgments

The author is gratefully indebted to many journalists past who observed and recorded the early Open championships with zest and style. I heartily thank the photographers who have permitted the use of their pictures here: athletes all, they work even harder than the golfers. Among Joe Dey's expert U.S.G.A. staff at Golf House I owe a particular bow to Frank Hannigan, Don Weiss and Janet Segal for their courtesy and assistance. Last and largest is my admiration for the combination manuscript typist, grammarian and first reader: Sally Stockum Flaherty.

T. F.

Contents

Illustrations

Foreword

The U.S.G.A.'s Frank Hannigan won an award last year from his fellow golf writers for recording an imaginary interview with the New Golf Fan of the 1960's. Judging from this interview the New Fan has been created and, for the most part, educated by the weekend golf programs on television. He has a fascinating, if slightly cockeyed, view of the sport that can be summed up like this:

Golf is an outdoor game invented about ten years ago in a little town outside Pittsburgh by a young millionaire named Arnold Palmer. Palmer can play better than anyone but sometimes he is challenged by a big scowling meanie named Jack Nicklaus and by Gary Player, a little guy with a funny accent. Often they finish in a tie and when this happens everybody goes back to the fifteenth hole, where the first cameras are set up, and play starts all over again from there.

If you happen to be an Old Golf Fan, the temptation is to laugh off the New Fan with contempt. But when you stop think about it, golf *did* begin for millions of American fans just a few years ago with the coming of television. Arnold Palmer, the heroic golfer who happened along at just that time, has certainly become a millionaire. Golf is enjoying a marvelous boom: in audience appeal, in participation and in the quality of play. The truth is that golf has had booms before, in fact several of them in the seventy-five years or so since we appropriated the sport from our British cousins. Each boom has expanded the popularity of golf to new horizons and each, by more than coincidence, was inspired by the heroics of an individual player. Golf barely was mentioned in the sports pages until Francis Ouimet beat the Britishers Vardon and Ray in 1913. Radio listeners of the 20's eagerly waited for the newsflash that would tell them whether Bobby Jones had won or lost. Ben Hogan convinced

9

a whole postwar generation by his example of dedication and determination that golf is a pursuit which demands all a man has to give.

The showcase for these heroes each year is the Open championship conducted by the United States Golf Association. The Open started small, practically as an afterthought. Now it is the most important tournament in the world, and the man who wins it is guaranteed fortune and lasting fame. In this book we have started at the first tee and tried to bring to life all the heroes of the Open, from the immigrant Scot clansmen of the 90's to the Big Three of the 60's. And as for the next generation's hero, who knows? He may have been that likely looking young fellow who toted your bag at the country club this very afternoon.

[1895–1912]

•

•

CHAPTER ONE

The Beginnings

Golf, the marvelous malady, is growing so explosively as a game both to play and to watch, that the beginnings of the sport in the United States, just three generations ago, read today like ancient history. The story of those early days, though well-documented, has the faraway ring of a fairy tale.

Today, golf might well be called the national pastime. Its heroes can earn as much as $50,000 in two days by playing in a televised exhibition match, and they have become some of the most celebrated professional athletes in the nation. After watching the pros, seven million Americans swarm over the nation's 8,000 courses. Armed with 10 million new clubs a year, they spray 85 million shiny new golf balls over real estate valued at $2 billion. Then they turn back to the pros for lessons and inspiration.

As recently as 1888 there were no golfers or golf courses in the United States. When a group of friends in New York, anxious to try out a set of clubs which one of them had brought back from Scotland, set out to play, they first had to lay out a course. They set up three crude holes in a Yonkers cow pasture which they named St. Andrews, although their

11

course bore little resemblance to the famed Scottish links. That pasture was golf's first permanent beachhead in the United States. But the enthusiasm of the early players was infectious and the golfing malady spread like influenza. In 1893 there were 16 courses in the nation; by 1900 the number had swollen to more than 1,000. In that first pioneer decade before the turn of the century a national golf association was formed, national championships held, and the first crop of professional players emigrated from Scotland and England to teach the royal and ancient game to awkward but eager Americans.

Three nights before Christmas in 1894 nine men, representing the five most influential golf clubs in the country, met for dinner at the Calumet Club in New York City to discuss the problems facing the infant game of golf in the United States. From this meeting emerged the organization that became the United States Golf Association, created to "promote interest in the game of golf, establish and enforce uniform rules. . . . to be a court of reference as final authority in matters of controversy. . . . to hold annual meetings at which competitions shall be conducted for the amateur and open championships in the United States."

The founders and the original member clubs were:

John Reid and Henry O. Tallmadge from St. Andrews Golf Club, Yonkers, New York;

Theodore Havemeyer and Winthrop Rutherford from Newport Golf Club, Newport, Rhode Island;

Laurence Curtis and Samuel Sears from The Country Club, Brookline, Massachusetts;

Charles Macdonald and Arthur Ryerson from Chicago Golf Club, Wheaton, Illinois, and

Samuel Parrish from Shinnecock Hills, Southampton, Long Island.

The choice as first president of the organization narrowed to two men. One was John Reid, a Scottish-born Yonkers businessman who had laid out and first played those three original holes and who is generally considered to be the father of American golf. The other was Theodore Havemeyer, a captain of commerce known in the daily press as "The Sugar King" because of his extensive interests in that industry. Havemeyer had been infected by the golf bug during a holiday trip to Pau, France. He brought that bug back to Newport where in 1890 he built the first nine-hole course in the United States and introduced his friends, the Astors, Belmonts, Vanderbilts and other Newport summer colonists to the game. Havemeyer was elected first president; one officer was selected from each of the five founding clubs; and the association dedicated itself toward expansion of the game and toward solving the golf problems of the day.

The United States Golf Association was born out of controversy—a fact which should surprise no one who is acquainted with the nature of golf. At the center of the storm stood the imposing figure of a man who more than any other left the stamp of his forceful personality and colorful character on the early American development of the game. Charles Blair Macdonald, Chicago-born but educated at St. Andrews, Scotland, had sat at the knee of Old Tom Morris and the other nineteenth-century high priests of golf. Almost single-handedly he introduced the game to the midwestern United States. Forced it down the Midwest's throat might be a more accurate description, for Charlie Macdonald was the General Bullmoose of his time: a strong man, bluntly outspoken, who considered himself not only the best player in America, but also the ultimate authority on the game this side of the Firth of Forth.

Macdonald built the Chicago Golf Club, the first 18-hole course in the United States and the first to approach in quality the classic links of Great Britain. He also designed himself or influenced the design of many more new courses. Although he was a fine player, Macdonald was a consistent slicer. So when Architect Macdonald designed a course, he kept Golfer Macdonald's slice very much in mind and always laid out the holes in a clockwise pattern around the perimeter of the club property. Thus, when Charlie Macdonald sliced, the worst that could happen to him was to land in the rough between fairways, and a big slice would carry him to the comparative safety of the adjoining fairway. On the other hand, hookers who played Macdonald's courses had to watch their errant shots sail over the fence into Farmer Jones' corn field. Even today hookers pay a price in strokes on many courses because the pioneer United States golf architect had a slice.

In 1894 Macdonald suffered two defeats on the links that were more than his outsized ego could swallow in peace. The Newport Golf Club had opened a new nine-hole course, complete with such man-made hazards as mounds and bunkers and low stone walls that ran directly across the fairway. To show off the new course the club invited the best players in the country to Newport in September, 1894, for a 36-hole match to decide the champion amateur and professional players in the United States. Twenty amateurs teed off but only eight were able to complete two rounds on consecutive days over the ruggedly primitive course. Macdonald, representing the West against the Eastern dandies, was a heavy favorite; and after shooting an 89 on the first day, he was four strokes ahead of his closest competitor, W. G. Lawrence, a member of the Newport club. But on the second day Macdonald came acropper. He shot 100, for a 189 total, while Lawrence finished with 95–188 to win the tournament by a stroke. The shot that undid Macdonald was a skuffed drive which came to rest at the base of one of the stone walls. He was forced to take a two-stroke penalty to move it.

In the post-mortem Macdonald complained loudly that stone walls in the fairway are not proper hazards and that, at any rate, the only legitimate way to select a champion was by *match* play, not medal. Largely to assuage Macdonald, the St. Andrews club invited 27 players in October to a match play competition. The pressures of an expanding New York City had by this time pushed St. Andrews to its fourth new home in six years, a site called Grey Oaks on the Saw Mill Road. It boasted nine holes and a farm house converted into a clubhouse. Macdonald again was favored and he charged like a firehorse through the early rounds. In the semi-final round he took revenge on W. G. Lawrence, winning 2 and 1. But in the finals Macdonald lost again, this time to Lawrence Stoddard of the home club. The two had finished 18 holes all even, but on the play-off hole Macdonald sliced his tee shot into a farmer's field (St. Andrews was *not* a Macdonald-designed course). It took him three shots to regain the fairway and he lost the match.

This time Macdonald offered the alibi used by many a visitor to New York, before and since: lack of sleep and what amounted to a massive hangover. Besides, he argued, the St. Andrews tournament was the project of only a single club: it could not be considered a national championship.

The handwriting was there on the clubhouse wall in the large bold script of Charles Blair Macdonald: golf needed a governing body with national authority to conduct championships and settle disputes. Into this breach stepped the new U.S.G.A. The association issued a call for the first national match play championship to be held at Newport on the first three days of October, 1895. The tourney originally had been scheduled for September, but it was moved up to avoid competing with a more established Newport spectacle, the America's Cup sailing races.

The first U.S.G.A. championship brought out the flower of East Coast society. The gentlemen golfers strutted in their shiny-buttoned jackets of British Redcoat red, winged collars and checkered caps. The ladies, for the most part, stayed behind on the clubhouse lawn. But a few tucked up their full skirts and followed along in the informal galleries. From the West came the rambunctious Macdonald with a retinue of supporters, well-heeled and ready to bet their money on Charlie's putter. U.S.G.A. president Theodore Havemeyer spared no expense to make the first championship a success. Havemeyer donated a $1,000 championship cup (the winner could take the cup home but under U.S.G.A. rules was required to give security for its "safekeeping"). He paid the expenses of all the entrants and made sure there was at least one lively party in progress at all times.

Almost as an afterthought, in the small print of its charter, the U.S.G.A. established an "open" championship to be held in addition to the amateur competition. This secondary tournament would be "open" to amateur players *and* to the handful of young Scottish and English professionals who had come over as employees of the newly-formed golf clubs to teach the game to Americans. There was no particular stigma attached to being a golf professional in 1895. It was considered honest work, requiring skill and even a certain deftness in the pro's handling of his employer-pupil who, then as now, often brought to the game more money and determination than natural ability. Good pros were sought after as good riding masters or key household employees might be. But socially an ocean of difference separated the early United States gentlemen golfers, many of whom were among the wealthiest men of the day, and the foreigners they hired to teach them the new game. The pros kept clannishly to themselves. They had, in fact, a haughty disdain for the novices they were stuck with as pupils and perhaps an even lower regard for the primitive playing conditions in this country, which compared poorly to their home links in the British Isles. But the early pros liked the Yankee money and the opportunity, so to the new land they came, by family and by clan, brother encouraging brother.

The U.S.G.A. had drawn a clear line between amateur and professional in its first set of rules:

*An amateur golfer shall be a golfer who has never
made for sale golf clubs, balls or any other article con-
nected with the game, who has never carried clubs for
hire after attaining the age of 15 years and who has not
carried clubs for hire at any time within six years, and
who has never received any consideration for playing in
a match or for giving lessons in the game.*

In the three days of amateur play at Newport Charles
Macdonald cut a swathe through the starting field of 32
players like the Grim Avenger. This time avoiding stone
walls and other hazards, Macdonald overwhelmed Charles
Sands, a comparatively green golfer, 12 and 11, in the
36–hole final match on October 3 and took Havemeyer's new
trophy home with him to Chicago.

The following day, as a side attraction to the main amateur event, the professionals held their "open" tourney. It
called for 36 holes of medal play—or four times around
Newport's nine holes—on a single day. There was no trophy
for the winning pro, although the club he represented would
receive one. The winner himself would be presented with a
gold medal and $150 cash. Second place was worth $100;
third place, $50; fourth, $25 and fifth place, $10. (Fifth
place in the U.S. Open today, it might be noted, is worth
over $4,000.) The favorite was Willie Dunn, a Scot with a
reputation as a player and golf architect in Great Britain and
in continental Europe. Dunn had been lured to the United
States four years earlier to direct the building of the Shinnecock Hills course in Southampton, Long Island. Dunn had
won the unofficial championship and a gold medal at St.
Andrews the year before. In that 1894 tournament only four
professionals had entered. Dunn defeated W. F. Davis of
Newport, 3 and 2, in the morning round. In the finals he beat
Willie Campbell of Brookline, 2 up. But this time when the
11 starters had finished banging their gutta percha balls

around Newport's well-bunkered links, Dunn could claim no better than second place.

The winner of the first U.S.G.A.-sponsored Open was a young Englishman named Horace Rawlins, who shot 91–82–173. Rawlins had come to the United States just nine months earlier, in January, 1895, to take a job as assistant professional at Newport. At age 19 he became not only the first man to win the U.S. Open, but also the youngest ever. Dunn was two strokes behind Rawlins with an 89–86–175. The lone amateur in the field, A. W. Smith of Toronto, managed a tie for third place at 176 with Jim Foulis, professional at Chicago Golf Club. Rawlins' victory was a distinct upset—the first surprise in a U.S. Open, but positively not the last.

In July, 1896, the championships were renewed at Shinnecock Hills in Southampton, N.Y. Shinnecock Hills was a very posh social club. It had, in fact, been the first formally incorporated golf club in the United States and the first to have a waiting list for membership. The clubhouse had been designed by the renowned architect Stanford White and the course itself, a full 18 holes, covered 4,423 yards along the Long Island shore. The competition at Shinnecock Hills became another triumph for the Midwest. Charles Macdonald was defeated in the amateur tournament, but his successor as champion was H. J. (Jim) Whigham, an Englishman who played out of Onwentsia Club in Lake Forest, Illinois. Whigham eventually became Macdonald's son-in-law, thus keeping the amateur title tidily within the family.

The second Open, like the first, was a sideshow to the amateur tournament, and it attracted 35 entrants for one day of medal play. Of the 28 who finished the two rounds the winner was Jim Foulis, the Scot whom Macdonald had hired as pro at Chicago Golf Club. Foulis shot a 78–74–152 to defeat Rawlins, the defending champion, by three strokes. With his closing 74 Foulis set a record for a championship round that lasted until the passing of the gutta percha ball seven years later.

Chicago, which was enjoying an expansion boom in golf to match the one on the Atlantic seaboard, hosted the national championships for the first time in 1897. Jim Whigham again won the Amateur over the rolling meadows of the Chicago Golf Club. The Open was captured by Joe Lloyd, an Englishman who may have been the first golf pro to exploit the idea of following the sun. In the summer Lloyd taught at the Essex Country Club in Manchester, Massachusetts. Winters he held forth at a plush resort at Pau, France. To finish first in a field of 35 at Chicago, Lloyd turned in a card of 83–79–162. In second place, playing in his first Open, was a young Scot named Willie Anderson, of whom more was to be heard later.

The British Open had been extended to 72 holes in 1891, so the U.S.G.A., which in those days frankly patterned itself after the standards of Great Britain, extended Open championships to 72 holes in 1898. It also for the first time separated the time and place of the Amateur and the Open. As a result, the Open took its first step toward becoming an independent attraction. In June, 1898, the pros gathered at the Myopia Club in South Hamilton, Massachusetts and as usual the affair was pretty much a gathering of the Scottish clans, both off and on the course. To play their 72 holes, the contestants had to go around Myopia's nine holes eight times in two days. When they had finished, the new champion was Fred Herd, a Scot who worked as professional at the Washington Park Club in Chicago. Herd's score was astronomical to the modern eye: 84–85–75–84–328.

In 1899 the Open moved to the Baltimore Country Club, and total purse money was increased to $650. The winner still received $150 and a gold medal, but the low eight scorers instead of the low five shared in the pot. The winner was Willie Smith of a famous clan of golfing Smith brothers from Carnoustie, Scotland. Willie, representing Midlothian Country Club in Chicago, fired rounds of 77–82–79–77 for a total of 315 which gave him a winning margin of 11 strokes

—a margin, incidentally, that has never since been equaled.

In 1900 the A. G. Spalding Company sponsored an exhibition tour of the United States by Harry Vardon, the impeccable British shotmaker. Vardon made the game look easy, or at least sublimely graceful with his perfectly-timed swing and his exceptional control over the ball—he could pick a brassie shot out of the rough and drop it dead on the green. Vardon was at the top of his career in 1900. He had won three British Opens, then the most important professional championship in the world, and was eventually to win three more. Spalding sent him across the U.S. as part of a campaign to promote its new golf ball, named the Vardon Flyer, and the effect he had on an admiring public might best be compared to the reaction accorded Arnold Palmer and Gary Player sixty years later on their visit to another golf-hungry nation, Japan. Wild.

As he was in the country anyway, Harry Vardon turned up in October at Chicago Golf Club to try his hand at the U.S. Open, and it soon became apparent that his only competition would come from another highly-skilled visitor from Britain, J. H. Taylor. No American-based pro could do anything to stop them. In the end Vardon prevailed, with rounds of 79–78–76–80–313. That was good for a 2-stroke margin over Taylor despite a whiff by Vardon on the final green when he stabbed carelessly at a short putt. So, for the first time, the U.S. championship went out of the country.

There was no Vardon on hand when the pros reconvened at Myopia in June, 1901. Harry chose not to return to defend his title so the leading roles fell to a pair of club pros who were clearly the best in the nation during the early years of the century. After 72 holes at Myopia the Open was a standoff at 331 strokes. Tied were Willie Anderson, of the Pittsfield, Massachusetts, Country Club, who had missed the title by a single stroke in 1897, and Alex Smith, whose brother Willie Smith had won the Open in 1899. Anderson was the stereotype of the somber Scot: dour of countenance, always all-business, and a hard man to shake when the pressure was on. Alex Smith was the opposite, a hearty man with an outgoing disposition and a robust sense of humor. But he, too, was unruffled by pressure. In the 18-hole face-off at Myopia, the first of many Opens to be settled by a playoff, Anderson defeated Smith by one stroke, 85 to 86.

The 331 strokes which Anderson and Smith had required for four rounds in 1901 were the highest winning totals on the books, and theirs is one record that never has been threatened. In 1902 a new ball was introduced to championship competition that revolutionized the game. It added some twenty yards to each drive and consequently cut several strokes off the score. Developed jointly by the Goodrich company and a Cleveland amateur golfer named Coburn Haskell, the ball had a hard rubber core. It soon replaced the old gutta percha ball, just as the guttie had replaced the feather-stuffed ball half a century before.

Ninety entrants signed up for the 1902 Open at Garden City, Long Island, attracted perhaps by the increased prize money: $200 for first place and $970 to be distributed among the first ten places. The winner was Laurie Aucherlonie of the Chicago Golf Club. His 307 total included rounds of 78–78–74 and 77. Progress. For the first time the winner broke 80 in all four rounds. That Haskell ball did make a difference! In second place was Walter J. Travis, the best U.S. amateur player of the era and the man who had designed the Garden City course on which the tournament was played. Two years later Travis was to strike a key blow for American golf by bringing home the British amateur championship, the first Yank to do so.

It was Willie Anderson again in the 1903 Open, played at Baltusrol in Springfield, New Jersey. Anderson, now playing out of Apawamis in Rye, New York, scored a record low 73 in the first round, but his 307 total was only enough to put him in another playoff, this time with David Brown. Willie won it, 82 to 84. Anderson won his third Open the next July at Glen View in Illinois. This time no playoff was necessary. Willie scowled his way through four smashing rounds of 75–78–78–72 for a 303 total that was five strokes better than Gil Nichols, who finished second.

In September, 1905, at Myopia Hunt Club Willie Anderson won his fourth U.S. Open and his third in succession. It was a feat that in years to come only the truly great would ever approach. Twenty-five years later Bobby Jones won *his* fourth Open title and 23 years after that Ben Hogan won *his* fourth. No one has won more, or seems likely to.

Even Willie Anderson's reign eventually had to come to an end, and in 1906 it was Alex Smith, still as congenial a personality as Anderson was dour, who did the job. At Onwentsia in Lake Forest, Illinois, Smith put together four hot rounds of 73–74–73–75 for a 295 that outdistanced by seven strokes his closest pursuer, who happened to be his own brother, Willie. Alex's 295 total was considered a breakthrough, the first crack in the 300 barrier for four rounds and the lowest score to win either the British Open or the U.S. Open up to that time. For winning Smith received a purse of $300.

In 1907 it was the turn of another family of golfing Scotsmen, the brothers Ross, to win an Open. This one was played on the St. Martin's course of the Philadelphia Cricket Club and Alex Ross from Brae Burn Country Club in Boston won handily with cards of 76–74–76–76–302. The following year Myopia Hunt Club played host to the Open for the fourth and final time. After four rounds, tied for the lead at 322 were the tough, durable Willie Smith and a tiny Scot from Midlothian Country Club in Chicago named Fred McLeod. At 108 pounds McLeod was the first hero of the world's pint-sized golfers. In the playoff McLeod easily outshot Smith, 77 to 83, to become the smallest man ever to win the Open. Fifty-five years later Fred McLeod, grown no larger but none the worse for it, was still teeing off first in the Masters tournament at Augusta, Georgia.

For the first dozen years of its existence, the Open had been the private preserve of the Scottish and English pros who had taken up residence in America. Now, as the game caught hold in the United States, the first generation of homebred players was appearing. The amateurs were mostly the sons of wealthy men who had both the leisure time and the opportunity to perfect their game. The professionals were young graduates of the caddy yard who became assistants in the pro shop and eventually decided to try to make a living at this uncertain but fascinating game. At first the homebreds did little but build character for themselves when they challenged the foreign-born pros. But their day was coming. In the 1909 Open at Englewood, New Jersey, Tommy McNamara, a homebred pro from the Wallaston Golf Club near Boston, fired a sensational 69 in the second round to take the first-day lead with 142 for 36 holes. On the second day he battled George Sargent, an English pro from Hyde Manor, Vermont, down to the wire before succumbing 290 to 294. Sargent's 290, composed of rounds of 75–72–72–71 over the fairly easy Englewood course, set a scoring record that was considered untouchable. McNamara's 69 and a 68 in the first round by Dave Hunter, who blew to 84 in the next round, were the first sub-70 performances the tournament had seen.

The next year, 1910, the homebreds came even closer. When Alex Smith fluffed a sure three-foot putt on the 72nd green at the Philadelphia Cricket Club, it threw him into a three-way tie for first place at 298 with his kid brother, Macdonald Smith, and a cocksure little American-born pro from Atlantic City named Johnny McDermott. Alex Smith pulled himself together the next day and won the playoff with a 71 to McDermott's 75 and brother Macdonald's 77. But by now the breakthrough by a homebred player appeared inevitable.

As an underdeveloped golfing nation, the United States had for two decades benefited from a kind of Lend-Lease in reverse. From the British Isles our golfers had received their instructors, course designers, rules, equipment and traditions. It was inevitable that eventually the Colonials should turn and beat the British at their own game. Walter Travis, the grand old man of United States amateur golf, had broken through in 1904 to win the British Amateur. But not until 1911 did a United States–bred player win the U.S. Open. The one who did it was as American as they come. Johnny McDermott was 130 pounds of Bantam-rooster confidence, a graduate of the caddy yards around Philadelphia, where as a young player he learned to back up his golf bragging with dollars—and then win the bet if he expected to eat that day. When the 1911 Open began at the Chicago Golf Club in Wheaton, Illinois, Johnny McDermott, representing the Atlantic City Country Club, was at the top of his game; he feared no man on the golf course. In the opening round he shot an 81, but the next three days he was 72–75–79 for a 307 total. That put Johnny in a three-way tie with Mike Brady and George Simpson and set up an 18-hole playoff the following day. Johnny was no stranger to playoff situations, having lost a playoff to Alex Smith the year before. This time there was no denying him. McDermott won the playoff with an 80 to Brady's 82 and Simpson's 85 over the rolling Illinois prairie to become the first homebred winner of the U.S. Open.

Some called McDermott's victory a fluke, but in August of 1912 at the Country Club of Buffalo, there was Johnny primed to show all comers he could do it again. By winning in 1911, McDermott had encouraged United States players and the impetus he provided brought to Buffalo 131 entries, a record number. This large field soon found itself chasing McDermott again. He turned in cards of 74–75–74 and after three rounds the only man within striking range—four strokes back—was another young American, Tom McNamara. In 1909 McNamara had become the first player to break 70 in Open competition. On the final day at Buffalo,

McNamara did it again, shooting 69 for an aggregate of 296. But McDermott was equal to the challenge. He shot a closing 71 to save half of his lead and beat McNamara by two strokes with 294. That 294 enabled McDermott to earn a special line for himself in the record book: the first man to play 72 holes in fewer strokes than a new standard called "par," which at the Chicago Golf Club was 74–296. Just a year earlier the term par had come into official use when the U.S.G.A. defined it as "perfect play without flukes and under ordinary weather conditions, always allowing two strokes on each putting green." Golfers have been struggling with par ever since, seeking it in all kinds of weather and accepting with thanks any and all flukes they can get.

Now Americans had won the Open twice running and had, in fact, finished one, two each time. But Johnny McDermott, the double champion, was to have little more success in golf or in life itself. Within a very few years the nerves that had carried him to the championship collapsed. Johnny had a mental breakdown and he disappeared from the competitive scene. In time his fame was eclipsed by the exploits of another young ex-caddy who came along in 1913 to turn the golf world upside down.

[1913]

CHAPTER TWO

The Magnificent Upset

Half a century and more has passed since the September Saturday in 1913 when Francis Ouimet, amateur, ex-caddy, American and unknown, won the United States Open by firing what author Herbert Warren Wind christened "the shots heard round the world." As long as golf is played, the story will be told about the boy from Brookline who brought low the British champions—largely because there is much pleasure in the telling of the story. But also because Francis Ouimet (pronounced *wee-met*) never let his idolators down. Ouimet the man always lived up to Ouimet the legend: modest, soft-spoken, candid, a man who would rather play the game than talk about it. Although not wealthy, Ouimet never turned professional. In 1914, the year after he won the Open, Ouimet won both the French Amateur and the U.S. Amateur, both of which were then still considered more important events than the U.S. Open. Francis never won another Open, although he came as close as second place in 1925. He reached the semi-finals of the U.S. Amateur seven more times—on three occasions losing to Bobby Jones—and finally capped his playing career in 1931 by winning the Amateur for a second time.

While pursuing a successful career as a stockbroker in Boston, Ouimet continued to contribute his time and his name to the best interests of golf. After the Walker Cup series began in 1922, Ouimet represented the United States for 27 years as player or captain in a long sequence of victories over the British. As patron saint of all caddies, Ouimet established a scholarship fund bearing his name which has raised more than $300,000 and has given college scholarships to some 500 young men. Finally in 1951 the British gave their highest accolade to the gentleman who had upset their champions that day so long ago and had given United States golf the page-one heroics it needed to become a major sport. At an elaborate "driving in" ceremony the Royal and Ancient Golf Club at St. Andrews initiated Francis Ouimet, in formal red tailcoat, as honorary captain of the club, the first American to be so honored.

Young Francis Ouimet would not have believed it could happen to him. When he awoke to the sound of rain slashing against his bedroom window on the morning of the great playoff in 1913, more than enough had already happened to strain his credulity. By some fluke, or miracle, he had tied Harry Vardon and Edward "Ted" Ray for the U.S. Open championship. Vardon and Ray had been barnstorming the country that summer on a tour sponsored by the London *Times,* just as Palmer and Nicklaus today might tour Lower Burundi or Pago Pago to amaze the natives. Vardon, the stylist supreme, had already won four British Opens. He had a perfect foil in Ted Ray, winner of the 1912 British Open and a hulking bear of a man with a bush mustache who swung his club like an angry giant, lurching furiously into the rubber-center ball and propelling it farther than any man alive. In addition to these two the Open at Brookline had attracted a third British star, Wilfred Reid, and the French champion, Louis Tellier. Johnny McDermott, the defending champion, Mike Brady, Tommy McNamara and Jerry Travers were on hand to represent the homebreds along with the immigrant pros like Macdonald Smith and Jim Barnes. The Open had become big league and this 1913 tournament was a clear challenge to American prowess.

Because of the large number of entries the 36-hole qualifying round was divided into sections with play spread over two days. Vardon led the first-day qualifiers with 151. One stroke behind him was Ouimet, the hometown boy. Francis had recently turned 20 and his credentials were painfully slight. His father, a French-Canadian immigrant, had moved the Ouimet family into a modest house across the road from The Country Club when Francis was a small boy. He first stepped on the course as a trespasser, taking a shortcut to school. When Francis reached the age of 11, he followed in the footsteps of his older brother Wilfred and became a caddy, toting the bags of Country Club members for 20 cents a round. The two boys became obsessed with the game, and when they eventually managed to get hold of some used balls and hand-me-down clubs, they laid out a rough three-hole course of their own on some unused land behind their house. The holes were short, but they encompassed within their bounds a swamp, a brook, a gravel pit and large patches of long, thick grass. Once Francis had learned to hit a brassie shot safely over the brook, 100 yards away, he never worried about a tee shot again. As a teenager Ouimet did well in tournaments around Boston. After failing three times to qualify, he finally made it into the U.S. Amateur in 1913 and reached the semi-finals before losing. He also won his first championship of any note: the Massachusetts State Amateur. Now, suddenly, here he was with the experienced name players. But the pros were too concerned with the struggle among themselves to pay attention to him, and this anonymity was Francis' great ally. On the second day Ted Ray led the qualifiers with 148, three shots better than his countryman, Wilfred Reid. Macdonald Smith had 154. McDermott played poorly, but qualified, and a young pro named Walter Hagen, playing in a national tour-

nament for the first time, hit the ball well enough to qualify
and turned in a 36-hole card of 157.

Then the qualifiers began their championship test—72
holes of medal play spread over four days on the difficult par
71 Country Club course. After two rounds Vardon and Reid
shared the lead at 147. Ray was two strokes behind at 149;
Mac Smith and Jim Barnes were within rallying distance at
150. The two youngsters, Hagen and Ouimet, were in the
running at 151, as was the French champion Tellier at 152.
But McDermott, Brady and the other homebreds had fallen
too far behind. On the third round Ouimet fired a 74 and
found himself in a tie for the lead with Vardon and Ray at
225. Reid had blown up and the others had not made up
enough ground to challenge the leaders.

With the fourth day came soaking rain. Ted Ray, among
the earlier players to tee off, slogged around in 79 strokes.
He posted his 304 and waited to see how his rivals fared.
They were not faring very well. Vardon's putting stuttered
on the wet greens and he barely managed a 79 to tie Ray at
304. The others staggered and fell back. The pressure and
the bad weather had apparently also reached young Ouimet. He took 43 strokes on the first nine and used up five
more on the short tenth hole. To get his 304 now Francis
would have to play the final eight holes in one stroke under
even fours, a nearly impossible challenge under the best of
conditions in 1913, and rain made these hardly the best.

But Ouimet did not realize he was beaten, even when he
took another bogey 5 on the 12th hole after parring the 11th.
Ouimet did realize he must get two birdies on the last six
holes to tie. He got the first one on the 13th, a short par 4
hole on which he chipped into the cup from the edge of the
green. On the 14th Ouimet took his par 5. The 15th was a
tough par 4 and after a nice drive, Francis hit his second
shot into the rough. Now to stay alive he had to get down in
two from a thick lie. He did it by lifting a superb pitch shot
to within a yard of the cup. Ouimet had counted on the

short 16th as the place to pick up the second birdie he
needed. But he was wrong. It took a nine-footer there to
salvage his par. The birdie did come at the 17th, a dogleg
par 4. Ouimet slapped his drive straight down the fairway
and placed a jigger-shot approach 20 feet from the pin. With
the confidence of youth he ignored the blaring horns of
automobiles on the road nearby that upset the gallery
around him. He blithely stroked a sidehill, downhill putt
against the back of the cup and in. The birdie 3 brought
him even and sent the gallery of some 3,000 fans splashing
excitedly to vie for vantage points along the 18th fairway.
Francis' drive on the home hole was straight and long. His
approach hit the soft bank in front of the green and stopped
short. His chip from there covered all but the last five feet to
the cup. Five feet from a tie with Vardon and Ray! Ouimet
did not stop to dwell on it; he hit the ball into the cup for his
79–304. The partisan Boston crowd allowed itself a shout of
enthusiasm and would probably have mobbed its new hero
but for one sobering thought: Ouimet still had to face Ray
and Vardon in the morning.

Francis was abed by nine-thirty that night and he slept
until eight A.M. After breakfast at home he walked to the
club. He had come this way many times before, at five in the
morning, to sneak a few holes of golf before the greens-
keeper arrived. It never had occurred to him then that he
could be a serious rival to the world's two best-known
professionals. "I was an amateur who played for fun," he
recalled in later years. "I looked on professionals as magi-
cians who knew all the answers. This was to be a match
between Vardon and Ray. I was there by mistake."

On the first tee Francis might well have been mistaken for
somebody's caddy, slender and boyish-looking in his
knickers, white shirt, striped tie and checkered cap. He
looked particularly young standing between the dapper
Vardon and the burly Ray. But Francis was a full-grown
man compared to his caddy. The youngster who had ap-

pointed himself to the job of carrying Ouimet's light canvas bag and 10 clubs was a somber-faced 10-year-old who wore knickers and a four-in-hand tie, like his boss, with the sleeves of his shirt rolled up to the elbows in a businesslike manner and the brim of his sailor's hat turned down around his ears. Caddy Eddie Lowery kept one eye peeled for the truant officer (he had played hooky from school to caddy for Ouimet the day before). Little Eddie would eventually grow up to become a millionaire auto dealer in San Francisco and patron of young golfers, including another Open champion, Ken Venturi. On this day his duty, besides toting the bag, was to recite two lines to Ouimet before practically every shot. One was, "Take your time: you've got all day." The other was, "Keep your head down and your eye on the ball."

In the starter's tent at the first tee the three finalists drew straws for the honor of teeing off first. Ouimet drew the long straw and with Eddie Lowery's two admonitions echoing in his ears sent his first drive flying through the drizzle that still was falling. Ouimet held the honor through the first four holes. Vardon, playing consistent picture golf but not hitting quite as long as the youngster, stayed right with him. Ray was having trouble with his slugging tee shots, and on the third hole he went down a stroke to the other two.

The fifth, a long par 4 from an elevated tee with woods on the right, became an important hole. Ouimet continued his steady driving. "I was just numb," he explained later. "It was a wonderful mood to get into." But numb or not, Ouimet's brassie shot for the green was a complete miss that sailed off to the right and out of bounds. It was the youngster's first poor shot, and by rights it should have shaken him badly. But without hesitating, Francis dropped a new ball over his shoulder and hit his third shot. This time the brassie streaked to the edge of the green and Ouimet scrambled home in two from there for a 5. That earned him a tie on the hole, surprisingly, for both Vardon and Ray had required three to get on and two putts for bogeys of their own. Ouimet had survived his first bad hole and, more importantly, he realized that his opponents were playing a very human brand of golf themselves.

On the sixth hole Vardon placed an elegant pitch shot next to the cup for a birdie 3 that gave him the lead. The seventh, a long par 3, was Ray's hole—he parred it and the others took bogey 4's. This pulled Ray even with Ouimet and just a stroke behind his rival Vardon. The threesome drove into a valley on the eighth hole and Ouimet hit a mashie 160 yards up the slope to the green. His shot was dead to the pin—18 inches away for a sure birdie. Ray matched his birdie by sinking a 35-foot putt and Vardon took his par 4. That left the match all even after eight holes at 33 strokes apiece. Each man had to settle for his par 5 at the 520-yard ninth hole, and at the turn the match was still as close as it had been on the first tee.

"Ouimet was playing against tremendous odds," according to one eyewitness. "He was the hometown hero and all his friends were there to root him home. Which was wonderful, except that they dogged his steps from hole to hole, talking with him, patting him on the back, giving him advice and even cleaning the ball." One club member went so far as to stop Ouimet on the way to the tenth tee and ask for help in curing his own slice. But nothing bothered young Francis or disturbed his concentration.

On the 10th hole Ouimet took the lead for the first time. All three hit the 140-yard green with irons from the tee, with Francis on the inside. The two Englishmen three-putted, but Ouimet needed only two putts and went one stroke up. Both Vardon and Ray missed birdie putts on the 11th which would have brought them even. Instead they halved the hole with Ouimet in 4. "The pressure on them and myself was entirely different," Ouiment recalled. "Their prestige was at stake. It had finally dawned on them how terrible it would be if I beat them."

Ouimet had been consistently outdriving Vardon and on the 12th hole he outdrove Ray as well. Then he hit a fine mashie 12 feet from the pin and earned a solid par 4. Vardon was short with his approach and Ray was off to the left. Both took 5's to fall another stroke behind. Vardon got that stroke back with a birdie on the 13th. Now he was one stroke off the pace with five holes to play—the ideal position for a stretch run. But on the long 14th hole Harry hooked his drive, recovered, then hooked again on his mashie third shot and had to scramble for a par 5. It was a most un-Vardonlike performance. Ray was still wild and had to recover brilliantly through the trees for his par. Ouimet topped his fairway brassie shot but put the next one right on the green. All 5's and no change.

Ray went down flailing on the 15th, despite a lucky break. His drive was headed for the rough until it hit a spectator's derby and rebounded onto the fairway. But his next shot landed in a bunker and he took two to get out. A 6 on the hole left him four strokes behind. Vardon and Ouimet got their fours, but on this hole Vardon did something no one had ever seen him do before in all his years on a golf course. He lit up a cigaret and started puffing away. Harry's end came on the 17th, the left-hand dogleg. He decided the time to gamble had arrived and tried to cut the corner with his drive. The ball hooked into a bunker located at the corner of the dogleg. Vardon could not go for the green on his recovery shot and settled for a bogey 5. Ouimet, just as cool as though he were playing alone on caddy day, hit one straight down the middle and laced a lovely mashie to the top of the green. Francis now called on his long-shafted, narrow-bladed putter to get him down in two putts from 18 feet for a par. Instead he tapped the ball gingerly downhill and into the cup for a birdie 3.

Now Francis had a three-stroke lead going into the 18th. Right up to the green he played as though unconscious. Ray finished with a futile birdie 3 for a 78. Vardon closed ingloriously with a 6 for 77. That left Ouimet standing poised over a four-footer that would give him a par 4, a 72 and golf immortality. "For the first time I thought about the championship," he later recalled, "and it was almost too much. Suddenly I couldn't get my breath. The green began heaving beneath me. I could not even see the hole." Despite this last-minute attack of the shakes, Ouimet managed to make his winning putt. The click of his ball dropping into the cup triggered the first great groundswell of mass participation in American golf.

There were 350,000 golfers in the United States on the day Francis Ouimet won his championship. Ten years later there were two million, and American golfers, following in his footsteps, became the best in the world.

CHAPTER THREE

The Hagen Touch

A squarely-built young fellow with black hair walked into the locker room of The Country Club at Brookline. Johnny McDermott, the defending national champion, was holding forth among a crowd of his fellow professionals at one end of the room. The newcomer strode over to the champ and extended his hand. "The name is Hagen," he said. "I've come over from Rochester to help you boys take care of Vardon and Ray."

Thus did Walter Hagen, the fabulous and irrepressible Sir Walter of sport's Golden Age, launch himself into big-time golf at the U.S. Open of 1913. Hagen, like Francis Ouimet, was only a stripling of 20 that September. The son of a blacksmith, he had started caddying at the Country Club of Rochester, New York, when he was seven—the bags were lighter in those days—and soon he was saving most of his caddy fees, 10 cents an hour plus a nickel tip, to buy golf balls and clubs. When he was 12, Walter followed the siren call of a sunny spring day right out the window of his seventh-grade classroom, and he never went back to school again, at least not on any regular basis. At 15 he became assistant professional at the Rochester club and at 19, already a veteran of 12 summers' employment, he was promoted to head pro. The young Walter Hagen of the Rochester days had yet to meet his first European royalty or Hollywood movie star, but he already had the easy manner and the special flair—the ability to be remembered—that was to make him an international idol for two decades. It was this Hagen style which eventually served to elevate every professional golfer from a back-door hired hand to a front-door equal and, in fact, a celebrity.

Young Walter did not yet smoke and had not tasted his first drink, but he already had a lively taste for clothes. For his debut at Brookline he blew most of his savings on what he thought was the perfect tournament outfit: a rainbow-striped shirt of pure silk, a red bandanna knotted casually around the neck, white flannels with the cuff turned up just once, no more no less, and white buckskin shoes with thick red rubber soles and the widest white laces he could find. How could anyone forget a sight like that?

It was Francis Ouimet, not Hagen, who stopped Vardon and Ray in that 1913 Open, but Walter did well enough even though the Boston newspapers misspelled his name, Hagin. He shot a strong 73 on the first round and was well up with the leaders until the rain-soaked final nine holes. Then he slipped and skidded on those red soles to an 80 that included one awful 7 on the 14th hole. Even so, he finished with 307 in a four-way tie for fourth place with some of the biggest names present, Jim Barnes, Macdonald Smith and Louis Tellier, and one stroke ahead of Johnny McDermott. Hagen headed back to his pro shop without even staying over to watch the playoff. But he offered a parting shot, "I'll see you next year, fellows."

Hagen almost didn't make it back the next year. That winter while playing golf in Florida, Walter tried playing baseball for the Philadelphia Phillies. As a pitcher and outfielder, he had been the best player in the district around Rochester. More importantly, he believed that if he were ever to make a name for himself, it would have to be in baseball which was then the national pastime.

Pat Moran, the Philadelphia Phillies manager, had offered Hagen a tryout for the 1915 season. So as the 1914 U.S. Open came near, Hagen decided to pass up the long and expensive trip to Midlothian Country Club in Blue Island, Illinois. But one of the club members at Rochester, Ernest Willard, editor of the *Rochester Democrat and Chronicle*, took Hagen aside and argued that Walter had time for both golf and baseball. When Willard offered to pay his trip expenses, Hagen decided to give the Open another try.

In August Walter caught the day coach for Chicago. To his wardrobe he had added the snappiest straw skimmer that five dollars could buy and a pair of hobnail shoes to replace the ones with slippery red soles. At Midlothian he qualified readily enough with 152 for 36 holes. Then on the eve of the first round Hagen treated himself to dinner at a downtown Chicago restaurant which featured a dish he had never tried before: lobster. Before the evening was out, Hagen's stomach was killing him. Through the night he tossed and groaned in the grip of an attack of ptomaine. Next morning he thought seriously about withdrawing from the tournament, but he decided that it would be too hard to explain to Mr. Willard and the folks back home. So out he went to play.

At this stage of his career Hagen did not exactly possess a picture swing. One observer wrote that his swing "started with a sway and ended in a lurch." Throughout his career, in fact, Hagen's game rested mostly on a superb putting touch and magnificent short and middle iron shots that could put him dead to the pin from any briar patch. And, of course, he had the ability to come up with the superlative shot when everything depended on it. Hagen's recovery irons got a workout on the first day of the 1914 Open. When Walter didn't hook off the tee, he sliced. Weakened and still in pain, he gave little thought to anything except whether he could live out the round. But when it was over, he had somehow shot a 68, a new record for the 6,355-yard Midlothian course. It was enough to cure him quickly. That and the fact that Francis Ouimet, the defending champion, was only a stroke behind him at 69. But Ouimet fell off to a 76 on the second round and Hagen never surrendered the lead. A 74 and a 75 had kept him in front, four strokes ahead of Chick Evans, as the final round began.

Charles Evans, Jr., a brilliant young amateur from the Edgewater club on the North Side, was the pride of all Chicago. And all Chicago, it seemed, was out to applaud his belated rush to catch Hagen. Playing three holes ahead of Evans with no gallery to speak of, Hagen could hear one distant shout after another that could only mean Evans was hot and gaining. Walter went out in 38, but Evans shot a 35 and shaved Hagen's lead to one stroke. On the 13th hole Hagen hooked a mid-iron shot but recovered and sank a 12-footer for his par. On the 16th he pulled a brassie and scuffed his chip shot but sank a long putt for a birdie. On the last green Hagen dropped an eight-footer for a 73. That brought him home in 290, equaling George Sargent's 1909 record for low total in the Open. Hagen came back from the locker room to watch Evans finish. The Chicagoan needed an eagle 2 on the 18th for a tie. Chick almost got it with a perfect pitch shot that struck the back of the hole only to come to rest a foot from the cup. This time the newspapers spelled it right. *Hagen!* All the way home to Rochester in the day coach Walter clutched the victory gold medal in his hand. He had won his first title, and for the next 20 years he would win at least one big one a year, every year. Almost never would he be without a current golf title of some kind behind his name. The Phillies had lost one promising outfielder.

Despite the breakthrough by domestic players in the Open and the impressive debut of Walter Hagen, American

pros in the years just before and during World War I were
not the best golfers in the world. In 1913, for instance, a
quartet of the best professionals in the United States—Mc-
Dermott, McNamara, Brady and Alex Smith—invaded
France for a challenge series and were soundly thumped by
the French pros in both singles and team matches. The
increasing popularity of the game was creating a generation
of very good and very ambitious young players, but many of
the best of them never did turn professional. In those days
there was not all that much money to be made in golf, and
until Walter Hagen showed his fellow pros where the front
door to the clubhouse was, it was considered something of a
social comedown for a young man of good family to turn
pro. The result was an era in which amateurs could hold
their own with anybody, and often they dominated the
game. In 1913 Francis Ouimet, an amateur, had won the
Open. In 1915 it became Jerry Travers' turn.

The Travers family lived in Oyster Bay, Long Island, and
when Jerry's father joined the Nassau golf club, the youngster came in as a junior member. The pro at Nassau was
canny old Alex Smith whose eye soon fell on the 15-year-old
Jerry. "If you want to make something of your game, meet
me on the tee tomorrow morning," Smith told him. Jerry had
been slugging golf balls since he was nine. His homemade
course was the tree-lined front lawn of his family's Long
Island estate, more pretentious perhaps than the swampy
back lot that Francis Ouimet had played on as a boy, but
equally effective as a training ground. Under Smith's tute-
lage Jerry Travers brought his swing under control and
within two years—the year was 1904—he won the Inter-
scholastic Championship. Jerry attracted his first national
attention that year by defeating Walter Travis in the finals
of the Nassau Invitation tournament. Travis was the toast of
American golf at that time. With his Schenectady putter, a
mallet-headed club with its shaft in the center, the gifted
Travis had just returned triumphant from the British Ama-

teur. At 17 Travers was aching for a crack at the old master. For their match in the Nassau finals young Jerry borrowed a Schenectady putter that was a duplicate of Travis'. He was two holes down with five to play, but he caught Travis on the seventeenth hole and sank a 12-foot putt for a birdie to beat him on the 21st hole.

Travis, the old master, and Travers, the young one, met head-to-head many times after that, each winning his share. And from the crucible of their competition Jerry Travers emerged as a match player of practically invincible skill. He won the United States Amateur four times, beginning in 1907, a record that only Bob Jones surpassed.

When 141 entrants gathered in June, 1915, at Baltusrol in New Jersey for the U.S. Open, Jerry Travers was not among the favorites. Although fearless and ruthless in match play, Jerry had never been particularly brilliant in medal competition. Besides, he had been losing matches lately, and at 28 he was on the verge of giving up championship golf, after a full decade of remarkable success, to settle down to business. But after 36 holes at Baltusrol, Travers had a 148 and stood fourth, just two strokes behind Jim Barnes and Louis Tellier, the co-leaders, and one behind Mike Brady. Walter Hagen, the defending champion, was in close contention at 151. A 73 on the third round put Travers into the lead as Barnes, Tellier and Hagen all required 76's.

Holding a one-stroke lead going into the last round of a big championship is a position that many golfers dread. Like the flushed fox, he is the target of every snarling pursuer. But for an old match-play veteran like Travers the pressures of being out in front in medal play were just enough to make the game interesting. Travers was among the last to start on the final day, and by the time he reached the 10th tee, he knew exactly what he had to shoot to win. Tom McNamara of Boston had closed with a 75–298. To beat McNamara, Travers had to play the home nine in one under par. The

10th hole was a drive-and-pitch par 4. Attempting to play it safe Jerry switched to a driving iron for his tee shot. But instead he sliced out of bounds. Slugging now, like the boy Alex Smith had once taken in hand, Travers hooked his second tee shot into the tall rough. It looked like Travers had done himself in with the two loose shots. The green on the 10th hole was entirely surrounded by a water hazard. Travers was facing a double bogey 6, and possibly worse, if he should try for the green and fail. But Travers thrashed out of the rough with a magnificent pitch shot that carried the water and bit into the green two feet from the flagpole. He holed out for his par 4, a remarkable recovery.

On the 11th hole Travers had to scramble for a duffer's par. He switched back to his wooden driver but topped his tee shot barely off the tee. Two mashie shots brought him to the edge of the green, and from there he rolled home a 35-foot putt for his 4. Three more pars carried him to the 15th hole and a chance to get the vital birdie. On this par 5 hole a deep bunker cut across the fairway protecting the green, which lay some distance behind it. Travers challenged the bunker on his second shot, a long mid-iron, and won his gamble by the margin of four yards. He chipped on and one-putted for his birdie 4. Three cool pars on the three final holes brought Travers in with 297, one stroke up on Mc-Namara. Not long after this victory Travers gave up championship golf. Jerry stepped out a winner, with the Open to top off his long string of amateur accomplishments.

The third member of the ranking amateur triumvirate, with Ouimet and Travers, was Charles (Chick) Evans, Jr., the pride of the West. Chicago golf partisans always had at least one local hero to back with cheers and betting money in their perennial rivalry with the East. For many years their Lancelot was Chick Evans. Chick, the son of a librarian, had learned his game as a caddy at the Edgewater Golf Club on

Chicago's North Side. On his 16th birthday, in 1906, the tousle-haired youngster had ended his caddying career and embarked on a brand new one as a tournament player. He qualified for the Western Amateur that year, and the next year he entered the U.S. Amateur for the first time. By 1909 his game had made him one of the outstanding players in the United States, and his good-natured stage presence on the golf course as he waved and bantered back and forth with his gallery (much the opposite of most of the sober-sided competitors of the day) had made him a sectional hero. But Chick Evans had a problem: he could not win a big one. Particularly in match play he had a way of falling apart in the late rounds. Nine times Evans won the Western Amateur, but in the U.S. Amateur he managed to get beat (or to beat himself) time after time in the semi-finals. On the surface the fault appeared to lie with Chick's putting. Its eccentricity drove him to try every new putting grip and stance and clubhead style that came along. This was long before the 14-club limit was established, and Evans would carry as many as four putters at once in his bag. He would miss a putt with one, brood over it, then miss with each of the others in turn.

Evans' putting woes became exaggerated in his own mind. He certainly putted well enough to set any number of course records, to win sectional championships and to come close to winning the big ones. But, eventually, the idea that he was destined to be ever a bridesmaid fixed itself in his consciousness and bothered him deeply. When his friends told him he was the fairest golfer in the land, better than Ouimet of Boston or Travers of New York or any of the others, Evans, in his frustration, would agree with them out loud. In 1914 Chick came within an eagle of catching Hagen for the Open championship and finished second. In the U.S. Amateur that year for the first time he was eliminated before he reached the semi-finals. In the 1915 Open he was second low man among the amateurs but 10 strokes behind Travers, the

winner. In the U.S. Amateur he was upset in the first round
by a man he had been trouncing all summer.

For the 1916 Open championship, scheduled for the last
week in June at Minikada Country Club outside Minneapolis, Evans brought along his own caddy from Chicago
and, for the umpteenth time, a new putting style. A summer
rainstorm had softened the turf and left the course eminently playable. In the morning round of the opening day's
36 holes Evans streaked to the turn in 32. He cooled off to a
38 on the back nine but sat down to lunch with a 70 that tied
him for the lead with Wilfred Reid of Wilmington. In the
afternoon, relaxed and apparently unmindful that he had
ever had a putting problem, Evans shot a 69 for a total of
139 and a three-stroke lead over Reid, his nearest competitor. It was as impressive a day's work as golf had ever seen.
The next day turned hot and Reid crumpled to a 79. Evans
slipped to a 74 as the field closed in, but Chick managed to
go into the last round with an edge of three shots over Jim
Barnes. On the fourth hole Evans caught a bunker, then
three-putted and took a 7. This was the logical time for a
typical Evans collapse. But it never came. At the turn Chick
got word that Barnes, playing three holes behind him, had
caught him. Then came the news that Barnes had lost a
stroke on the ninth. Evans was on the 12th hole by now and
decided to press his advantage. The 12th at Manikada was a
par 5 with a creek running in front of the green. Evans went
for the green and made it with two fine wood shots. Two
putts gave him his birdie and steady play from there in put
him beyond reach.

Evans three-putted the last green for a 73, perhaps just to
show that he still knew how to miss a putt. But his total for
four rounds was 286, a new Open scoring record that was to
stand for 20 years. Barnes dropped to third place, four
strokes behind Jock Hutchinson, who finished with a flash-
ing 68 and wound up second, two strokes behind Evans.
Hutchinson earned $500 and the gold medal as low pro, but

the title stayed in amateur hands for the third time in four years.

To make his year complete Evans went on to win the 1916 U.S. Amateur at Merion in September. That made him the first player to win the Open and Amateur crowns in the same year. With the entry of the United States into World War I in 1917 the U.S.G.A. suspended its championships for the duration. So Evans, who had waited so long for his first national crowns, got to wear them both for three years.

The Open championship was officially in limbo during the war, but in June, 1917, the U.S.G.A. did sponsor a Patriotic Open at the Whitemarsh Valley Country Club in Chestnut Hill, Pennsylvania. The winner was Jock Hutchinson, a fidgety Scot who was born in St. Andrews but developed his game in the United States and was considered a strictly American pro. Jock was capable of streaks of great golf and at Whitemarsh he outdistanced the field with a total 292. That beat Tom McNamara, who finished second, by seven strokes. Hutchinson had finished second to Chick Evans in 1916 and was among the leaders several times after the war. But his only Open victory was an unofficial one.

Meanwhile golf and golfers were earning new respect for themselves by their volunteer work in the war effort. Exhibition matches between the name players attracted sizable crowds and became a popular way to raise money for Liberty Bonds, Red Cross and War Relief. The fledgling Professional Golfers Association, which had been founded in 1916 and had crowned its first champion in Long Jim Barnes, sponsored a series of team matches. The Western Golf Association pioneered the fund-raising effort and found a willing workhorse in Chick Evans, who spent most of his weekends playing charity matches. Walter Hagen was a box-office attraction in the team matches along with Francis Ouimet before Francis joined the army. From the Deep South came a hot-blooded and precocious 15-year-old to join the exhibition circuit. His name was Bobby Jones, and he delighted in defeating name players twice his age.

The postwar era began on June 9, 1919, at Brae Burn Country Club in West Newton, Massachusetts. Chick Evans was on hand to defend the national championship he had won three years earlier. But among the 141 pros and amateurs determined to take it away from him were the names of all the familiar challengers: Brady and Hutchinson, McNamara and McLeod, Tellier and Ouimet, Barnes, Sargent and Hagen. Mike Brady, the old pro Bostonian, was the popular favorite of the galleries. Walter Hagen had become the best known of the pros for his colorful style on the course and his stylish color off it. In 1918 Walter had moved from Rochester to Detroit where he took the job as professional at Oakland Hills, an ambitious new, and as yet unfinished course in suburban Birmingham. Postwar Detroit and Hagen were made for each other. The automobile city was a boom town then, lusty and full of life. Chrysler and Ford and Fisher were the names of living men, not just companies, and they adopted Sir Walter as one of their own.

Hagen was determined to win another Open to prove that his unexpected 1914 victory was not a fluke. He arrived early at Brae Burn, but found little time for practice. Al Jolson and his musical company were in Boston playing in *Sinbad*, and most of Hagen's time was devoted to partying with them. "Practice always took the zip out of me anyway," Hagen later wrote. "I preferred to be keen, fresh and eager when play actually started."

Prize money had been increased to $1,745 with first place still worth $500 and the low dozen pros sharing in the purse. For the first time play was scheduled on three days with 18 holes to be played on each of the first two days and 36 holes on the third day. Brae Burn was a rugged, demanding course that did little to promote low scoring. On the first day Willie Chisolm earned his notch in history when he took 18 strokes on the eighth hole, which was only 185 yards long. Hagen could do no better than 78 on the first day, but he followed that with a 73–75 while almost every other contender had at least one round in the eighties. With 18 holes to play Hagen trailed Brady, the local favorite, by five strokes. But Brady skidded to an 80 and Hagen played the final six holes in one under 4s in one of his patented Hagen finishes and overhauled Brady with a 75 to tie for the lead at 301.

The tie set up a playoff of 18 holes for the following day. But Walter had a previous and pressing engagement that evening in Boston: a farewell party with Al Jolson and all of the troupe. "Naturally I wanted to be there," Hagen recalled later. "The party lasted all night with champagne, pretty girls, jokes and laughter . . . and no sleep."

In the dawn Hagen rolled back to his hotel room for a shower, breakfast and a change of clothes. Then he wheeled his big Pierce Arrow out to Brae Burn to meet Brady who had been hitting shots on the practice tee for more than an hour. Hagen wanted the championship every bit as badly as Mike Brady did, but he succeeded in concealing his feelings under a cloak of magnificent casualness. Brady won the toss for honors on the first tee, and while he took a few more warmup swings, Hagen slipped into the clubhouse for a quick pick-me-up. Both men took par 4 on the first hole. As Brady prepared to tee off on the second hole, Hagen accosted him, "Mike, if I were you, I'd roll down my shirtsleeves."

"Why?" asked Brady.

"Everyone in the gallery will see your muscles quivering," said Hagen.

The needle did its job. Brady promptly hooked his tee shot into the trees and took a 6 on the hole while Hagen made his 4 to go two strokes up. By the 17th hole Walter was still clutching that same two-stroke lead. By then he was far from the "fresh, keen and eager" player he had described, but was instead just a tired young man struggling to finish the match on his feet. The playoff had been marked by an unusual double penalty involving a rule technicality. On the 10th hole as Hagen had looked over his short approach shot, he had picked up a matchbox, which lay near his ball, and tossed it away. An official, Fred Hoyt, invoked a rule which forbade any such ground improvements when the ball lay within 20 yards of the hole. The penalty was two strokes. Hagen always claimed his ball was more than 60 feet out and that the matchbox was more than the maximum two clublengths from his ball. Later on it developed that Brady had committed a similar infraction on the ninth hole when he cleared away a small stone. After some discussion both men accepted their penalities, which in effect cancelled each other out.

On the 17th hole Hagen skied his drive into a patch of sandy loam off the fairway and the ball disappeared from sight. Under the rules only the two players and their caddies were allowed to hunt for the ball while the official stood by, watch in hand, ready to declare the ball lost at the end of the five minutes the rules allowed for searching. Before the five minutes were up, Brady spotted the ball almost completely covered with earth and called his opponent over. Hagen insisted on his right to identify the ball. Under the rules then in effect, if Hagen had played the ball, taking more than two shots, and it turned out not to be his ball, he would be disqualified. Many years later, in 1953, the U.S.G.A. modified the rule to allow a player to uncover only enough of a buried ball "as will enable him to see the top of the ball." If he plays the wrong ball from the hazard, there is no penalty. But under the old rule, Hagen insisted and won permission to lift the ball, identify it as his own, clean it off and then gently, ever so gently, place it back in its hole. After doing all this he then managed to hit it back onto the fairway. Hagen wound up with a 5 on the hole while Brady took a 4.

That brought Brady within one stroke, but he got no closer as both players took 4's on the final hole.

Hagen had won the playoff, 77 to 78, and at the age of 26 he possessed his second Open championship. As it turned out, it was to be his last though he kept trying until 1937. Hagen was immediately faced with the decision of whether to fall exhausted into the nearest bed or to mount the convivial hustings once more to celebrate. History does not record which course Walter pursued that evening, though he could be forgiven for choosing either one.

The Open championship of 1920 came in August at the Inverness Club in Toledo and attracted a record 265 entries. Two days of qualifying play were required to bring the field down to 70 starters. The two-day format was restored for the tournament proper, with 36 holes of medal play each day. On the roll of qualifiers appeared for the first time the name of Mr. Robert T. Jones, II, and farther down, Gene Sarazen. (Even the youngest of amateurs were listed as "mister," a title withheld from the pros.) But this was not to be a year for the youngsters. Among the oldest men in the field were the famed British combination of Harry Vardon and Ted Ray. Vardon and Ray had returned to the United States that summer for a farewell exhibition tour. They were older and grayer now. Vardon, in fact, was the grand old man of British golf at 50, and Ray was no chicken at 43. But Vardon was still a master shotmaker and Ray had not lost his power. The crowds still flocked to see their exhibitions, and if America, having developed a generation of champions of its own, no longer looked upon the Britishers with awe, it continued to admire and applaud them. The burly Ray had never been one for style, nor was he one to accept criticism well, although Vardon was always more than willing to point out his colleague's flaws to him. The story is told that at one stop on their tour both men submitted to having their swinging styles recorded by a movie camera. That evening in the clubhouse they were invited to watch themselves on film. It was a moment of triumph for Vardon. "Just as I've been telling you for years, Ted," he exclaimed. "You lunge so badly at the ball you can't help but finish off balance." Ray stormed from the room and immediately wrote a note to the promoter resigning from the tour. But by next morning he had cooled off and the series continued, sans cameraman.

In the first round at Inverness Jock Hutchinson shot a 69 to assume the lead, three strokes ahead of young Leo Diegel of the Lake Shore club in Chicago. Ray and Vardon each had 74. A 76 in the afternoon left Hutchinson still in the lead at 145. Diegel and Long Jim Barnes were a single shot behind at 146. Vardon, Ray and Walter Hagen, the defending champion, were two strokes off at 147. The next morning Vardon, playing the same immaculate golf that he had shown a quarter of a century earlier in winning his first British Open, took over the lead with a 71. At 218 he was one stroke up on Hutchinson and Diegel, two up on Ray. A sentimental gallery swarmed around to root the old master home, and after nine holes of the afternoon round it looked as though Harry would make it. He had gone out in 36, and he could take as many as 41 shots coming home to beat the 296 posted by Jack Burke, Sr., who had finished early with a 72. Vardon parred the 10th, birdied the 11th. But as he prepared to play the 12th, a big 522-yard hole, the sky grew dark and a vicious windstorm swept across the links. Vardon had never been a power golfer. Now he bent into the gale and tried to find some untapped source of strength for the run home. He found none. Vardon needed four shots to reach the 12th green and he took a 6. On the 13th hole he set himself to sink a two-foot putt for his par. He missed. He three-putted the 14th, again on the 15th and again at the 16th. Weary and beaten, Vardon hit his second shot on the 17th hole into a brook in front of the green. On the final seven holes Vardon had gone seven over par. His 78–296 was worth only a tie with Jack Burke. Still out on the course were Hutchinson, Diegel and Ray. For Diegel it was his first test in a major championship, and he did well enough until the 14th hole. There he topped his drive, hooked a brassie and took a costly 6. His eventual 77 tied Burke and Vardon at 296.

Hutchinson's downfall was a putt at the 15th green. It was only a three-footer but he jabbed it wide of the cup. "That shot cost me the championship," said Jock and with 77 he joined Vardon, Burke and Diegel at 296.

Ted Ray shot a 75 and beat them all. On the first four holes he dropped putts of 35, 25, 40 and 15 feet. On the seventh his booming drive for the fourth time in as many rounds carried the trees at the corner of a dogleg 275 yards away, and for the fourth time in as many rounds he got his birdie 3. He was out in 35. On the finishing nine he struggled through the wind and used 40 shots. But his 295 was sufficient to win by a stroke and to take the championship away from the United States for the second time—and last for 45 years. At 43 Ted Ray was the oldest man to win the National Open until Julius Boros came along more than 40 years later to push the age limit upward.

Jim Barnes was a long and angular immigrant from Cornwall. When Barnes curled over a putt, he gave the appearance of a giant question mark dressed up in sweater, flat cap and slacks. Long Jim won the very first P.G.A. championship in 1916, and during the war years he ranked with Hagen and Hutchinson as the three best pros in the United States. As late as 1925 he won the British Open, and in the intervening years he became one of the first pros to discover the secondary commercial potential that can come with success in golf. *Guide to Good Golf* and other pioneer instruction books for the edification of aspiring players were written by Barnes. They were the first of an eventual avalanche of words written by golf champions and their "ghosts," all purporting to unravel the mystery of the game for any who would read them.

In 1921 Jim Barnes, representing the Pelham, New York, Country Club, made the National Open his personal party. The field of 258 who teed off at Columbia Country Club in Chevy Chase, Maryland, included two respected British invaders, George Duncan and Abe Mitchell, as well as Jock Hutchinson who had just returned from winning the British Open in his home town of St. Andrews, and all the other name players of the day. But Barnes immediately took charge with an opening round of 69. No one else was under par. Hagen played himself entirely out of contention with a 79. Barnes shot a 75 for his second round and at 144 he was three strokes better than little Fred McLeod who was the home pro at Columbia. Hutchinson fell out of sight after shooting a horrendous 83. Barnes still held the lead after a 73 on the third round. Of the two Englishmen, Mitchell had withdrawn and Duncan, after an opening 72, had shot two 78's and could no longer threaten. A closing 72 gave Long Jim a 289 total and an easy nine-stroke victory over Hagen and McLeod who finished in a tie for second place at 298. Bob Jones and Gene Sarazen, each 19 years old, had both come back for a second whack at the Open. Sarazen, who was working as an assistant pro in Titusville, Pennsylvania, finished 17th with a score of 311. Jones tied for fifth at 303. But both were well in the background when President Warren G. Harding motored out to suburban Chevy Chase from Washington to present the championship trophy to Long Jim Barnes.

The 26th U.S.G.A. Open championship, which began July 10, 1922, at Skokie Country Club in Glencoe, Illinois, was memorable in many ways. For the first time spectators were charged admission to watch the play. The number of entries reached a new high of 323, and the qualifying rounds to select a starting field of 77 had to be stretched over three days, a development which convinced many observers that some new method of limiting the field must be found. And not the least of the events that year at Skokie was the bursting in full bloom of Gene Sarazen into the select corps of golf's elite.

Born Eugene Saracein in suburban Harrison, New York, in 1902, the young Italian-American had, in a way, bet his life on the chance of becoming a golf champion. At Apawamis Golf Club near his home Gene worked as caddy No. 99, and on countless mornings he would slip onto the old course at sunrise to play a few furtive holes before he went to school. Even when he was imprisoned in the classroom, Gene's mind would roam free, assaying the bunkers and hills of Apawamis. During World War I Gene took a job in an ammunition factory and contracted a disease named empyema. The cure, said the doctors, was to find a job that would take him out into the open air. Gene knew just the job to fill that prescription. He turned to golf and caught on first as an assistant clubmaker at the Brooklawn club in Bridgeport, Connecticut. Soon Gene began to show signs of the insatiable lust for travel that has made him a world traveler for half a century. He has played in almost every golf capital worth mentioning. But his way-stops in those days were more modest. From Bridgeport he moved on to jobs as assistant professional at Fort Wayne, Indiana, Titusville, Pennsylvania, and by 1922, Highland in Pittsburgh.

Sarazen had only recently turned 20 when he turned up at Skokie for the Open. Very young, certainly, but not many months more or less in age than Hagen and Ouimet had been when they crashed through to national prominence. Gene had already competed in two U.S.G.A. Opens but he was still practically unknown, this dark-complexioned youngster who measured little more than 5 feet 5 inches in his stylish knickers. Even after he fired an opening round of

72 the only expert who gave him any chance to win was Gene Sarazen himself.

Walter Hagen, the newly-crowned British Open champion of 1922, shot a first round 68 and had all eyes fastened on him. By the end of 36 holes Sarazen, with a second round 73, had caught Hagen at 145. Meanwhile John L. Black, a little-known 43-year-old grandfather from Oakland, California, had put together a pair of 71's and had taken a surprising lead on the field. Then came the morning of the final day Bob Jones, the spectacular young amateur from Atlanta, produced a third-round 70 that earned him a share of the lead with William Mehlhorn of Shreveport, Louisiana.

Sarazen, after a morning 75, began his final round four strokes behind the leaders. He had no gallery to speak of and was under no particular external pressure. After playing two shaky holes, Sarazen made a vital decision—the kind that was always to mark his style of play just as it marked the style of Hagen, Hogan and a few others who in their own way reached the same conclusion: he who finishes second is soon forgotten. Sarazen decided never to settle for second best if he could help it. He decided to hit full-out on every shot, to give every putt a chance to drop. On the third hole he went for the cup on a 40-foot birdie putt and it plunked in. On the next hole he scored from 25 feet away. On the 18th, a long par 4, he used his driver twice to reach the green in two. Then he knocked in another birdie putt for a 68. His total of 288, eight strokes over par, was good enough for the early lead.

Most of the favorites were still on the course. But it is said that the best way to win any big championship is to post a low score early and then sit it out in the clubhouse. This was the day that axiom was proved. A friend who found Sarazen sitting alone on a rail fence warned him that several players were making a run at his 288. Gene answered brashly, "I've got mine. Let them get theirs."

No one did. Old John Black managed a 72 on the final

round, but that left him with one stroke too many at 289. He tied for second place with Jones who finished with 73. Mehlhorn took a 74 for 290 and even the heralded "Hagen finish" fell short as Walter shot a 72 for 291. Sarazen, the kid from Harrison, survived the late charge and was crowned national champion at 20. He followed this up by winning the 1922 P.G.A., and promptly challenged Hagen to a 72-hole match for the unofficial world's championship. "The Haig" was a man-killer in match play and was at his prime—four P.G.A. titles and three more British Open victories still lay ahead of him. But Sarazen matched Hagen snarl for withering stare and stroke for magnificent stroke. Sarazen won the challenge series, three up and two to go, and his place among the gods of golf was assured.

CHAPTER FOUR

The Golden Age of Bobby Jones

Bobby Jones and Bobby Cruickshank stood all even as they came to the 18th hole of the Inwood Country Club on Long Island. The date was July 15, 1923, and the match between Jones and Cruickshank was an 18-hole playoff to determine the winner of an Open championship that already had stretched over seven days of suspenseful play. Four days of qualifying rounds had been needed to trim the number of entrants from 360, a new record, to a starting field of 77. The tournament proper was played in two days of 36 holes each, and it had ended in a deadlock between Jones and Cruickshank. Now after 17 playoff holes the two Bobs still were as even as they had been a week before.

Cruickshank was a hardy little Scot who had come to the United States just two years earlier. During World War I as an infantryman in the British Army he had demonstrated convincingly that he was not a man to fold under pressure, no matter how great. Cruickshank had been in the thick of the fighting, was captured, eventually escaped and rejoined his regiment. After the war he had turned professional golfer and had come to America to seek his fortune. Now he was on the brink of finding it.

Jones was only 21 but already he was a veteran of a long series of tournament challenges and disappointments. Bobby had swung his first golf club as a frail toddler of five at the East Lake Club in Atlanta. One old record shows that he won a local tournament in 1910 when he was only eight years old. But until 1913 golf to young Jones was just another pastime that ranked somewhat above fishing and somewhat below baseball in his esteem. Then like thousands of other American boys he read and was impressed by the news of Francis Ouimet's astonishing victory over Vardon and Ray in the Open at Brookline. Later when the two touring Britishers put on an exhibition in Atlanta, Bob tagged along in the gallery. That year Bobby Jones shot his first 80, and that year he began to think seriously about golf. He was a chubby youngster with a determined set to his oval face. He had learned to do a deadpan mimic of the various swinging styles possessed by certain East Lake club members of limited skill. But, fortunately, he had also learned to imitate the flat, full swing of Stewart Maiden, the club professional, and from a distance the youngster was often mistaken for the pro.

Bobby's ability grew with amazing swiftness, and during the 'teens he became the infant prodigy of the game. In 1916, after Bob swept the Georgia amateur tournaments, his father allowed him to go to the National Amateur at Merion. Wearing his first pair of long trousers and carrying a pair of high-button golf shoes, he arrived unsung in Philadelphia. There he qualified for one of the 32 starting places with a score of 163 for 36 holes. Jones won his first match, 3 and 1. He won the second, 4 and 2. In the quarter finals against Robert Gardner, the defending champion, Bobby carried the match 31 holes before he succumbed, 5 and 3. At the time he was 14 and a half years old. His performance was a sensation. Later, in winning match after match, he proved that his introduction to national championship golf had been no fluke. The golf world soon beat a trail to his door. Walter

Travis, the revered old master, watched Jones play and announced that Bob's swing could not be improved upon. Long Jim Barnes went to Atlanta for an exhibition with the youngster and predicted that he could not miss at greatness. But young Jones still had a lot to learn, particularly about gaining control over himself. His temper tantrums on a golf course were a sight to behold. When Bob missed a shot, his golf clubs were apt to be sent flying in all directions and the air would turn blue with his schoolboy curses. Bobby never appeared angry at anyone except himself—in fact, he was remarkably courteous to others—but for himself he had no tolerance: every shot must be a jewel, every round a perfect day. It was the kind of temperament that, once brought to harness, could produce a champion. But until it was brought under control, it cost young Bob some victories and made him less than an ideal playing partner. Bob himself remembers as his worst performance a match at Brae Burn Country Club in Boston. It was one of many exhibitions he played during the war to raise funds for the Red Cross. In the foursome was Alexa Stirling, the national women's champion who also came from the East Lake club. When his game fell apart, Jones started tossing clubs and finally threw away his ball. "I read the pity in Alexa's soft brown eyes," Bob wrote later, "and I finally settled down, but not before I had made a complete fool of myself. That experience had its proper effect. I resolved then that this sort of thing had to stop."

When the Great War ended and championship competition resumed, Jones quickly established himself as the most consistent player among the amateurs and one of the few amateurs who could any longer hold his own with the pros, who were getting better every year. But through 10 national championships, victory eluded him. In 1919 Bob reached the finals of the United States Amateur at the tender age of 17, but lost to Dave Herron in the final round. In 1920 Jones played in the U.S. Open for the first time and tied for eighth place with a total of 299. The next year he tied for fifth with 303.

In 1921 Bob ventured to Britain to enter their championships for the first time but with dismal results. In the British Amateur he was eliminated in the fourth round. And in the British Open at St. Andrews he suffered through the most inglorious moments of his career. Bob had by this time outgrown his unpleasant club-throwing habit, but little things could still upset him mightily. On the third round at St. Andrews Bobby took 46 strokes for the first nine holes and was a prime candidate for a blowup. He took a six on the 10th hole, and when five shots on the 11th left him still shy of the hole, he picked up his ball and quit in disgust. Quitting was a plain breach of sportsmanship and when he cooled off, Bob was so ashamed of himself that he never again let his temper get the best of him during a tournament. Though he never entirely got over the urge to berate himself for a mistake, the memory of his pickup on the 11th at St. Andrews helped him to maintain control of himself. That he succeeded is demonstrated by the fact that he went back to play in three more British Opens. He won them all, and in doing so he became as much a hero in Britain as he was at home.

In 1922 at Skokie Jones tied for second place at 289, just one stroke behind the victorious Gene Sarazen. But in the United States Amateur that September, Bob, who was by now a graduate student at Harvard after having earned a bachelor's degree from Georgia Tech, lost in the semi-finals to Jess Sweetser, an outstanding young player who was in his sophomore year at Yale. The score was 7 and 6. Match play, head-to-head combat with another golfer, was still giving Jones trouble. Over and over again Bob and O. B. Keeler, his biographer and confidant, analyzed the fine points of his losing matches. Bob was learning the hardest lesson of match play: your only opponent is par—ignore the other fellow and play your own game.

By the end of the 1922 season Jones had appeared in, and failed to win, no less than 10 British and American national tournaments. It was written that he approached the 1923 United States Open at Inwood with an attitude of "give it one more try," and that if he did not finally break through this time, he was seriously considering quitting. Jones himself says no thought of quitting ever entered his mind. "Those so-called lean years were the years when I most enjoyed competition," he said later. "I enjoyed playing to make a good showing, or to win as many matches as possible. Tournament golf only began to gall me in later years when anything but an outright win looked like failure to me and to everyone else."

When the 77 qualifiers at Inwood finally got their first 36-hole day under their belts, the number of serious contenders had been drastically reduced. Gene Sarazen had a disastrous 79–78–157 and blew his chance to repeat as champion (it would be 10 years before Gene won another Open). Hagen was far back at 152. The leader at 142 was little Jock Hutchinson. Jones was in second place at 144, even par, and Cruickshank had 145. The next morning Hutchinson shot an 82 and eliminated himself. Jones shot a 76 and took the lead at 220. Cruickshank slipped three strokes back after a 78. In the final afternoon round Jones was even par for the first 15 holes. The day appeared to be his. Cruickshank, playing behind Jones, was having an erratic time and was making no particular move to overtake him. But on the 16th hole and again on the 17th Jones slipped to bogey 5's. Now a par 4 on the finishing hole would bring him in at 294, a figure beyond the reach of anyone left on the course. All week Jones had played the 18th at Inwood as though it were his private domain. In three rounds he had scored two birdies on it and just missed a third. But the hole was anything but a push-over: 425 yards long, fringed by thick rough and shut in by trees with its green effectively guarded by a rather large lagoon. Jones rifled his drive up the narrow fairway against the rising wind. He chose a spoon for his second shot and managed to carry the lagoon with it. But the ball hooked into the rough. It came to rest green-high but needing a short pitch shot over a bunker separating it from safety. Jones hit the pitch and dribbled it right into the bunker. It took him three more shots to get down for a 6 and a 72-hole total of 296.

Out on the course Cruickshank now was enjoying a hot streak. He played seven holes, from the sixth through the 12th, in 22 strokes, just one over even threes. He cooled off somewhat after that but came to the 16th hole needing only to par in to win. But on the 16th Cruickshank took a 6 of his own which included three putts. Now suddenly he needed a birdie just to tie Jones. He failed to get it at the 17th where he had to come up with a fine recovery from a hooked drive just to salvage par. On the 18th hole the doughty Scot whistled his drive down the middle. Then with a mid-iron he slashed the ball across the lagoon and onto the green six feet from the cup. Cruickshank lined up his putt and rolled it in for the birdie 3 that tied Jones at 296 and set up a playoff.

The advantage of impetus belonged to Cruickshank the next morning, and he teed off as a 10 to 7 favorite over Jones in their 18-hole match. Head-to-head contests still were not considered Jones' best game and after watching him take that disappointing 6 on the 72nd hole, most of the gallery were convinced the young Georgian would have to wait still another year for his first big win. After all, he was only 21.

It was anybody's match. In the first five holes Cruickshank collected three birdies and Jones got one. Jones caught up and by the 13th hole had taken a two-stroke lead. Cruickshank got one of those back at the 14th hole and the other at the 15th. Jones went ahead again by a stroke at the 16th hole, but Cruickshank got down in two from a bunker next to the 17th green and squared the match. Now they had run out of holes and the next slip would be fatal. Cruickshank had the honor at the 18th tee and hit a low, hooking drive into the rough. Jones was long but his drive caught the edge of the right-hand rough. From his lie Cruickshank could not hope to carry the lagoon, so he played his second shot safely short. That left the pivotal decision to Jones. Should he play it safe from his not-very-good lie and settle for a probable tie on the hole, or should he hit out for the flag which rippled temptingly in the breeze almost 200 yards away? For Jones there could be only one decision. He dug in and laced a mid-iron across the water, onto the green and almost up to the pin in perfect position for a birdie putt. That shot beat Cruickshank, who finished up with a 78 to Jones' 76. At last the Era of Bobby Jones had truly begun.

In the eight seasons that followed his breakthrough at Inwood in 1923 until his retirement late in 1930, Jones built a fantastic record of victories. He won the U.S. Amateur five times beginning in 1924. He won the British Open three times and the British Amateur once. In the U.S. Open during this span Bob once finished in 11th place, but in no other year was he lower than second. Twice he won the Open without a playoff; twice more he won after a playoff; twice he lost in a playoff, and once he finished alone in second place. In six years out of eight he either won the Open or finished in a tie for the lead. From a promising prodigy Jones grew in stature and reputation until he became the scourge of the links. The haunting cry, "How is Jones doing?" echoed from one tournament gallery to another across two continents. The question cut like an icy slash into the consciousness of the men playing against him, for Jones usually was doing all too well. Amateurs and professionals alike admitted to a "Jones complex," and few tournament players could concentrate completely on their own game with the sure knowledge that somewhere on the course Bobby Jones was streaking home behind them. It was Jones against the field. When the stretch run began, the worry and wonder over "how Jones was doing" reached universal proportions that were not matched until decades later when Ben Hogan and, still later, Arnold Palmer came along to psyche the competitors of another era.

Even Jones did not win them all. In the 1924 Open at Oakland Hills in Birmingham the wind blew at gale strength and scores went soaring upward. After three rounds 222 was good enough for a share of the lead, and the two men who shared it were Jones and Cyril Walker, a 120-pound mite from Englewood Country Club in New Jersey. Walker was not a big-name pro and he had never come close to winning the big one before. But a few weeks before the tournament he had told his wife Elizabeth that he felt absolutely certain of winning this time. Walker had developed his game on the gusty English seaside links at Hoylake, and this early education in how to play in high winds served him well at Oakland Hills. Keeping his shots low and under control, Walker started with three consecutive rounds of 74. His fourth round was a 75. At 297 he was the only man in the field to finish below 300. Jones skied to 78 on the final 18 and finished in second place with an even 300, three strokes behind Walker.

Later in that summer of 1924 Jones won his first U.S. Amateur, thus setting up a pattern of winning either the Open or the Amateur, or both, every year.

In order to accommodate the growing number of golfers who wanted a crack at the national championship, regional qualifying rounds were held for the first time in 1924 at courses other than the site of the championship itself. Qualifying competition at Worcester, Massachusetts, Country Club for eastern-based players and at Oak Park Country Club near Chicago for players in the West and Midwest served to cut the original 319 entries to 85. In 1925 a Pacific Coast site was included. Qualifying rounds were held for 445 hopefuls at Lido Country Club in Long Beach, New York, Onwentsia in Lake Forest, Illinois and at the San Francisco Golf & Country Club. The Open proper was set for early June at Worcester—two playing days of 36 holes each.

Jones opened with a sloppy 77 at Worcester and found himself straggling in 36th place in a field of 96. Bobby got down to business in the second round with a 70 that lifted him to 10th place. Another 70 had him running in fourth place as the final round began. The final round at Worcester turned into a golf promoter's dream, the kind that modern television producers pray for but seldom get. It was a stampede finish with no less than eight accomplished golfers still having a chance at the title as they came down the stretch. Each of the eight was a recognized name: Jones, Hagen, Sarazen, Ouimet, Willie MacFarlane, Leo Diegel, Johnny Farrell and old Mike Brady. As the afternoon wore on, Brady slipped a stroke or two behind the others, but when the stampede reached the final hole, the hopes of all the other seven were very much alive. The 18th hole at Worcester was only 335 yards long, but its sloping, raised green was surrounded by a squadron of deep bunkers. The pitch shot would be a mean one.

First came Diegel. The bunkers caught Hard Luck Leo and he took an embarrassing eight for 296. Next came Farrell and he got his par 4, which was good enough for a total of 292 and the lead among the early finishers. Amateur Francis Ouimet—his 70 had led the tournament after the first round—played a smooth par 4 and tied Farrell at 292. Sarazen came in needing only a birdie 3 to tie for the lead, but he had to settle for a par and 293. Now came Hagen needing a par to join Farrell and Ouimet in a tie for the lead. But the gallant Hagen had other ideas: namely, a birdie and a 291 total. Hagen scorned the center of the green and tried ambitiously to drop his pitch shot next to the flagpole near the front of the green. His gamble failed. The ball fell short into the side wall of the trap, and Hagen took a bogey 5 for his trouble, which put him out of contention. Jones' turn was next and for him a par 4 would mean 291 and the lead. He got it: on in two and two putts for his par. Now only Willie MacFarlane could catch him. Tall, gaunt MacFarlane, who looked like a college professor in his rimless glasses, was the least known of the contenders that day. Willie was not a tournament regular. He preferred his teaching chores at Oak Ridge Country Club in Tuckahoe, New York, or playing the game for fun. But he was a brainy player and was capable of great scoring streaks—his 67 in the second round was a new one-round low for the Open. Needing a 4 to tie Jones, he planted his approach shot on the top side of the green, leaving himself a 40-foot downhill fall to the cup. Willie watched his playing partner tap his downhill putt well past the cup. Then Willie barely nudged his own putt and it dribbled down the slope until it ran out of gas just a foot from the cup. It looked like a kick-in, but by accident the ball had stopped in a small hole dug into the green by some earlier player's approach. So Willie faced a new problem. He solved it by calling for his mid-iron instead of his putter and chipping the ball into the cup to tie Jones at 291.

MacFarlane and Jones squared off the next morning at Worcester to resolve their tie, and the excitement of the day before carried over into their match. MacFarlane went out in 37 and Jones in 38. On the 14th green Willie still had his one-stroke advantage and he appeared certain to pick up another stroke or two on this hole. MacFarlane lay two on the green with an eight-foot putt waiting for him. Jones was 20 yards away, chipping his third shot out of the rough. But Bobby chipped dead into the cup for a birdie 3. A startled MacFarlane missed his eight-footer and the match was all even. It stayed that way through the 18th hole where Jones dropped a tense five-footer for a 75 that matched Mac-Farlane's 75 and sent the playoff into still another 18-hole round after lunch. In the afternoon Bobby got off to a fast start and at the turn he had MacFarlane four strokes down, 35 to 39. No one lately had picked up four strokes on Bobby Jones in nine holes, so MacFarlane's task seemed hopeless.

With their collars off and their sleeves rolled back, pioneer champions Willie Anderson (*left*) and Alex Smith made a twosome to be reckoned with. In 1905, the year this photograph was made, Anderson won the Open for the fourth time, a record that has since been equaled but never surpassed. Smith won the title in 1906 and again in 1910. (*Culver*)

At Brookline in 1913 young Francis Ouimet and his schoolboy caddy, Eddie Lowery, played early rounds in almost complete privacy. But after Ouimet's incredible upset of Vardon and Ray in the playoff he became a national hero overnight. (*Underwood & Underwood*)

ve. Slender and natty in his striped shirt and ankle-topper shoes, Walter
gen, a blacksmith's son from Rochester, N.Y., won the Open in 1914 at age
and ruled the hearts of golf fans for the next quarter century. BELOW. A
mpionship foursome faces the camera in 1920. From left, Bob Jones, Ted
, Chick Evans and Harry Vardon. Their styles were as different as the put-
they carry in this picture, but among them they won the Open seven times.

The winner and new champion, Gene Sarazen clutches his trophy as the gallery hoists him in triumph at Skokie in 1922. Gene was only 20 when he won his first Open. Exactly a decade later he won it again.

But Willie proceeded to pick up not four but five strokes on the second nine. He shot a pair of deuces on his way to a sparkling 33–72. Jones came acropper at the 15th hole where he went for a birdie 3 on his long approach but caught the rough instead and wound up with a 6. Bobby finished with a 73. To show for the long day's work Willie MacFarlane had $500 and the Open championship. Bob Jones had second place and, as usual, a gold medal as the low amateur.

The year 1926 was Bobby Jones' greatest to date although it began in a way that was anything but promising. In a highly-publicized 72-hole challenge match in Florida between the Big Two players of the day, Jones the amateur and Walter Hagen the outstanding professional, Hagen manhandled Jones. Walter won the match 12 holes up and 11 to play. A month or so later Jones sailed for England and another whack at the British Amateur. This time Bobby made it to the fifth round. Then, on a day in which he woke up with a painfully stiff neck, he was eliminated by Andrew Jamieson, 4 and 3.

Next came the Walker Cup matches and Jones helped the United States team defend the cup. He won his singles match and teamed with Watts Gunn to win their foursome. Then, on a last-minute decision, Jones made up his mind to stay on in England and enter the British Open for the first time since he had quit at St. Andrews five years earlier. It was the right decision, for in the next few weeks Jones played some of the best golf of his career and some of the best ever seen anywhere. The high point came in the qualifying rounds for the British Open at Sunningdale, a proud 6,500-yard course. Jones smashed all records with two rounds of 66 and 68 for 134. His 66 is still considered one of the most perfect rounds ever played and it was certainly the most symmetrical. It consisted of 33 strokes on each nine; 33 shots from tee to green and 33 putts. There were no 5's or 2's on Jones' card. Every hole was a 3 or a 4.

In the British Open itself seven of the first nine finishers were Americans. Jones was on top with 291. By winning he gained a degree of vengeance over Hagen, who finished third with a score of 295. But, more importantly, he made up for his earlier collapse at St. Andrews and won the hearts of the British with his superlative performance.

Three weeks later the United States Open began at Scioto Country Club in Columbus, Ohio. There was much that was new in this 30th renewal of the national championship. Play again was extended to three days with 18 holes on each of the first two days and a final test of 36 holes. This format was to survive without change until 1965. Sectional qualifying rounds were played at 17 sites from Atlanta to Seattle to accommodate all the entries, which rose to a new high of 694. The total purse was increased to $2,145 with eight places added so that the low 20 professionals at the finish were in the money. But first prize remained an unlordly $500. A 36-hole cut was instituted for the first time to reduce the starting field of 147 to 62 for the final day. As has been the case in every cutoff situation since then, several former champions and name players failed to shoot the 159 or better required to make the cut. Among the casualties were Jim Barnes, Fred McLeod, George Von Elm (who later that summer defeated Jones in the final match of the U.S. Amateur) and Jock Hutchinson.

Bob Jones had returned from Britain to a hero's welcome in New York. With Mayor Jimmy Walker at his side he paraded through the city in a shower of ticker tape and confetti. Almost before Bob could catch his breath, he was on the first tee at Scioto and rapping out a two-under-par 70 in the first round of the Open. That put Bob two strokes *behind* the leader, Wild Bill Mehlhorn, but the vast majority of spectators and reporters present were ready to concede the victory to Jones. They called him "The Scoring Machine." But despite the deceptively easy appearance of his swing and the near-perfection of his shots, Jones was anything but a machine. Pressures were building inside him—the drive to do ever better and better—and the next day these pressures made their presence known. Bob shot a wild and woolly 79. It was the kind of day that happens all too often to duffers and happens just often enough to the Bob Joneses of this world to remind us that they, too, are human. On the 10th hole Bob's drive landed hard by a stone wall which was ruled to be part of a water hazard. Penalty stroke. On the 15th green he lowered the blade of his putter *in front of* his ball as he lined up his putt. Cut off from the breeze that helped to hold it in place on the sloped green, the ball moved a fraction of an inch. Jones was the only one who saw the motion, but he called it on himself. Penalty stroke.

By the time he reached the long 18th hole, Jones was striving to rescue a 76. He pushed his drive into the rough. He tried an ambitious mid-iron out of the rough but the shot backfired. The ball dribbled 20 yards forward, still in the rough. Another slash with the mid-iron sent the ball hooking to the other side of the fairway. An approach chip shot died short of the green. Another chip shot brought Jones, at last, to within five feet of the cup. And Bob missed the putt. Instead of a birdie 4 and a respectable 76, Bob had a foolish 7 and 79.

In the 36-hole finale Jones was faced with the challenge of making up six strokes on Mehlhorn, who led the field with 143, and four strokes on Joe Turnesa, who was in second place at 145. Joe, who represented the Fairview Country Club, was the best swinger among the Turnesa family of fine golfers who were earning a name for themselves in West-chester County, New York. Joe shot an even par 72 on the third round to usurp the lead from Mehlhorn. Wild Bill faded to a 76 and never threatened again. Jones gained ground on them both with a 71 that put him three strokes off the pace with 18 holes to go.

Bobby took up the chase again in the afternoon, but for the first eight holes he gained not an inch on Turnesa, and on the ninth hole where Jones failed to get his par for the fourth time in four rounds, Turnesa opened up a four-stroke lead. Joe, who was playing two twosomes ahead of Jones, then parred the 10th and 11th holes. So did Jones. On the 12th, a 545-yarder, Turnesa gambled with his second shot, a brassie that did not quite carry a plot of rough. He took a bogey 6. Jones moved quickly to take advantage of the slip; he reached the edge of the 12th green with two long, hard wood shots and earned his birdie with a chip and a putt. With six holes to go, Jones trailed by two.

Bobby picked up another shot at the 13th when Turnesa again missed with a long wood and bogeyed. Jones missed the green, too, but he managed to roll his ball out of a shallow trap onto the green and drop a short putt.

Turnesa held his lead until the 16th green. There he was a bit long on his approach, chipped back carefully but missed a nine-foot putt that would have given him a par 4. Jones was on in two and down in two more for his seventh straight 4. Now the match was even. The 17th was a par 3 and here Turnesa made his last mistake. His iron from the tee was short of the green. He chipped on and needed two putts for a 4. Jones got his 3 and went out in front for the first time in the tournament.

Turnesa showed he was anything but a quitter as he finished with a classy birdie on the 480-yard 18th hole, canning an eight-foot putt for his 4 to keep the pressure on Jones. Responding in championship style, Jones let out a notch on his backswing and laced a drive 290 yards down the home fairway. His approach iron was dead on the pin and 15 feet past it. Bobby lagged his first putt up close and sank the second one for his winning birdie. Jones' finishing kick, 35 on the last nine, to produce a 73–293, was exactly what he needed to defeat Turnesa by a single stroke. The victory made him the first man to win both the British and the United States Opens in the same year.

In the players' locker room afterward, a frustrated Walter Hagen unleashed a remarkable lecture to his fellow professionals. "Whenever I fail to stop Jones," said Hagen, who had finished in sixth place, "the rest of you curl up and die too. All that blooming amateur has to do is show up on the first tee, and the best pros in the world throw in the towel. What are we going to do about it?"

Meanwhile, downtown in the privacy of his hotel room, Jones unwound from the demands of a memorable day by dissolving into a teary state of exhaustion and relief.

Hagen's appeal to their collective pride was not taken lightly by the pros. In June, 1927, when 148 qualifiers gathered for the Open at Oakmont Country Club near Pittsburgh, each man was determined to finish ahead of Jones if he did nothing else. As it turned out, this was not to be Bobby's week. His game was anything but sharp, and he failed to turn in any score lower than 76. Bob finished in a tie for 11th place at 309. (The slump did not last for long, however. Before the summer was out, Jones had again won both the British Open and the United States Amateur.)

With Jones out of contention, for a change, the pros turned their attention to another tormentor, the Oakmont course. For the Open tournament the course had been extended in length to more than 6,900 yards. Each hole became a tortuous pathway through sand and bunkers—more than 200 traps in all. Oakmont more than lived up to its reputation as "The Monster." The terrors of the course turned the tournament into a scramble for survival. Par was 72 and on the first day not one of the starters matched it. More than half the scores, in fact, were above 80. On the second day Tommy Armour managed to chip one stroke off par with a 71. That turned out to be the only sub-par round of the tournament except for a bizarre finishing-round performance by Al Espinosa of the Glencoe Country Club in

Illinois. Espinosa, after shooting himself entirely out of contention with rounds of 83, 80 and 79, somehow played the final 18 holes in 69. Golf is that kind of game.

Armour's 71, which followed his opening 78, put him just off the lead with 149. Gene Sarazen, with a pair of 74's, was on top at 148. Walter Hagen and Harry Cooper were close behind at 150. The third round was notable mostly for an 80 committed by Sarazen, which knocked him out of the lead, and a 74 by Cooper, which put him in front by one stroke over Armour. Coming down the stretch, half a dozen players had an equal opportunity to take command, but the course was too much for any of them. Cooper seemed to have the championship won when he reached the 71st green. He was faced with a delicate downhill putt of 12 feet or so for his birdie. Harry had been putting well and he tapped this one boldly for the cup. The ball missed the lip and rolled well beyond the hole. Instead of a safe kick-in putt he now had a pressurized four-footer coming back. He missed this one, too, and took a bogey 5 on the hole. Cooper finished up with a 77 and 301, a total that looked like it might stand up. Armour, the last contender still on the course, took a 7 at the 12th hole, which appeared to finish him. But instead of folding, Tommy found one last hot streak in himself and played the final six holes in two under par. On the final hole he drilled a three-iron approach to within 10 feet of the flag. It was the kind of rifle-shot iron that was to become Armour's trademark. Then, as Cooper looked on, Armour ran home the birdie that earned him a tie with Harry for the lead. Their totals of 301 strokes for four rounds were the highest of modern times and were never approached again except in 1935 when the Open was once more played at Oakmont.

Although they had not yet made their full reputations, the two contestants in the 1927 playoff were no mean golfers. Armour, known admiringly as the Silver Scot, had seen heavy duty as a tank machine-gunner in the British Army in World War I and had come out of the war a wounded hero. He lost the sight of one eye and carried eight pieces of shrapnel in his left shoulder. In 1921 he had come to the United States as a member of the British Walker Cup team. He decided to turn professional and seek his fortune in America. Tommy had the shots as well as the battle-tested disposition for championship golf, and although he could be as inconsistent as he was brilliant, Armour at one time or another won all of the big ones.

Harry Cooper, on the other hand, was as consistent a scorer as his era produced, and over the full decade of 1927–37 he was probably the best professional golfer in the United States. For one reason or another, Cooper was never to win a major tournament. But this was something Harry could not have suspected as he teed off against Armour for another go at Oakmont in 1927. A congenial and colorful personality, Cooper at 23 was the most promising young pro in the game. English-born and a naturalized American, Harry had been raised in Texas. His father Sid was a professional at a municipal course in Dallas. In 1926 Harry had launched himself into the big time by winning the rich Los Angeles Open. He hit the ball with an apparent disdain for tedious concentration and went chasing after his shots with such enthusiastic speed that the press quickly dubbed him "Light Horse Harry."

The match remained even as both Cooper and Armour made the turn in 39. By the 15th green Cooper had gone ahead by a shot. Armour's ball lay a full 50 feet from the pin with Cooper well inside him. But Tommy stroked the 50-footer into the hole for a birdie 4 and pulled even with Cooper, who settled for par. Armour went ahead on the 16th hole, a 226-yard par 3. Cooper went for the pin on his tee shot and caught a bunker instead. In a desperate final stab Cooper placed his approach on the 17th hole just 18 inches from the cup. But Armour responded by putting *his* approach eight inches closer than Cooper's, and that settled the issue. Cooper finished with 79 and Armour with 76 to clinch the championship.

In 1928 the entry total climbed past 1,000 for the first time, and once more the name that stood out in red capitals was Jones. Bob believed that too much tournament golf was as bad for his game as too little, and in 1928, while devoting more time than before to his new law practice, he decided to pass up the defense of his British Open title and concentrate on the two American championships. Jones was the name that brought paying customers by the thousands in late June to Olympia Fields, the big layout south of Chicago.

When Bob started fast with rounds of 73 and 71 to assume the lead after 36 holes, all but a handful of his opponents were willing to concede it was another Jones year. Bob was having trouble with his driving, usually one of the strongest parts of his game. But another 73 in the morning of the final day carried him into the last 18 with a margin of three strokes on his closest pursuer, Walter Hagen. Jones needed every shot of it. He had been struggling all week for his pars, and now the strain was getting the best of him. The best he could do was a closing 77 for 294. This was enough to beat Hagen, but Johnny Farrell of the Quaker Ridge Country Club in Scarsdale, New York, gained five strokes with a 72 to tie Jones at 294.

Farrell was a stylish Irishman who dressed the part of a posh Westchester County pro. He also had finished close to the top in each of the past six Open championships. Having to meet Jones head-on did not appear to faze Farrell. The playoff route had been extended to 36 holes. Johnny started the day with a sharp 70. Jones still was having trouble straightening out his drives and could muster nothing better than a 73. In the afternoon Jones finally found himself and started to apply the pressure. Farrell stumbled but caught himself in time. He finished strong to defeat Jones by one stroke. The card read Farrell 70–73–143, Jones 73–71–144.

Now the pros had stopped Jones, their amateur nemesis, twice in a row. But one year later as he stood on the 15th tee at Winged Foot Golf Club in Mamaroneck, New York, Jones once more appeared to be the invincible player. Bob had immediately stamped his mark on the 1929 Open by firing a 69 on opening day, the only sub-70 round of the tournament proper. A 75 and a 71 followed, and Jones once more had the professional gallants: Hagen, Sarazen, Armour, Diegel, young Horton Smith and Denny Shute, bobbing unhappily in his wake. One who managed to stay close to Jones was Al Espinosa, a big and ponderous Spanish-American from Monterrey, California. Al had started with excellent rounds of 70 and 72, but a 77 in the third round left him four shots behind Jones, an apparently insurmountable margin.

Playing his final round ahead of Jones, Espinosa had started off well, but he slipped to a 38 at the turn. On the 12th hole everything went wrong and he took an 8. That left him so far behind with six holes to go that he gave up all hope of finishing first. With only a small gallery compared to the 5,000 who were marching behind Jones, Espinosa finished his round in comparative privacy. The fans did not know what they were missing, for Espinosa played the final six holes at Winged Foot in a blistering 22 strokes. He was surprised to discover when he turned in his score, a 75, that he stood first among the early finishers at 294.

Jones had run into trouble early at the eighth hole, where he blasted out of one sand trap clear across the green into another trap and then back again to the first one. It was an experience that almost everyone who has challenged the bunkers at Winged Foot has shared with Jones. The result was a 7 on a par 4 hole. After that Bob played conservative golf, staying shy of the traps but not getting any birdies either. With four holes to play Jones needed only pars for a

75 and a four-stroke victory. But, as the gallery shuddered, Bob flubbed the 69th hole completely. His approach was short on this routine par 4 hole. His next shot was too strong and carried over the green. The return required a short loft over a little knoll, but Bob skuffed the shot right into the side of the knoll. He was on at last in 5 but then took two putts for his second embarrassing 7 of the afternoon. At the next hole Jones three-putted from 20 feet, and the last remnant of his four-stroke lead was wiped out.

Bob got his par on the 71st and needed another par on the final hole to tie Espinosa. After two shots he was green high but off the left-hand edge of the putting surface. A chip left him with a twisting 12-foot putt that had to be made. Jones made it, curling the ball through a slow slide into the dead center of the cup. Bob's score was 79–294 and he had thrown away a big lead, but at least he was still alive. The next morning, for the fourth time in seven years, Jones turned out to play off against a single opponent for the national championship. This time it was no contest. Jones shot a 72 followed by a masterful 69. Espinosa had 84 and 80 and lost the title to Jones by 23 strokes.

By July, 1930, Bob Jones had arrived at the threshhold of an accomplishment which would elevate him forever above all other men who play the game of golf. Since 1926 when he won his first British Open, Bob had been privately contemplating the possibility of winning the Amateur and Open championships of both Britain and the United States in a single year. It would be a unique grand slam. His next opportunity to compete in all four tournaments came in 1930 when a team of American amateurs, with Jones as their captain, sailed in the spring to Britain for the Walker Cup matches. This gave Bob his first chance in three years to play in the British championships. At 28 he was at the peak of his game. He swung his hickory-shafted clubs as though they were part of him. His putter, "Calamity Jane," had been the instrument of sinking so many crucial putts over the years that it had become famous in its own right. And Bob was mentally prepared to go all out in one final rigorous and climactic campaign. Then, if all went perfectly, he would seek blessed retirement from the oppressive demands of being a champion—demands that were threatening to ruin the joy of the game for him.

After leading the Walker Cup team to victory, Jones went on to win the British Amateur for the first time in four tries. Next he won the British Open. Then it was back to New York for another hero's welcome, with Jimmy Walker and Grover Whalen at his side and the band playing "Valencia" in a snowstorm of confetti. Two down and two to go. But the United States Open loomed only a week away and barely 24 hours after he had arrived in New York, Jones was on his way to Minneapolis and the Interlachen Country Club. Eleven hundred and seventy-seven golfers, almost everyone, it seemed, who could lift a club, had presented themselves as challengers to Jones for the Open championship, and the 150 best of these, survivors of the qualifying rounds, arrayed themselves at Interlachen. Bob arrived in time for three or four practice rounds, which left him feeling vaguely let down and uncertain about his game. On the day before the tournament was to begin, Bob tried to relax by staying away from the course. He went fishing with a friend on Lake Minnetonka. But by early afternoon the fishing soured, and Jones hustled back to the golf club for a final nine-hole warmup.

The opening-day weather was like a furnace. Both temperature and humidity hovered near 100. Jones, surrounded by the largest gallery a golfer had ever attracted, almost 10,000 avid and cloying humans, must have thought he was in hell. Bob started the day dressed in the links style of the day: light-gray knickerbockers, a white shirt with collar and a red four-in-hand tie. In his trousers pocket he carried a dozen or so red wooden tees. By the end of his round the trousers were so saturated with perspiration that they appeared to be black. The tie color had run all over his shirt and the tees had stained one leg of his trousers red. In the locker room he could not loosen the tie, and O. B. Keeler—always on hand in a pinch—finally had to cut it off with a pocket knife.

Nevertheless, Jones shot a 71, one under par, and held the lead for an hour or so until Macdonald Smith and Tommy Armour came in with 70's. On the second day Jones stayed close to the leaders with a 73, but his score would have been higher were it not for an unusual shot on the ninth hole. Bob's drive found the right-hand side of the fairway and left him with a long second shot over a pond to a green some 30 yards beyond the water. As he went up on his backswing, his eye was caught by a sudden movement in the solid wall of humanity that fenced the fairway. Two little girls had made a break as though to run out on the fairway. Jones flinched but swung anyway, and he half-topped his shot. The ball hit on the surface of the water, bounced a few times like a flat stone being skipped across the water and safely reached the grass on the far shore. From there Bob pitched up next to the flag and made his putt for a birdie 4. The danger was past almost before it began, and instead of a 6 or 7 with a water penalty, Jones had a lucky 4.

Horton Smith, a young flash from Joplin, Missouri, who had recently set the winter tour on its ear, held the lead with 142 going into the final day. Jones was bracketed at 144 with Harry Cooper and Charlie Lacey. Macdonald Smith, Tommy Armour, Wiffy Cox, Johnny Farrell and Walter Hagen were bunched within five shots of the lead. It was the perfect situation for anyone to take command who could come up with a hot hand in the third round. The hot round belonged to Jones. His first break came at the long fourth hole where he came nicely out of a bunker in front of the green and dropped his putt for a birdie 4. Two more birdies followed at the sixth and seventh holes and he was out in a scorching 33. Bob turned on the power at the 11th and 12th holes, both par 5's, and he birdied them both. A sixth birdie followed at the 16th hole, and now Jones was gunning for a 66, a better score than had ever been made in the Open. But he slipped one over par at the 17th hole, a 260-yard par 3, and again at the 418-yard, par 4 18th hole. With a 68 Bob had failed to close the door, but he had taken a commanding lead. Now if anyone in the field wanted to stop Jones' bid for the Slam, they had to catch him first.

Jones started the afternoon round a full five strokes ahead of Harry Cooper, who had moved up to second place. Horton Smith and Mac Smith had fallen six and seven strokes behind, respectively. Jones played the front nine in a safe 38. Three orthodox pars followed. But from there in the shrieking gallery saw him play six of the wildest and most unorthodox holes ever committed in public. The short par 3's, which often bothered Jones, almost derailed him completely on the home stretch at Interlachen. The 13th hole—the 67th of the tournament—was only 194 yards long. Jones took a 5 on it. Bob quickly got hold of himself and dropped a 15-foot putt for a birdie 3 on the 14th hole. Another good drive and iron combination on the 15th hole left him putting from eight feet away for another birdie, which he missed. But at 16 he was exactly on target with a mashie-niblick approach and tapped in a one-foot putt for another birdie 3.

That should have put him safely out of reach of any last-minute charge. But the 17th hole was another one of those par 3's, and that meant more trouble. Jones caught his tee shot with the heel of his clubhead and the ball wheeled far off line into a marshy water hazard. Penalty stroke, followed by a chip and two putts and Bob had suffered his third double-bogey 5 of the round on a par 3 hole.

Behind him on the course, Macdonald Smith, a 20-year veteran of the Open, was gaining ground. Smith had gobbled up four strokes of Jones' lead and was still coming. Bob could afford no error on the finishing hole, a 402-yard par 4. A drive and an iron brought him barely onto the front edge of the big green. The massive crowd walking with Jones mashed together with the stationary gallery already jammed around the edge of the home green, and all settled down to watch the final shots. Bob paced off the 40 feet from his ball to the hole and then walked back again. "As I stepped up to the putt," he wrote later in his autobiography, *Golf Is My Game,* "I confess that my most optimistic expectation was to get the thing close."

Bob did better than that. His putt climbed the top of a gentle rise, broke to the right and spun the last five feet into the cup. Birdie 3. The shout from the gallery let everyone still on the course know that the Emperor Jones had once more shut them out. With a 75 for 287 he had the lowest total he had ever recorded in the Open, and now had won the title for the fourth time in eight summers. Mac Smith finished gamely, but he came to the 18th needing an eagle to tie. He parred the hole and wound up two shots back at 289.

Three down and one to go. Ten weeks later Bob Jones completed his unprecedented grand slam by winning the United States Amateur at Merion. He promptly retired from tournament competition.

[1931–1941]

•

•

CHAPTER FIVE

The Surprising Thirties

Suddenly golf was fighting for its very survival. For 40 years the game had enjoyed an uninterrupted boom. It grew in every direction. American players reigned supreme in the world. Hagen and Jones had achieved a broad popularity that put them up on the same pedestal with Rockne, Dempsey, Ruth, Tilden and other sports idols of the Golden Twenties. In 1929 eight of the first 10 finishers in the hallowed British Open were Americans. From that single cow pasture in Yonkers in 1889 golf courses in the United States by 1931 had grown in number to 5,700. At the same time there were 2,000 courses in the British Empire and another 1,300 in the rest of the world. Of the American courses, 4,450 were private clubs, 500 were municipal courses and the remaining 750 were privately-owned public courses. Many of the new courses had been built as adjuncts to plush resorts and social country clubs. Constructed with Babylonian abandon, they were grand and glorious temples dedicated to the pursuit of leisure. It was the kind of booming opulence that could not last forever. In 1931 the full weight of the Depression combined with the retirement of Jones to send the game reeling. The number of golf clubs and golf players went into a five-year decline and it would take almost three decades before golf regained and surpassed the levels it had reached during 1930, the year of the grand slam. From 1931 to 1935 the number of member clubs in the United States Golf Association decreased by one-third, from 1,154 to 767. Many tournament sponsors were forced to cut the size of their purses. Others went out of business altogether. Each year in the past the number of players who entered the U.S. Open had increased until in 1930 a record 1,177 applied for a shot at Bobby Jones. Now the numbers decreased and six years were to pass before the 1930 turnout was topped. Without Jones as a drawing card, tournament attendance dropped off too. Often as not the promoter was lucky to take in enough cash at the gate to pay the promised prize money. Only a few of the champions of the twenties were still competing regularly, and the new crop of tournament players, while they were very fine golfers, somehow lacked the magic spark required to arouse the public.

But there were certain developments in 1931 that augured well for golf's future. In that year the august St. Andrews Society formally approved the use of steel shafts for golf clubs, thus opening the way for the mass production of these high-quality clubs. The U.S.G.A. had been experimenting for some time with a larger and lighter-weight golf ball. Now it officially adopted the "balloon ball," which measured 1.68 inches in diameter and weighed 1.55 ounces in contrast to the traditional ball of 1.62 inches and 1.62 ounces. The balloon ball lasted only one year. The next season the U.S.G.A. returned the ball to its heavier weight but kept the new larger size. Perhaps the most important change was that without the presence of Jones to dominate and demoralize the field, the national Open became truly "open" again. Each tournament became anybody's tournament to win—the form chart of the twenties was no longer valid. The result was that surprise Open winners appeared (and often disappeared again) faster than in any period before or since.

The 1931 championship was played at Inverness in Toledo and it turned into the longest marathon in the history of the Open. One hundred and forty-four holes—twice the normal number—were required to produce a successor to Bobby Jones, and at the end the new champion's winning margin was only a single stroke. After the regular three days and 72 holes, Billy Burke and George Von Elm were tied for the lead with scores of 292. Von Elm was a trim, cocky little blond from California who had played most of his career as an amateur. In 1926 he had defeated Jones for the U.S. Amateur championship and, like Bobby, he could hit the ball far enough and straight enough to hold his own with the pros.

After the 1930 season Von Elm had announced that he no longer could afford the luxury of playing without pay, and he turned professional as what he called a "businessman-golfer." In his first pro season George had been eminently successful: he won $8,000 in purses during the winter tour alone.

Billy Burke (born Burkowski) was in his fifth year as a professional, but until recently he had devoted himself mostly to his job as the club pro at Round Hill in Greenwich, Connecticut. Before he became a golfer, Billy had worked as a puddler in an iron mill. In an accident at the mill the fourth finger of his left hand had been cut off at the second joint and the little finger also was damaged. So Burke wore a piece of sponge inside his golf glove to help him strengthen the grip of his injured hand. Burke was a cigar-chewer, a stolid sort of plodder who could hit a mean iron shot and was unflappable around the greens.

On the 72nd green at Inverness Von Elm dropped a 10-foot putt for a birdie to earn his tie with Burke. The next day this contrasting pair went out to play 36 holes more in the fierce July sun. Burke shot 73–76–149. Once more Von Elm sank a birdie putt on the final hole to earn a tie. His card read 75–74–149. Still another 36-hole playoff was decreed for the next day. For this second playoff the midsummer heat drove all but about 200 of the gallery to cover. But the two opponents kept at it: Von Elm outdrove Burke by 20 to 30 yards a crack, but Burke made up for it with sharp play around the greens. At one stretch Von Elm, trailing by four shots, clicked off four straight birdies to catch up. On the morning round, the seventh of the tournament, Von Elm put together a 76 to take the lead by one stroke. But George was not putting well enough to pull away. In the afternoon Burke caught Von Elm and, on the 14th hole, passed him. This time Burke came into the 18th with a lead of *two* strokes, and it was more than Von Elm could overcome. Von Elm parred the hole. Burke reached the green in two and carefully used two approach putts to get his ball within a few inches of the cup for his final tap-in. Billy's 71 gave him 148 for the day and a one-stroke victory over Von Elm after five sweltering days and 144 holes.

The man who did more than anyone to give tournament golf a splash of color and vitality during the doldrums of the thirties was Gene Sarazen. Gene carried with him some of the glamorous aura of the Golden Twenties—he had won his first U.S. Open in 1922 and had been a contender in most of the major championships since then. He was an inveterate traveler, touring the world with his golf bag and his inevitable knickers, making friends for himself and for the game of golf. Gene was by instinct a showman: short, stocky, darkly handsome, nattily dressed in matching brown sweater and knickerbockers, he was one player whom any spectator could recognize on sight without benefit of a scorecard. And Gene had a knack for making news. One season he livened up the sports pages with a one-man campaign to double the diameter of the hole from four and one-quarter inches to eight inches. In 1932 Sarazen's personal manager, Ray McCarthy, guaranteed Gene $250,000 for his services for two years—a pretty good figure for 1932. Then McCarthy made another headline by insuring Sarazen's health for every cent of the $250,000, including a $100,000 policy on Gene's hands alone. Sarazen, meanwhile, was busy with a project of his own. Like most golfers he realized that all too often matches are won and lost in sand traps and he was not satisfied with the conventional niblick as the best club for getting the ball out of the sand. In a Florida machine shop during the winter of 1932 Gene developed a new club that eventually became a standard weapon and one of a golfer's best friends: the sand wedge.

With the wedge rattling confidently in his bag, Sarazen in 1932 accomplished a long-time goal by winning his first British Open at Troon in Scotland. A few weeks later, back in the United States, he was trying for a double by winning the National Open at Fresh Meadow Golf Club on Long Island. In his earlier years Sarazen had been the home pro at Fresh Meadow and he had a great respect for the course. Perhaps too great, for even with the new sand iron in his arsenal Gene decided that the way to overcome the dangers of Fresh Meadow's tightly-trapped greens was to play a safe and cautious game. This was surprising strategy for Sarazen; his natural style was to gamble all-or-nothing. It soon became apparent that the conservative approach was unsound. In the first round Sarazen played a cautious 74. Big Olin Dutra shot a 69 to take the lead. On the second round Sarazen played a careful 76 which left him still five strokes behind the leaders.

Sarazen kept to his conservative plan through the first eight holes of the third round. He came to the ninth needing a par 3 for a 39. Instead of par he rolled in his first putt for a birdie deuce. That was the clarion signal for a change in tactics. Caution suddenly became a dirty word, as Sarazen at last threw himself into every shot without restraint. He lashed out with his woods and punched his irons boldly toward the pin. The immediate result was a 32 for Sarazen on the back nine which gave him a 70 and brought him up among the leaders for the first time. T. Phillip Perkins, a British amateur who had recently become an American pro, was the low man after three rounds with 219. Sarazen was just one shot behind at 220 and Bobby Cruickshank, who had turned in a third round of 69, was two strokes back at 221. On the final round Perkins and Cruickshank made determined bids, shooting 70 and 68 respectively to finish in a deadlock at 289. Sarazen knew he had to keep attacking to win and attack he did with every shot. He went out in 4–5–3 2–5–3 4–4–2 for a front nine of 32. In the home stretch Gene continued his streak until with three tough finishing holes to go he was seven strokes under even fours. He parred the last three for a second-nine card that read 4–4–3 4–3–3 5–4–4 for 34. That gave him a 66, the lowest score ever unleashed in the Open up to that time. The spectacular charge gave Sarazen a 286 and made him a clear winner by three strokes. To capture his second national championship Gene had highballed through the final 28 holes at Fresh Meadow in an even 100 strokes. It was a nice round number and not an easy performance to forget.

After the tense Burke–Von Elm marathon of 1931 and Sarazen's exciting stretch run of 1932, it remained for a comparatively unknown player to make the Open of 1933 a memorable one. Johnny Goodman was merely an amateur— and not even a highly successful one at that. With Bobby Jones safely retired, the pros thought they had gotten the amateurs out of their hair for good. But they reckoned without Goodman, a modest youngster from Omaha, Nebraska, who had a pleasant, well-scrubbed appearance and an efficient, compact swing. Johnny was the fifth of ten children in a family of Polish-Americans who lived on the wrong side of the tracks in Omaha. Young John knew some hard knocks as a teenager, but through the medium of golf, first as a caddy at the Omaha Field Club and later as a player, he earned himself a permanent place in the sun. Goodman first attracted national attention in 1929 at Pebble Beach when he eliminated Bob Jones in the first round of the National Amateur. It was an astounding upset and the only match Jones lost in the Amateur in the last four years of his career. Goodman himself was eliminated in the very next round, however, and he did not win the Amateur championship until 1937. In the 1932 U.S. Open Johnny won a gold medal as low amateur, but his score of 302 was a world away from Sarazen's winning 286.

The U.S.G.A. thought so little of Goodman it did not even select him for the Walker Cup team in 1932. So Johnny, at age 23, was not exactly one of the favorites when the 1933 Open championship began in June at the North Shore Golf Club in Glenview, Illinois, and his opening round 75 did little to attract attention. Sarazen, the defending champion, was having trouble with his drives and he resorted to taking a lesson from a fellow pro, Jock Hutchinson. But the lesson did little good and Gene soon played himself out of contention. Tommy Armour set a blistering early pace with a 68. But the second day Armour, playing with a sore thumb that had to be taped up, putted poorly and shot a 75. Meanwhile, Goodman was putting as though it were against the law to take more than one putt per hole. Johnny used only 25 putts on his second round, and on one hole, the 15th, he needed no putts at all. His approach shot there bounced three times on the green and came to rest stuck between the flag and the rim of cup for an eagle three. A final birdie on the 18th hole, where a 170-yard iron shot carried him from the edge of the rough to within three feet of the pin, gave Goodman a 66. That equaled Gene Sarazen's record for a single round and put Johnny two strokes up on Tommy Armour, his nearest challenger.

The next morning Goodman's putter was infallible again. He took 28 putts and finished his third round with a 70. At 211 he was now an astounding six strokes ahead of the field.

Ralph Guldahl, an obscure 22-year-old from Texas who had played steady golf through the first three rounds, was closest to Goodman with 217. Craig Wood, who had been the leading money winner on the 1932 winter tour, was one stroke behind Guldahl. Armour was a stroke behind Wood.

After a brisk lunch of cottage cheese, Goodman launched his final round as though he were going to run away with the tournament. He played the first three holes in 4, 3, 2—a par, an eagle, a birdie. But at that point Johnny Goodman must have realized how close he was to winning the championship. To protect his lead he began to play ultraconservative golf. The putts that once had eyes now refused to fall and the strokes began slipping away. Johnny wasted six shots on the next six holes and made the turn in 39. The final nine was a struggle all the way. But on the 69th hole, a 501-yard par 5, Goodman rallied. He was 30 feet off the green in two strokes, chipped to within five feet and holed a much-needed birdie. At the 70th hole he saved a par with a 10-foot putt after exploding out of a trap. On 71 he slipped to a bogey, but on the last hole, 429 yards long, he held on to get his par 4 for a 76. Then Johnny lay down in the locker room to rest and wait. He had posted a total of 287, just one stroke higher than the Open record held jointly by Sarazen and Chick Evans. Out on the course, 40-year-old Walter Hagen was titillating the gallery with one of his oldtime fast finishes. Even with a drive out of bounds at the 17th hole, Walter closed with a fine 66. But his 292 total was good enough only for a fourth-place tie with Tommy Armour. Craig Wood finished three strokes off the pace at 290. At last the only man who had a chance to overhaul Goodman was Ralph Guldahl, the shambling, unexcitable Texan. With 15 holes to go, Guldahl had trailed by nine strokes. But Ralph was pounding the ball great distances down the narrow North Shore fairways. With a steady run of pars and birdies he made up all nine of the shots he needed to pull even and reached the 72nd tee needing only a par 4 to tie Goodman.

Guldahl hit a mighty drive down the middle. But his second shot spurted off the bank of the green into the right-hand bunker. Attacking with his niblick, Ralph laid the ball up within four feet of the pin. A crowd of 8,000 shouted its approval and tensed for the putt that would tie the match. But Guldahl pulled the ball and it trickled off to the left of the cup. Bogey 5. So Johnny Goodman, who had started his career riding to golf tournaments in boxcars and had been passed over for the Walker Cup, won the National Open by a stroke. Goodman was the eighth amateur to win the big cup—and the last.

One of the basic truths of championship golf is that it is easier to catch up than it is to hold a lead. When the going gets rough down the stretch the easiest shots can become monumentally difficult for the fellow out in front. The same man, when he is charging from behind, can make impossible shots look easy until finally he himself slips into the lead. Then the shoe changes feet and the hot challenger is transformed into the harassed leader. Gene Sarazen won the Open of 1932 with a classic late charge. In 1935 he won the Masters tournament with another late rally that included his fabled double eagle 2 on the 15th hole at Augusta. But in the Open of 1934, at the Merion Cricket Club, this same Sarazen found himself in the role of a front runner. He failed to hold an impressive lead and kicked away his chance to win a third National Open. Sarazen was favored in a field that included Bobby Cruickshank, Harry Cooper, Wiffy Cox, Guldahl, Diegel, Burke, Von Elm, Horton Smith and a dozen other serious contenders. After 36 holes the leader was Cruickshank at 142. Sarazen was well-placed at 145. After a third round 73 Gene took over the lead. Olin Dutra, a large and bearish man playing out of the Brentwood Country Club in Los Angeles, had started the day at 150, a full eight strokes behind the leader. A dozen or more players separated him from the top. Olin felt so ill with an aching stomach that if it had been any other day but the final of the U.S. Open, he would have been home in bed instead of trying to play 36 holes of golf. But while no one was looking, Dutra fired a 71 on the morning round to move within reach of the leaders. In the afternoon, while Sarazen struggled to hold his lead, Dutra edged steadily upward. Waterloo for Sarazen came at the 11th. On this hole a stream called Baffling Brook runs close along the left side of the fairway, then twists sharply and almost encircles the plateau green. Gene elected to play safe off the tee with an iron and then powder his second shot for the green. But Gene pressed for a little too much distance with his iron and the ball hooked into Baffling Brook. He lifted out and hit again—right back into the brook at the bend where it guarded the green. Sarazen took a 7 on the par 4 hole and this indiscretion opened the gate. Dutra sailed through it, upset stomach and all. Olin's shots avoided Merion's hazards with inspiring regularity and his final round of 72 gave him a 293 total, 13 strokes over par but one stroke better than Sarazen, who finished with a 76–294. The eight-stroke deficit that Dutra wiped away on the last 36 holes was the biggest handicap to be overcome by any champion in modern times, until 1960 when Arnold Palmer made up a similar eight-shot deficit to win the Open at Cherry Hills.

In 1935 the Open returned to Oakmont outside Pittsburgh and once again the monster course dominated the mere mortal men who played it. Designed by William Fownes, the 1910 Amateur champion, and his partner Emil Loeffler, Oakmont represented the epitome of the "penal" system of golf-course design in which the slightest error is immediately and harshly penalized. At 6,981 yards, the course was oppressively long for its day. Its deep traps numbered almost 300, and most of them had raked-in furrows which made an explosion shot the only possible way to get out. And the greens. Ah, the greens. Slick as ice, hard and fast, they had come to be known as the notorious "skinless wonders" of Oakmont.

Opening day of the battle of man-against-course brought out a hefty crowd that included such nonplaying celebrities as Dizzy Dean of the baseball world champion St. Louis Cardinals, Olympic track heroine Babe Didrickson, and the popular lawyer from Atlanta, Bobby Jones. The galleries missed the only sub-par round of the day, a 71 by Alvin Krueger, a very dark horse from Beloit, Wisconsin. On the second day Krueger shot a 77 and slid straight back into obscurity. Jimmy Thomson, who could hit a golf ball farther than any man in the world, turned in his second 73 in a row and took the lead. The highlight of Thomson's round came at the 621-yard 12th hole. A drive and spoon put him hole high but in a bunker. Jimmy blasted out and his ball stopped one inch from the cup for a cinch birdie. Close behind Thomson were some familiar threats: Sarazen, Hagen, Shute, Espinoza, Runyan, Horton Smith, defending champion Olin Dutra and his brother Mortie. Also in contention, four strokes behind Thomson at 150, was an unfamiliar contestant named Samuel McLaughlin Parks, Jr.

Sam Parks was a local boy of 25, well-dressed and well-mannered, the son of a Pittsburgh real estate man. Sam had received his first golf lesson from Gene Sarazen in 1922, the year Gene won his first Open. Later Sam had captained the golf team at Pittsburgh University and, turning professional after graduation, he became pro at nearby Southern Hills Country Club. In three years as a professional Parks had never won a tournament. He had entered this Open because it was being played close to home and because he knew the Oakmont course by heart. Sam's approach to The Monster was a strategy based on sour experience: play it safe—take no chances and the bogey man won't get you. The result was modest scoring, but at Oakmont few other contenders could produce even that. On the third round Parks shot a 73 and surprisingly enough found himself tied for the lead with

Thomson, who had slipped to a 77. But very few onlookers took the upstart seriously. Henry Picard, youngest of the favorites, had shot a 70, the lowest round of the tournament, and Ray Mangrum had shot a 72 to move within striking distance with one round to go.

The gallery at last discovered Parks and the biggest crowd of the week jammed around to root for the hometown hero. On his final round Sam fussed endlessly over his putts on the bald greens. He lost one stroke to par at the second hole, another at the third, still another at the fourth. Then he steadied and finished the front nine in 38. Parks clicked off five pars in a row to begin the final nine. But Sam bogeyed the 15th hole and when he took three putts at the short 16th, he appeared on the brink of a collapse at last. But he managed a par on the tricky 17th and, despite a missed three-footer at the 72nd green, he posted a 76 for a total of 299. Not a figure to brag about, but then no one else was having any better success at conquering Oakmont's horrors. Picard took a ruinous 41 on the front nine. Thomson was in perfect position to win, but he three-putted at 16 and again at 17 and finished with 78 at 301. Not a single player among the 20 leaders was able to break 75 in the last round. Finally only Walter Hagen had any chance of catching Parks and the old swashbuckler made a gallant try. Six strokes behind at the 15th tee, Hagen made up three of them, but he was still three down at the end. By sticking faithfully to his conservative tactics, unknown Sam Parks had stolen the Open.

In 1936 as the nation was struggling to emerge from five years of depression, the fortunes of golf took a turn for the better. Club membership in the U.S.G.A. started to climb upward again. Fred Corcoran, a skilled and inventive promoter, became tournament director of the P.G.A., and total prize money for the tour reached $100,000. The purse for the 40th U.S. Open, held at Baltusrol in Springfield, New Jersey, was $5,000, and the number of entries who attempted to qualify at 28 sectional sites reached 1,277, breaking the old record for participation set in 1930. Golf was embarking on a new era of steady expansion that is still going strong to this day.

The Upper Course at Baltusrol played remarkably fast that June, and it was apparent from the start that the Open scoring record was in danger. Chick Evans had set the record at 286 in 1916 and his mark had been tied only once—by Gene Sarazen in 1932. At Baltusrol three players broke 70 on the opening day, an unheard-of feat. After 36 holes Vic Ghezzi and Ray Mangrum were tied for the lead at 140. Sam Parks, the defending champion, failed to make the cut at 152. Another who was eliminated after 36 holes was a rookie from Texas named Ben Hogan. As the final two rounds began, a dozen players were bunched within four strokes of the lead. One of these was Harry Cooper, the popular Englishman from Texas. Harry was a wiser and sadder man than the rollicking youngster who had lost the title in 1927 at Oakmont to Tommy Armour. At the age of 32 Cooper's hair was thinning and he had taken to wearing spectacles. But he still swung as confidently and quickly as ever, and his shots were almost always true. Consistently a top money-winner on the pro tour and winner of the Vardon trophy for best average score per round, Cooper had captured just about every honor in sight except the Open. When he stuck his nose in front with a fine 70 on the third round at Baltusrol, it was widely conceded that this, at last, was Harry Cooper's Open. Cooper's third-round score included an explosion shot that dropped into the cup at the 16th hole and a 45-foot putt that did the same thing at the 17th hole. His 211 was a new record for 54 holes and put him two shots up on Vic Ghezzi, three up on Denny Shute and four up on Ky Laffoon, Henry Picard, Clarence Clark and Tony Manero.

Now the beat of Cooper's pulse gathered speed as he tried

to hold his precious lead through the final 18. On the front nine his game turned erratic, but for every error he made he treated the gallery to a matching brilliant recovery. Harry eagled the first hole and then three-putted the second for a bogey. He missed the green on each of the fourth, fifth and sixth holes, but got down in two for his par each time. He bogeyed the tough seventh hole but got that stroke back by birdieing the eighth, and he made the turn in a solid 35. A new challenge presented itself on the 340-yard 12th hole. After a long drive, Cooper dropped his short pitch shot about four feet from the cup. A birdie here would add a vital stroke to his lead and for once Light Horse Harry slowed down and lined up his shot with care. He made it! No question about it now. Old Harry was holding up nobly under pressure while practically all the other contenders were cracking (Ghezzi had an awful 81). True, Harry let a couple of shots get away from him after that birdie on 12. He missed a three-foot putt on the 14th, plopped his pitch into a bunker on 15 and took three from the apron on the 18th. That brought him in with a 73—higher than the 70 or 71 he should have had—but low enough to earn the backslapping plaudits of the crowd and shouts of "Hiya, champ," which must have rung like sweet music in his ears. Cooper's total of 284 was two strokes below the old Open record held by Evans and Sarazen. Even so, Harry was slow to believe he had finally landed the big one. "I haven't won this thing yet," he said cautiously.

And indeed he hadn't. Just 20 minutes behind Cooper on the course and stringing birdies together like so many beads was Tony Manero. Who? asked the crowd. Anthony Manero, that's who. Tony was an obscure young professional who was currently employed by the Sedgefield Club in Greensboro, North Carolina. But, like the famed Turnesa brothers before him, he had learned most of his basic golf on a ragged plot of grass behind the caddy house of the Fairview Country Club in Elmsford, New York.

After two rounds of 73 and 69, Manero, a small and dark man with a neat black mustache, had been two strokes behind the leaders. For his final two rounds Manero was paired with Gene Sarazen, another of the golfing Italian-Americans who seemed to thrive in Westchester County. In the morning Manero shot an undistinguished 73 and trailed Cooper by four strokes. Sarazen had played himself out of contention, but on the outgoing nine of the afternoon round he gave Manero something to shoot at: a sparkling 33. Manero matched it with a 33 of his own. On the back side Sarazen started poorly, but he kept "talking Tony home" with relaxed and friendly conversation. Manero birdied the 12th and 13th holes to go five under par. On the 14th he played it safe—on in two and two putts—for his par 4. After 68 holes he had exactly the same figure Cooper had had at that point, and Cooper had missed his par on two of the four remaining holes. So a score of one over par on the last four holes would win for Manero: a requirement that sounds easy enough. But many players better established than Manero had found par an impossible obstacle when they were faced with the chance to win a major title. Cooper waited nervously at the clubhouse, but his gallery backtracked down the fairways to find Manero. The sudden people-jam forced Tony to slow down and wait as much as 10 minutes between shots, but each time Sarazen eased the tension by filling the gaps with light conversation.

On the 15th hole, a par 3, 140 yards downhill, Manero fell short of the green in a bunker. He blasted out and took two putts for a bogey 4. Still, even par would win. On the 439-yard 16th hole Tony drove well and placed his iron 12 feet from the hole. He sank the birdie putt. On the par 5 17th hole he was putting again for a bird but missed from seven feet. On 18 Manero hit his second shot to the front edge of the green, and as he paraded down the fairway, he tipped his cap to the applause of the largest crowd to gather on a gold course since the days of Jones. Manero now could allow himself three putts from 40 feet and still win by a stroke. Instead he put his first putt up to within five feet and ran home the second. His 67 was a new course record and gave him a total of 282, four shots under the old tournament record and two shots better than Cooper, the runner-up. Once more Light Horse Harry had been had.

Enter, Samuel Jackson Snead. Through the lean years after the abrupt retirement of Bob Jones, American golf fans had been searching for a new hero. They found one early in 1937 when Sam Snead's star streaked like a rocket over the winter tour. Snead and Jones were poles apart in background, personality and style. But they shared the secret of popular appeal: a certain magnetism that makes people *care* whether they win or lose. Young Sam was a raw-boned Virginia mountaineer, just over six feet, 185 pounds with a masculine shyness that made hearts flutter. At 25 he had dark hair which already was receding at the temples and dark eyes that reflected the trace of Indian blood in his heritage. Snead was a perfect foil for Fred Corcoran, the energetic promoter of the pro tour, and with Corcoran's help the legends quickly began to sprout up around Snead. Sam had been the youngest of five sons of a powerhouse worker in Hot Springs, Virginia. He learned to play golf while roaming barefoot through the farm fields, with homemade clubs hewn out of sticks. Caddying jobs at Hot Springs and Cascade led to a job in the pro shop there and eventually at Greenbrier, the famed railroad resort across the state line in White Sulphur Springs, West Virginia. It was at Greenbrier one day in 1936 that Sam filled in on a foursome which included Lawson Little, winner of both the American and British Amateurs, and two former U.S. Open champs, Johnny Goodman and Billy Burke. According to legend, Snead shot a 61 that day and convinced both himself and his embarrassed victims that he was ready for a try at the big time. Sam has been scalping unsuspecting strangers on his Greenbrier course ever since.

With some financial backing from friends at home Snead joined the winter circuit and broke in by finishing 10th in the Miami-Biltmore Open. He was sixth at Los Angeles (where the newspapers spelled his name "Sneed"). Then he made headlines at Oakland, where he won with a sensational four-day total of 270. After this victory Snead's picture appeared in the New York papers. When Sam heard about it he is reported to have drawled in surprise, "How'd they get my picture? I ain't never bin to New York." Of such remarks, of course, celebrities are made.

A perfect swing helps, too, and Sam had been blessed with the most perfectly integrated stroke ever seen anywhere. Sam—and the other big hitters who followed behind him—arrived on the scene at exactly the right time. Golf courses in general were being made easier to score on. Bunkers were filled in and the rough was kept trimmed as the strategic approach to golf course design—as exemplified by Bobby Jones' new course at Augusta, Georgia—gained in popularity over the old penal design. Golf clubs were better made, mass-produced in steel-shafted sets with matching weights. Even the ball was hyped up to deliver greater distances. With his gargantuan drives of 300 yards and more Snead usurped the title of "world's longest driver" from Jimmy Thomson. Jimmy could sometimes hit them just as far, but he did not have Snead's consistency. Sam was also a marvel with his irons—a match even for Byron Nelson, another young player who was regarded as a wizard with the long iron. And Sam could drop his share of birdie putts. If he sometimes did not get as close as he might with his lag putts and if the easy two-footers seemed to bother him—well, that was just enough of a flaw to make Sam all the more interesting to watch.

Snead followed up his Oakland victory by winning the Bing Crosby Open and finishing second in the Houston

Open. Few players have come into their first National Open with as much advance fanfare and buildup as did Sam Snead in 1937. The Open was being held once more at Oakland Hills outside Detroit, still as tough a course as when Cyril Walker upset Bob Jones there in 1924. The purse was boosted to $6,000 by stretching the number of places in the money from 21 to 30—though first place was still worth $1,000. The sectional qualifying rounds attracted 1,402 would-be champions, a record that was to stand until after World War II.

Gene Sarazen predicted no one would beat par of 288 for the four rounds, but he admitted that Snead's big game adapted well to Oakland Hills' broad acres and raised, table-top greens. In the first round Sam lived up to his notices with a fine 69, three under par, accomplished despite bogeys on the first two holes. That tied Sam for the lead with Denny Shute. The next day belonged to Jimmy Thomson who arrived at the 17th green needing only a par and a birdie for an incredible 64. Typically, Thomson missed a two-footer at 17 and another short putt on the 18th to finish with a 66. The sensation of the third round was little bandy-legged Bobby Cruickshank—the same straightshooter who had been Bobby Jones' playoff victim in 1923. Cruickshank shot a 67 that elevated him from fifteenth place to fourth place after 54 holes. Snead, meanwhile, had added 73 and 70 to his opening 69. That was good enough for a second place tie at 212 with Ralph Guldahl, one length behind Ed Dudley who held the lead with 211. On the final 18 Sam needed a 71 for a 283 and he got it. When Snead walked into the locker room, he was congratulated as the new champion. "Laddie," said Tommy Armour, "you've just won yourself the Open." Word came that Dudley and Thomson had passed out of the picture. Cruickshank was safely behind at 285. That left only Guldahl between Sam Snead and the remarkable feat of winning the U.S. Open on his first try.

But Guldahl, a husky, slope-shouldered Texan with

Classic rivals of the Golden Twenties. Bob Jones, the superb amateur, and Walter Hagen, the flamboyant professional, created excitement whenever they met. Hagen won the U.S. Open twice; Jones won it four times.

Swinging at Winged Foot in 1929, Bob Jones won his third U.S. Open by routing Al Espinosa by a margin of 23 strokes in their 36-hole playoff. The next year Jones executed his Grand Slam and, at age 28, retired from competition.

ABOVE. Five former Open champions are photographed together on the first day of the 1938 Open at Cherry Hills. From left they are Tommy Armour (who won in 1927), Billy Burke (1931), Olin Dutra (1934), Willie MacFarlane (1925) and Tony Manero (1936). BELOW. Ralph Guldahl—and everyone else —watches engrossed as Guldahl's approach shot flies toward the final green at Oakland Hills in 1937. Ralph got his par and defeated rookie Sam Snead by two strokes with a record score of 281.

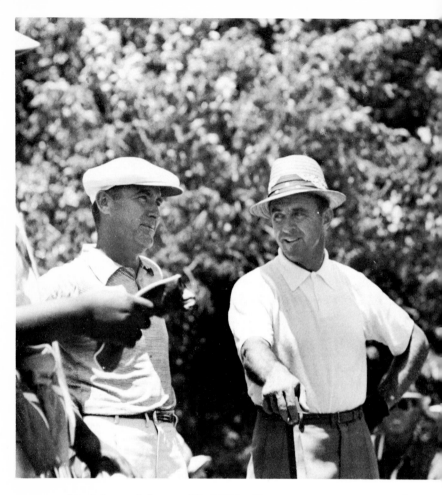

Rival titans of the post-World War II generation, Ben Hogan and Sam Snead were the focus of all attention when they played head to head, as they did in this round of the 1952 Open. Ben won the title four times. Sam never did. (*John Dominis—Life*)

tousled black hair and a somber countenance, was burning up the front nine. Starting out with the same score as Snead, Ralph had just missed birdies on the first four holes; then he holed a 50-footer for a birdie on the fifth. He took a weak bogey on the sixth and parred the seventh. On the eighth hole, a 491-yard par 5, Guldahl lay 65 yards from the pin after two wood shots. He chipped his next shot into the cup for a smashing eagle 3. On the ninth hole, a tricky 215-yard par 3, he reached the green with a two-iron and holed out from 25 feet for his birdie.

Having reached the turn in 33, Guldahl now could play the second nine in 37 strokes, one over par, and still defeat Snead. It was a fair test for any man who aspired to be champion, and at the 10th tee Guldahl said, "If I can't do it, I'm a bum and don't deserve to win the Open." But Guldahl lost one stroke to par on that hole and another on the 11th. All of a sudden he needed birdies to win. The crowd began to speak in whispers, as though anticipating a collapse. They remembered Oakmont in 1933 when Guldahl had gained nine strokes on Johnny Goodman only to miss the four-foot putt he needed for a tie on the final green. An even fresher memory was the 1937 Masters, played just two months earlier. Ralph appeared to have this one in the sack when he caught the water on two successive holes, thus losing six strokes and the title to Byron Nelson. But now Ralph Guldahl brought the gallery at Oakland Hills to life with a birdie 4 on the 555-yard 12th hole. He added another on the short 13th where he almost holed out his tee shot for an ace. After a routine par at the 14th hole, Guldahl got a break at the 15th. His approach shot went awry and was about to go into the deep rough when it struck the foot of a spectator and bounced instead into a smooth trap beside the green. A wedge and one putt from there and Guldahl had his par. Two more pars brought him to the final hole, a 537-yard par 5, two strokes up on Snead and needing only a bogey 6 to win. Feeling the pressure, Guldahl repeatedly stepped away from his ball; he wiped his hands on soiled trousers and peered at the murderous rough on his left as though if he stared at it long enough, it would go away. After several minutes of this he turned to his playing companion, Harry Cooper, and asked, "What should I do on this one?" Cooper responded, "Just don't drop dead."

Guldahl reached the green in three and got down in two safe putts for his par. He had played the last nine holes in 36 strokes for a 69. At 281 he had broken Tony Manero's Open scoring record, just 12 months old, by one stroke and defeated Snead, the precocious rookie, by two strokes. Snead, though he took the defeat graciously, was a severely let-down young man. One old pro observed, "He'll never be the same again."

Ralph Guldahl, as he walked across the green to make his final putt at Oakland Hills before an anxious gallery, had fished a small comb out of his trousers pocket and run it through his unruly hair. It was a characteristic gesture on Guldahl's part. "Combing my hair is part of the plan," he often explained. "Before an important shot I try to steady my nerves and slow down my breathing before I take my stance. That little pocket comb has saved me many a stabbed putt." But to many of the fans and some of the sportswriters who watched him, Guldahl's comb was a symbol of vanity and unconcern. When Walter Hagen came sailing home a winner, he could always be counted on to make some grand gesture. Even Tony Manero brandished his cap winningly in response to the applause. What did Guldahl do? He combed his hair for the cameramen.

This kind of misunderstanding was typical of Guldahl's career. By his background Ralph was every inch a man of the people and as a player he was a power hitter, courageous and willing to take a chance. But despite this he was slow to win his share of popular affection. Perhaps if that four-foot putt had dropped for him in 1933 at Oakmont, Guldahl's story would have been different. As it was the career of the big Norwegian ex-caddy from Dallas turned sour after his first near-miss at fame. For the next two years Ralph, with his wife LaVerne and their baby son, had struggled just to stay on the tour. They squeezed every dime, stayed in cheap rooming houses and piled onto all-night buses to get from one tournament town to the next. If Ralph appeared stolid and uncommunicative, it was because his only thought was to earn enough in today's tournament to get himself and his family to the next one. Finally Guldahl gave up. A budget cutback had cost him his job as a club professional in St. Louis. At one point he tried selling automobiles. But he sold just one—to himself. After the 1935 Open in which he shot a 318 and finished far out of the money, Guldahl loaded his family in the new car and headed to Los Angeles. There he picked up odd jobs as an assistant carpenter at the movie studios. For 1935 his total tournament winnings added up to $54.

By the spring of 1936 Guldahl's golf clubs were in hock. But his wife urged him to give the game another try. So did some friends at the Lakeside Club in Hollywood where Ralph was giving lessons. The friends offered to lend him enough money to make a new start. Meanwhile, Olin Dutra, the 1934 Open champion, had helped Ralph change his grip from palm to finger control, and after long hours of practice he was potentially a much-improved golfer over the Guldahl of 1933.

Ralph's first comeback appearance was the 1936 True Temper Open in Detroit. Playing with borrowed clubs, he finished sixth and collected $245, which looked to him like a million. Next stop was the Western Open in Davenport, Iowa. In the final round Ralph shot a gritty 64 to take the title away from Ray Mangrum. That was the turning point. Guldahl went on to win the Radix Cup for 1936 with a record low medal average of 71.63 shots per round. In the same competition a year before he had finished 45th. Ralph won two tournaments on the 1937 winter tour and finished second in the Masters before the strong finish that won him the Open at Oakland Hills. But to most people he was still that "other fellow" who had deprived Sam Snead, the new idol, of the championship. Guldahl has been called the "Depression champ," and perhaps he represented all too well a period that people desperately wanted to forget.

At any rate by 1938 Ralph had broken loose from his own economic depression. After winning $8,600 in purse money he had paid off his debts and had been hired as celebrity pro at the Miami-Biltmore in Florida and at Braidburn Country Club in New Jersey. Now his reputation for phlegmatic single-mindedness in tournament play actually started helping him. Players with more sensitive imaginations paused to worry, during their rounds, how the "dumb Swede" was doing. And sure enough, there came Guldahl, stalking them down the stretch. Guldahl could express his philosophy of the game in a single sentence. "All that matters in golf," he said, "is the next shot." That was a mouthful.

The Open championship never had been held west of Minneapolis. But golf was becoming more and more popular in the West and Southwest and in recognition of this the U.S.G.A. awarded the 1938 tournament to Denver. The club chosen for play was Cherry Hills, a young course and still pretty raw. Cherry Hills was selected because it had more parking space and roomier practice grounds than the swank Denver Country Club. Lawson Little, who had played Cherry Hills, figured that drives would carry farther than ever before in the rarefied Denver atmosphere, a mile above sea level, and predicted the Open scoring record would be lowered to 278 or less. But the tournament officials were counting on Cherry Hills' ribbon-thin fairways, heavy rough of alfalfa and dandelions and winding water hazards to guard the record. They were right. In the first round not a player scored in the 60's and only two, Henry Picard and Jimmy Hines with 70, were under par 71. Sam Snead's best round of the week was a 76. On the second day Picard, who had shared the favorite's role with Snead coming in, shot another 70 and led after 36 holes with 140. But on the final day Henry Picard folded with rounds of 77–78. Dick Metz of Chicago took over the lead after three rounds with a score of 211. That put him four big strokes up on Guldahl, the defending champion, who was second at 215 after rounds of 74–70–71. Every other contender had failed to get by the first three rounds without at least one bad score in the high 70's. Guldahl had run a 50-foot chip shot into the cup on the last hole of his third round to keep Metz's margin from being even larger than four strokes. As the final round began, Metz stumbled headlong onto a series of errors that melted his lead. Guldahl, playing directly behind Metz, stalked his man with four steady par 4's. At the 535-yard fifth hole Ralph rolled in a birdie putt for another 4 and pulled even with Metz. On the sixth hole, a mere 164 yards long, Metz took a 4 and Guldahl picked up a birdie 2 to take the lead for the first time. Metz never did get going and finished the round with a 79. Guldahl pulled farther and farther ahead as he rolled to a 69, the same fourth-round score he had won with the year before. This time, after starting the round four strokes behind, Ralph gained an astounding 10 strokes to defeat Metz by six, 284 to 290. It was the largest margin since 1921 when Jim Barnes had spread-eagled the field by nine strokes. And so to the exclusive roll of men who have won two consecutive Opens—Anderson, McDermott, Jones —was added the name of Ralph Guldahl.

History in reverse was made at Cherry Hills by a golfer named Ray Ainsley. Ainsley had shot a 76 on the first round, just two strokes behind defending champion Guldahl, and on the second day he was six over par when he reached the 397-yard 16th hole. On this hole a slender brook about five feet wide and two or three inches deep trickled close beside the green. Ainsley hit a good drive. Then he lofted a five-iron which hit the edge of the green but unfortunately spun back down into the water. It didn't look like too tough a shot, but after a couple of swipes Ainsley was wet all over and the ball was afloat—drifting slowly back toward the tee with the current. Now a large gallery that had been following Gene Sarazen along a parallel fairway came over to watch the fun. Ainsley stood in the stream, chopping away and then backing up to chop again. The scorekeeper stood over him like a referee, counting "seven, eight, nine." Finally the scorekeeper doubled up in laughter and he fell to the ground. Ainsley's playing partner, Bud McKinney, took up the count. McKinney had trouble keeping up because the unamused Ainsley wasted no time slashing away at the ball. Each time the ball would jump about a foot, then fall back into the stream. Soon the water got so muddy he could only guess where it was. At last the ball popped out onto dry land. By the time Ainsley holed out McKinney had counted 19 strokes and the unfortunate Ainsley went into the record book as the perpetrator of the worst single hole in the history of the Open. Several of the bystanders were sure they had counted more strokes, 22 or even 23. But somehow it didn't seem the time to quibble over a mere three or four strokes.

Guldahl could not keep on winning the Open forever and the man to beat him, obviously, would be Sam Snead. The popular mountain man had won $18,000 in P.G.A. purses in 1938, an all-time record, plus some pretty good extra pocket money by winning unofficial sweepstake matches and driving contests. In one well-publicized driving competition Sam averaged a mighty 307 yards for three drives. True, Guldahl had come from behind to give Sam another licking in the Masters of 1939. But all the best judges in the game—authorities like Jones, Ouimet, Hagen, Sarazen, and Grantland Rice—agreed that mechanically, at least, mankind had produced the perfect golfer in Sam Snead. Columnist Bob Considine wrote, "Sam is a greater driver than Jimmy Thomson, a better iron-player than Byron Nelson and a better putter than Horton Smith. He seems to have the perfect nervous system for golf, a hillbilly torpor, and the perfect lack of imagination—a helpful failing that makes it chemically impossible for him to imagine his ball coming to rest in a brook or trap."

For all this, Snead had somehow managed *not* to win a major championship in his short but meteoric career. But in the National Open of 1939, with just two holes left to play, this omission seemed about to be corrected. Defending champion Ralph Guldahl had played the sun-baked Spring Mill course of the Philadelphia Country Club in even 4's— 288—which was not nearly good enough to win. After 70 holes of sub-par golf Snead needed only pars on the two finishing holes for a 282, six strokes better than Guldahl and two strokes better than the 284 at which three players—Nelson, Wood and Shute—were tied for the early lead. Sam was a picture golfer in his sharply creased trousers, long-sleeved white shirt and soft hat with the brim turned down as protection from the sun. But Sam's game looked shaky as he bogeyed the 71st hole. His second putt from six feet away stopped a full foot shy of its goal. But never fear, a par 5 on the 558-yard last hole would crown Sam as the new champion. Even with a bogey 6 he would tie for low total.

But on the 18th tee something went wrong with the perfect Snead swing—too much right hand, perhaps—and Sam's drive hooked into the rough. Still a far piece from the green, Snead elected to play a brassie out of the trampled grass. It was a mistake. He pushed the shot into a bunker 100 yards short of the green. The smoldering volcano that is Snead's temper took control of him now. He swung; there rose a cloud of sand. But the ball rolled weakly across the trap. Sam swung again. This time the ball came out, but it hooked wide of the green. With his fifth shot Sam made the green. He putted once to three feet. He putted again. Then, before a gallery shocked into silence, he putted a third time.

Needing a 5 to win, Snead had taken an unforgettable 8. His 74–286 dropped him into fifth place.

Snead's demise was the most spectacular, but there were other heartbreaks that day at Spring Mill just as painful to the men who suffered them. Chicagoan Johnny Bulla moved close to the top with a third-round 68, then blew to a 76. Clayton Haefner, from Charlotte, North Carolina, one-time worker in a candy factory, was even more erratic. In the morning round Haefner shot a record-breaking 66. His afternoon score was 80. Marvin (Bud) Ward of Spokane, the strongest amateur player of the period, came down with a bad cold just before the final rounds and played in a heavy sweater despite the blistering heat. Ward needed only par on the final nine to win. But he came acropper at the short 11th hole, bouncing from one trap to another for a double bogey 5. He finished with 285, one stroke behind the leaders.

The blowups of Snead and the other unfortunates set up the first three-way playoff for the championship since the historic match in 1913 between Ouimet, Vardon and Ray. This time the protagonists were Craig Wood, a handsome 37-year-old New Yorker from the Winged Foot Club in Westchester; Byron Nelson, a moon-faced Texan, at 27 a superb technician and still not at his peak; and Denny Shute, a balding former British Open champion playing out of Huntington, West Virginia. Wood was advertised by the club manufacturer he worked for as "the man who can hit a brassie 300 yards." To earn his place in the playoff Craig did precisely that: he slammed his brassie second shot on the 558-yard final hole all the way to the green and got the birdie 4 he needed to tie. In the three-man playoff next day Denny Shute fell by the wayside early, shooting a 76. When the threesome came once more to the fateful 18th hole, Wood was leading Nelson by a stroke. But this time Craig hooked his brassie second shot. The ball struck a spectator named Robert Mossman on the head and knocked him unconscious. State troopers picked up the stricken Mossman and carried him, bleeding and still out cold, across the fairway directly in front of Wood. Craig was visibly upset and asked aloud, "What have I done?" Mossman soon recovered. But Wood did not, or at least not quickly enough to clinch his victory. Wood's next shot was over the pin. Coming back he missed an eight-foot putt but tapped the next one in for a par. Nelson, meanwhile, ticked off a birdie 4 that earned him another tie with Wood at 68.

The next day the two played again and the match was all Nelson. Byron was the son of a Fort Worth, Texas, feed merchant, and he had won the first important playoff of his career back in 1927 when both he and his opponent, a tough little guy named Ben Hogan, were 15 years old. The caddy championship of Glen Garden Country Club had been at stake in that match, and Nelson, winner by a stroke, had taken home a brand new midiron as his prize. Some lean years followed after Byron turned pro in 1930, but now he was an established star—winner of the Masters in 1937 and acknowledged as a nearly perfect shot with the tricky long irons.

On the fourth hole of the second playoff Nelson hit a long iron shot that *was* perfect. Using a one-iron, the most difficult club in the bag, Byron rifled his second shot 210 yards to the green. The ball rolled up to the hole and lodged between the flagstick and the rim of the cup for an eagle 2. After watching that magnificent shot, Craig Wood never got going and Nelson won the playoff and the title, 70 to 73.

The outbreak of war in Europe failed to dampen the enthusiasm for sports in the United States. Golf in particular was riding the crest of a period of expansion and as 1940 began the tournament scene was infused by a cadre of exciting new players who had both personal color and extraordinary skill. Many of them were Texans. Apple-cheeked Jimmy Demaret, for instance. Jimmy appeared on the links dressed like two rainbows competing with each other for attention, but he won half the tournaments on the winter-spring circuit of 1940 including the first of his three Masters championships. Even more consistent was bantam-weight Ben Hogan. Ben spent more time on the practice tee than any two of his colleagues put together—he actually seemed to *enjoy* practicing right through to sundown. In 1940 Bantam Ben started off on a streak of 56 straight tournaments in which he finished in the money every time.

Byron Nelson came prepared to defend his Open title when the field of 165 gathered in early June, 1940, at the Canterbury Golf Club outside Cleveland, but even Lord Byron took a back seat in the betting to the people's perennial choice, Sam Snead.

On the first day Sam defied the tricky winds off Lake Erie and made the dog-tiring trek over Canterbury's links in 67 strokes, the lowest opening-round score that had ever been shot in the Open. Maybe this would be the year Snead would overcome his U.S. Open jitters. Sam shot a 74 on the second round but retained a share of the lead along with lanky Horton Smith and beefy Lawson Little—all three tied at 141. Hogan, Nelson, Guldahl and Mangrum were bunched close behind. Also close was an old familiar hand, Gene Sarazen.

A storm moved in off the lake as the players hustled through their two last rounds. Horton Smith was making his last serious bid for a national championship. But he faded to a 78 on the third round and even a sterling final round of 69 earned him no better than third place. Snead and Little matched 73's on the third round to maintain their lead. Of the others only Sarazen, with a 70, gained enough ground to be a serious threat. Little, a bullnecked and broad-shouldered graduate of Stanford University, had won only two tournaments in the four years since he had turned pro. But in the wind and rain at Canterbury he discovered anew the mastery with which he had won the U.S. Amateur and British Amateur in 1934 and again in 1935. Lawson posted another 73 for 287 and stood by to see if anyone could match his score. Snead certainly couldn't. Needing a 72 to win, Sam shot a disastrous 81 and finished back in the pack with 295.

But Sarazen was yet to be heard from. It had been 18 years since Gene's first victory in the Open and eight years since his last. But here he came, nonchalantly plodding along on those familiar piano legs, still wearing the old-fashioned plus-fours and using a 40-year-old hickory putter. Sarazen needed a two-under-par 34 on the last nine to tie Little. He gave it all he had in a stretch finish every bit as exciting as the ones he had put on at Skokie in 1920 and at Fresh Meadow in 1932. This time Gene did not win but got the 34 he needed to tie.

The tournament would have ended in a triple tie except for an unusual incident. With the storm brewing, six players had started their final rounds half an hour ahead of schedule. For this infraction of the rules they were eventually disqualified. But before the ruling was handed down, the six played out the round provisionally, and one of them, Ed (Porky) Oliver, made an unofficial 287, which would have tied for first place.

As it was, the 18-hole playoff the next day paired Sarazen, who was then 38 years old, and Little, who was 29. Earlier in the week Sarazen had predicted that no man over 35 had any business winning the U.S. Open, and in the playoff the difference in age finally told: Little defeated Sarazen by three strokes, 70 to 73.

On the morning of May 22, 1941, Craig Wood was preparing to shave as usual. As he reached in the cabinet for his razor, an excruciating pain seared through his back. Craig had suffered a severe muscle spasm, as the doctor later explained it to him, in the lumbro-sacral region near the fifth vertebra. Back trouble was nothing new to Wood. In fact he could trace the intermittent pains back nine years to an automobile accident. During one tournament round in 1936 he had reached into the cup at the 18th hole to retrieve his ball and found he could not straighten up again. But after heat treatments and a night's rest Wood stayed in that tournament and won it. In a durable career that dated back to the Kentucky Open of 1925, Wood had won a fair share of tournaments, 17 in all. But he was far better known for the tournaments he had *lost*. At one time or another every one of the four major championships had slipped from his grasp:

The U.S. Open in 1939 when Nelson outlasted him in the playoff;

The Masters of 1935 when Sarazen fired his historic double eagle;

The British Open of 1933 when Denny Shute defeated him in a 36-hole playoff;

And the P.G.A. of 1934 when he reached the finals before losing to Paul Runyan.

All those near-misses were enough to discourage most fellows. But Wood had accepted each disappointment with such grace and philosophical calm that he had earned a special place in the hearts of the golfing public—even if they did call him America's No. 1 runner-up. Finally the tables turned. In April, 1941, Craig won his first big championship, the Masters, by outshooting Byron Nelson on the final nine holes. Wood was almost 40 years old by now and his days as a competitive athlete were fast running out. But this could be his year. What a time for that ornery back to act up again, just 14 days before the Open. But no matter, Craig would play anyway. He had his doctor fit him with a heavy and involved corset belt. When Craig tried to hit the ball while wearing the belt, he felt stiff and restricted. But when he took it off, the pain was so sharp he could not play at all. So back on went the corset and off went Wood to the U.S. Open at Fort Worth, Texas.

Never before had the national championship been held south of the Mason-Dixon Line. But Texans were clamoring to see their homegrown heroes: Guldahl, Nelson, Demaret, Hogan, Cooper and the Mangrum brothers. So when millionaire Marvin Leonard, who owned the biggest department store in Fort Worth, offered a $25,000 guarantee, the U.S.G.A. prudently decided it was time the Open be held in Texas. The course chosen was the new Colonial Club, barely five years old and hardly prepared to be the site of a major tournament. A 7,000-yard par 70 course, Colonial's narrow fairways were bordered by swamps, ravines and groves of pecan trees. The chocolate-colored Trinity River meandered over the course. Two of the 18 holes were being played for the first time. The tough Bermuda grass was an annoying novelty to many of the 163 players in the starting field. To add to their troubles, several days of rain had turned the course into a quagmire. The ground was not porous enough to drain quickly and the downpour made puddles of the greens and muddy seas of the fairways. To top if off the rain had brought out chiggers—those pesky little red bugs that burrow into human flesh and start an itch that is worse than a mosquito bite.

Under these conditions—and with both the fans and the gamblers making the two hometown boys, Hogan and Nelson, heavy favorites—many a Northerner in the field wondered why ever he had come. But on the first day of play under a blazing sun, the only player hot enough to crack par was no Texan but Denny Shute, who was then playing out of Chicago. Behind Shute's 69, Nelson shot a 73, Hogan 74, Demaret 75, Guldahl 79. Craig Wood, corset and all, had a respectable 73. On the second day play was held up for an hour by a rain and lightning storm that sent the gallery of 10,000 stampeding for shelter. When the last bedraggled, drenched and mud-caked player turned in his card at dusk, Craig Wood had proved to be the best mudder of the lot. By shooting a 71 he had moved into a tie with Denny Shute for the lead at 144.

For the 36-hole final next day the thermometer climbed to

95 degrees. But the non-Texans did not wilt. Hogan did fire
a 68 in the morning round, but could gain only two strokes
on Wood who fashioned a smooth par 70. That put Craig
two strokes up on Shute, his nearest competitor, who shot a
72. Under the scorching afternoon sun, Wood finished with
another 70. Middle-aged, tired and still encased in the un-
comfortable corset, Craig climaxed his round with a flourish.
On the 72nd hole he smacked out his best drive of the
tournament, lofted a seven-iron to the green and rolled home
an 18-foot putt for his birdie 3. There was no last-minute
challenge. Wood's 284 was good for a clear-cut triumph,
three strokes better than Shute and five strokes better than
third-place Ben Hogan, who finished first among the Texans.

CHAPTER SIX

The Wartime Heroes

After Pearl Harbor, world war once again forced suspension of the Open. Craig Wood, as the active champion for the duration, wore his crown for five years—long enough to wipe out the memory of his earlier years as a perennial runner-up. Originally the Open for 1942 was to be played at the Interlachen Country Club in Minneapolis. Instead, the U.S.G.A., the P.G.A. and the Chicago District Golf Association combined their resources to stage a tournament called the Hale America Open at Ridgemoor Country Club in Chicago. Part of the $6,000 prize money was awarded in the form of defense bonds and the net earnings of the tournament, which amounted to $25,000, were divided between the U.S.O. and Navy Relief. Captain Bob Jones of the United States Army came out of retirement to play and scored 290. It was an admirable performance but not enough to put Bobby in serious contention among the 96 starters who had been culled from a field of 1,540 entries. Ben Hogan, who was enjoying his third straight season as the leading money-winner among the pros, put his personal brand on the title in the second round as he turned in a fantastic 62. Hogan's 271 total for four rounds was three strokes better than the two runners-up, Jimmy Demaret and Mike Turnesa.

The Hale America was held only once. By 1943 most of the name golfers were in uniform. Porky Oliver, drafted early in 1941, had been first to go. Hogan and Horton Smith enrolled in officers' training school and found themselves in the ironic position of spending many hours on the familiar Miami Bayshore golf course which had been converted into a drill field for the troops. Sam Snead, having finally won a major title, the 1942 P.G.A., joined the Navy. So did Lawson Little and Jimmy Demaret. Jimmy Thomson went into the Coast Guard. Lloyd Mangrum, one of a dozen or more pros who served in the Army, was wounded twice in the Battle of the Bulge.

The Marines turned down Craig Wood because of his bad back. Byron Nelson was rejected by the services because he suffered from hemophilia. So Byron stayed home and became his country's outstanding athlete of the war years. Nelson and his "Gold Dust" twin, Jug McSpaden (who was 4-F with sinusitis), turned the golf tour into a two-man show. Along the way they raised thousands of dollars for war relief. In both 1944 and 1945 the Associated Press voted Nelson athlete of the year. In 1945 alone he won 19 tournaments, including one unparalleled streak of 13 victories in a row. The wartime competition was not always the best, but par was as tough an opponent as ever and against par Nelson was superb. In 1945 his stroke average for 120 rounds was a brilliant 68.33.

By late 1945 Snead, Hogan and some of the other familiar faces were turning up again on the tour along with a whole new generation of golfing ex-G.I.'s. All of them were eager and determined to make up for lost time and to build a name for themselves. By June, 1946, when the U.S. Open was resumed after a lapse of five years, the postwar golf boom was underway. In 1936 the touring pros had played 22 official tournaments a year for total prize money of $100,000. Now the tour lasted for 45 weeks, and, with tournament director Fred Corcoran demanding and getting a $10,000 minimum, the prize money for P.G.A. events surpassed $500,000. The U.S.G.A. boosted its Open purse to $8,000. The winner's end was increased to $1,500. But that was only the start. Because of the prestige of the tournament, it was estimated that victory in the U.S. Open was worth another $50,000 in exhibition fees and commercial endorsements.

A tense and unusually talented field of 170 gathered at Canterbury in Cleveland to contend for the honor of becoming the first postwar champion. The cofavorites, as they had been in every tournament that year, were Nelson and Hogan. The rivalry between Byron and Ben dated from their caddy days at Glen Garden in Fort Worth. By now it had become a majestic and not always friendly duel for pre-eminence. Nelson in 1945 had won a record $66,000 in defense bonds (cash value: about $50,000). Hogan, who had dominated the money lists before the war although he had yet to win a major title, was doggedly determined to prove himself better than Byron. The tour carried their duel across the breadth of the country. First one man gained the edge, then the other, until most observers had to admit the two great players were at a standoff. The crowds loved it. Hogan and Nelson, along with Sam Snead, attracted large and partisan galleries wherever they played.

The largest Open crowds in history turned up at Canterbury to watch Snead shoot an opening day round of 69, three under par on the 6,900-yard course. But once more Snead faded out of contention with subsequent rounds of 75 and two 74's. Vic Ghezzi, an ex-G.I. from Knoxville, Tennessee, and California's Lawson Little, who had won at Canterbury in 1941, shot 69's on the second day. Ben Hogan topped them with 68. Nelson made his move on the third round, shooting a 69 that put him in front of the pack with

211. He did it despite a penalty stroke incurred when his caddy accidentally kicked his ball into the swirling crowd. Lloyd Mangrum put together a 68 to move into second place, one stroke behind Nelson. As the field came down the stretch, only four strokes separated the first dozen players. Nine men were under par for the tournament, more par-busters than ever before in an Open. Vic Ghezzi finished early and set the mark for the others to shoot at: a 4-under-par 284. Both Nelson and Mangrum, playing together, were in position to beat Ghezzi's score. Nelson needed only three finishing pars to go ahead by two strokes. But Byron three-putted the 71st green and took a disappointing 6 on the 72nd hole to tie Ghezzi at 284. Mangrum shot a 72 and made it a three-way tie. Herman Barron, Jimmy Demaret and Dick Metz each played his last round in the 60's but couldn't quite catch the leaders. Then came Hogan, gunning hard and looking like a winner. Ben needed just three pars for a winning 283, but his putter turned cold and he failed even to get a tie. By missing a two-foot putt on the 72nd green Hogan missed the playoff by a stroke.

Next day Nelson, Ghezzi and Mangrum teed off for a tight-lipped extra 18 holes to resolve their tie. Mangrum, wounded at the Battle of the Bulge and holder of the Purple Heart, was golf's most celebrated war hero, although at 31 he had never won a major tournament.

Now Lloyd sprinted out to a four-stroke lead. But Nelson and Ghezzi whittled it down, and at the end of 18 holes all three were tied again with 72's. Once more the trio teed off for another full round, and this time Mangrum fell behind. With six holes to play he trailed Ghezzi by three strokes and Nelson by two. It was a time for birdies, and Mangrum found them. Lloyd birdied three of the final six holes despite a sharp thunderstorm that lashed the course as the tired threesome trudged down Canterbury's closing holes for the sixth time in four days. Mangrum scored a 72, his third 72 in a row, to defeat Nelson and Ghezzi by one stroke and become golf's first postwar champion.

Two months after the 1946 Open Byron Nelson declared he had a stomachful of full-time competitive golf and retired from the game. He was 34 years old.

Legions of fans love Sam Snead as much for his weaknesses as for his great talent. Perfection alone is not always much fun to watch, but if Sam is anything, he is human, and therefore imperfect. For three decades the cash customers have shoved each other and stretched their necks to watch Sam hit awesome drives and precise iron shots with his fluid, bred-in-the-cow-pasture swing. Then the fans stampede to the green. There they cheer for Sam, but secretly they are hoping for a glimpse of the great man in one of his moments of mortality: missing a dead cinch two-foot putt.

In 1947 Snead played the tournament that stamped him once and for all as the man who cannot win the Open. It had been a full 10 years since Sam had first come out of the Virginia hills to take the pro tour by storm. When the elite field of 164 gathered for the Open at the St. Louis Country Club, Sam was the current British Open champion, a title he had won the previous summer on his first try. But for one reason or another, Snead was in a grumpy mood as the tournament began. Talking to a reporter in the clubhouse as he scooped into an ice cream sundae, Snead said, "If I had another $100,000 in the bank, I'd give my clubs away. I'd stuff that golf bag over the caddy's head. Got no urge to play golf anymore." Sam may have been feeling blue because he had passed his 35th birthday just a month before. More likely he was goading himself into a proper fighting mood to take on the challenging grind offered by the St. Louis course: par 71, 6,532 yards closely bordered by bristling, ankle-high rough.

For the second year in a row the Open purse had been

increased, first prize to $2,000 and the total for the low 30 professionals to $10,000. A new championship trophy was at stake. During the winter the original cup had been destroyed by a fire that razed the clubhouse at Tam O'Shanter in Chicago where Champion Lloyd Mangrum was the club professional.

Snead apparently wasn't grim enough on opening day. He shot a 72, but eight other players shot in the 60's. A 70 on the second round brought Sam closer to the top. Dick Metz and Chick Harbert shared the 36-hole lead at 139. The third round produced some wild scoring. James B. McHale, Jr., an amateur from Whitemarsh Country Club in Pennsylvania, set a new 18-hole record for the Open when he played the course in 30–35–65. But that was McHale's only round under par; he finished far back in a tie for 24th place. One of those who tied McHale was Lloyd Mangrum, the defending champion. Mangrum had opened with a 77 and never really got into the fight.

Both the 36-hole leaders collapsed in the third round, Metz with a 78 and Harbert with an 81. Another 70 brought Snead into the clubhouse for lunch just one stroke off the pace. The new leader, at 211, was Lew Worsham, a sandy-haired 29-year-old pro from Washington, D.C. Bracketed with Snead at 212 was Bobby Locke, a South African visitor who wore knickers and could do wonderful things with his old wooden-shafted putter. Locke had arrived in America just two months before and was enjoying an eminently successful tour which would earn him $20,000 in purses before the summer was out.

Like Snead, Lew Worsham had been a sailor in World War II. Lew was a popular player but quite nervous. He had brought his wife with him to the tournament from Washington but instructed her to stay in the clubhouse while he played. Chainsmoking two cigarets a hole, Worsham had been remarkably consistent in the first three rounds with scores of 70, 70 and 71. In the final round Lew remained just as steady. At the 71st hole he faltered momentarily for a bogey. But he spit on his hands and, with newsreel cameras grinding in his ear, finished with a par. That gave him a 2-under-par 282 for the 72 holes. Worsham went off to the locker room for a beer and a wait.

Locke turned into the last nine holes needing even par to tie Worsham. But Bobby lost one stroke to par at the 10th hole and two more at 13 and 14. He finished three strokes arrears at 285.

Meanwhile, Snead was hanging on grimly—even par after 17 holes. To match Worsham's 282 he needed a birdie 3 on the 18th hole. Sam drove and pitched and still had an 18-foot putt to go. A gallery of 3,000, augmented for the first time by a local television audience, watched Sam pluck a leaf from the turf, then squat to survey the roll of the green. Finally, Snead putted. His ball rolled up to the cup and plunked in for the tying bird. The gallery shouted its pleasure and Snead grinned. This time things were going to be different.

For the fourth time in the past five Opens the championship went into a playoff round. For 17 tense holes Worsham and Snead were perfectly matched. All even. Their drives on the 18th were twin jewels, 260 yards apiece. Both men pitched up to within 25 feet on the pin, though Worsham was just off the green. Lew shot first; his ball rimmed the right edge of the cup and popped out. Snead's first putt stopped short, about the same distance from the cup as Worsham's. Sam prepared to putt again, but Worsham interrupted him and asked for a measurement. Whose ball was away? U.S.G.A. referee Ike Grainger measured the two balls. Snead was away, all right, precisely 30½ inches away from the hole to 29 inches for Worsham. The interruption over, Snead bent over his ball once more to putt. He stroked it quickly, not stopping to read the green. The ball missed the cup by two inches. Then Worsham stepped up and calmly tapped his ball in to win the playoff, 69 to 70.

A hero's welcome awaited Worsham at home. Official Washington met his train at Union Station and swept him in a parade to an honors ceremony on the front steps of the District of Columbia building. Among the gifts bestowed on the new hero was a Cadillac automobile.

Back in Bath County, Virginia, a snakebit Sam Snead still felt like stuffing his golf bag over somebody's head.

CHAPTER SEVEN

The Hogan Years

Ben Hogan was a hard man, hard mostly on himself. He was wholly devoted to making himself the most nearly perfect golfer of all time, and he succeeded. Hogan's swing was not naturally flawless like Snead's but was a manufactured article welded during countless hours of practice. Hogan had hit more golf shots than any man who ever lived. Until he came along, the tedium of hitting practice shots was anathema to professionals and duffers alike. But by his example Hogan made the practice tee the most "in" place in golf. Ben was not a rude man, nor without human qualities. In fact, the young pros who have received a friendly tip or an unpublicized helping hand from Hogan regard him as practically a god. But if his dedication to the game left little time for levity or personal indulgence, so be it. Championship golf had changed since the heyday of Walter Hagen when a pro played in about 15 tournaments a year. By now it was a year-around business and the potential rewards were great. Golfers who survived in the big time were mostly a businesslike gang who lived a life of tense desperation from hole to hole and tourney to tourney.

Ben was born in Dublin, Texas, the son of a blacksmith

who died when Ben was nine years old. When he was 12, his mother moved the family to Fort Worth and Ben got himself a job caddying at Glen Garden Country Club for 65 cents a round. For Hogan good things always came the slow and hard way. Caddy yard law at Glen Garden dictated that a new boy had to fight with his fists for his right to work there. Little Ben passed that test. Ben was a natural left-hander, but when he decided to learn golf himself, the only second-hand clubs available were right-handed. So young Hogan turned himself into a right-hander. Later when several of his teenage contemporaries, fellows like Guldahl and Nelson, were sweeping the Texas amateur tournaments with brilliant scores in the 60's, Ben was still struggling to break 80. In his early starvation years on the tournament circuit Hogan showed so little promise that people wondered how long he could stay with it and why he bothered at all. In the late 1930's when Guldahl and Nelson were winning their Opens, Ben was just beginning to climb to fame. But success could not escape forever from Hogan's relentless pursuit. After one early tournament round in which he had shot a 66, Ben went off to the practice tee and was still there hitting away at dusk when his friend Jimmy Demaret found him. "Ben, you had eight birdies today," said Demaret. "What are you trying to do?"

Hogan replied in all seriousness, "Jimmy, there is no good reason why you shouldn't get a birdie on every hole."

That, in one breath, was the philosophy of Ben Hogan. Except, of course, on holes where he had a chance for an eagle.

By 1948 Ben had won a potful of money but not a single major title had come his way. In May of that year he captured the P.G.A., but the long week of match play seemed to have worn him out. "I want to die an old man, not a young one," he told a reporter. Indeed, the little 137-pounder was no longer young. He had recently crossed to the shady side of 35 and a full dozen years had passed since he had qualified to play in his first United States Open. But the 1948 championship was to be played at the Riviera Country Club in Los Angeles, a 7,020-yard course made to order for Hogan's long shots and uncanny accuracy. Ben had won the Los Angeles Open at Riviera in 1947 and again in 1948, and his colleagues dubbed the place "Hogan's Alley." Hogan insisted, "There is no such thing as a course that fits a man's playing style." But the psychological edge was there anyway, and Hogan was easily the favorite in the field of 171 who had qualified for the Open from a record entry of 1,411.

Ben opened up with a 67, four under par. So did Lew Worsham, the defending champion, and this pair shared the first-day lead. Carefully, before each shot, Hogan would play it in his mind in order to get the tempo of the stroke. In effect he was rehearsing the shot before he hit the ball. He called it "muscle memory." On the second day a pair of runaway dogs joined the big Hogan gallery and went around the course yapping at Ben's heels. The tournament committee eventually managed to enforce the no-dog rule, but Ben shot a 72 and found himself in a second-place tie with Bobby Locke, the South African who had returned to the United States to make another haul of Yankee gold. In first place by one stroke after shooting a pair of 69's was none other than Samuel Jackson Snead. Sam's 138 was a new record for the halfway mark of the tournament. But by now it was taken for granted that something would happen somehow to keep Snead from winning, and sure enough, something did. Sam's putter cooled off and he finished with 73–72–283, good enough for fifth place but far off the winning pace. That pace was being set by Hogan. Ben turned Riviera in to his "alley" again with a 68 and fought his way back into the lead after 54 holes at 207. Jimmy Demaret matched Ben's 68 with one of his own but still trailed Hogan by two strokes. Hogan started his final round with a birdie and finished it by sinking a six-footer for another birdie and a 69. Demaret also had 69 but could gain no ground at all. Hogan's total of 276 sliced five strokes off Ralph Guldahl's 11-year-old scoring record for the Open. Demaret, second at 278, and Jim Turnesa, who was third at 280, also bettered the old record. Hogan's 276 was eight strokes below par for the four rounds, also a record. Ben had not birdied every hole. "Maybe next time."

There almost never was a next time. On the morning of February 2, 1949, Hogan and his wife Valerie were driving their Cadillac across western Texas. Ben had started the new winter tour by winning two of the first four events. In the Phoenix Open, just ended, Demaret had beaten him in a playoff for first place. Now the Hogans were heading home to Fort Worth for a few weeks of rest before picking up the tour again. On the highway near the crossroads town of Van Horn a Greyhound bus roared out of the morning haze and smashed head-on into the Hogans' car. In the crash Ben suffered grave injury: a double fracture of the pelvis, a fractured collarbone, a broken left ankle and a broken right rib. He was hospitalized in El Paso. A month after the accident his already serious condition took a turn for the worse. Phlebitis was causing blood clots in Hogan's legs. To halt the phlebitis doctors performed a two-hour abdominal operation on Ben and tied off the principal veins in his legs. The operation saved Hogan's life. But now there was no chance of Ben's being physically able to defend his Open championship. When the pros gathered in June, 1949, in suburban Chicago to challenge the Medinah Country Club's awesome No. 3 course, Hogan was at home recuperating and wondering if he would ever walk normally again.

The absence of Hogan at Medinah created a void, and into it stepped Cary Middlecoff, a lanky young Southerner who was rising fast into the first rank of golf talent. Cary was a refugee from a dentist's office. He had graduated from dental school in 1944 and went directly into the Army Medical Corps. "I'll bet I pulled 7,000 teeth," he later joked, "before I discovered the Army had another dentist." The Army experience was enough dentistry for Middlecoff, and after his discharge he turned seriously to golf, a game he had played with relish since the age of seven. Cary's father, who was a practicing dentist in Memphis, wanted his son to remain an amateur. He asked Bobby Jones to try to persuade Cary not to turn pro. Jones tried but to no avail, and in 1947 Middlecoff *fils* turned down a place on the Walker Cup team and gave up his amateur standing to join the pro tour.

Cary was a nervous player, an awful fidgeter. Until Jack Nicklaus came along he was probably the slowest player on the circuit. But when Cary had a hot streak going, particularly with his irons, he was a match for anybody. On the first day at Medinah Middlecoff shot a commonplace 75. But the course wasn't giving anything to anyone, and only one player broke 70. Next day Middlecoff got a hot streak going and put together a 67, which brought him up to a tie for second place. The following morning Cary was still hot, and a 69 in the third round put him out in front for the first time. In the afternoon round the strain started to tell on the 28-year-old dentist who had been a pro just two years. Clayton Haefner, a veteran from North Carolina who started the last round three shots arrears, caught Middlecoff, and the two battled through the back nine together. Haefner bogeyed the 15th hole and fell behind as Middlecoff got his par. Clayton had a putt for a birdie on the 72nd green but missed and finished with a 73 for 287. A 75 gave Middlecoff 286, two over par but one up on Haefner. The last threat to Cary's victory came from Sam Snead, who turned into the last nine needing a 33 to tie. The inevitable happened. Sam shot the birdies he needed to catch up. But on the short 17th hole his tee shot landed just off the green, and he took three strokes to get down from there. That bogey relegated

Sam to a second-place tie with Haefner. Hogan might be missing, but some things in golf never changed.

By 1950, miraculously, Hogan had returned. During the 16 months since his accident Ben had successfully completed a tedious and often painful convalescence: learning how to walk again by doing "laps" around his living room; the first shaky venture outdoors in April; gripping a golf club for the first time in August; then playing an actual round in December with his legs encased from ankle to thigh in elastic bandages. The golf world held its breath in January when Ben returned to competition for the first time in the Los Angeles Open at Riviera. The little man trudged down Hogan's Alley to a first-round 73 and followed up with three straight 69's for a stunning 280. It mattered little that Sam Snead sank birdies on the last two holes to tie Hogan and later beat him in a playoff. Hogan was back.

By June Ben had won one tournament. Fittingly, he won it on Snead's home course at White Sulphur Springs with a ridiculously low score of 259, which equaled the world record for 72 holes on a regulation course. But the pain in Hogan's legs still showed in his walk, and in the late rounds of a tournament his game obviously suffered from exhaustion. On the final day of the Open Hogan, for the first time, would have to ask his aching body to hold up for 36 holes. The betting was he couldn't make it.

This was the Golden Anniversary Open—the 50th renewal of the tournament—over the east course of the Merion Cricket Club near Philadelphia, a 6,696-yard par 70 layout noted for twisting fairways and greens as slick as skating ponds. Prize money had been increased to $15,000. First place was worth $4,000, and every professional who finished the 72 holes was assured of at least $100. In the opening round Lee Mackey, Jr., an unemployed pro from Birmingham, Alabama, set a new single round scoring record with a 33–31–64. Hogan had 72. The fans suddenly discovered

Mackey the next day and, unaccustomed as he was to public attention, the gallery finished him. He shot an 81 and finished eventually in 25th place with 297. Mackey wasn't the only one to blow. Sam Snead lost stroke after stroke on the greens and moaned, "I'm puttin' as though both my arms were broke." Hogan improved his position with a second-round 69, one under par. On the eve of the final 36 Ben was in the classic position to attack, two strokes behind the leader, E. J. (Dutch) Harrison, the old Arkansas Traveler. Ben started the long grind at a slow pace, limping noticeably on his left leg. But once Hogan poised over his ball his game was as strong as it had ever been. In fact, some observers thought it was better. Ben seemed to be able to "think" the ball right to where he wanted it almost every time. In the morning Hogan's 71 caught Harrison at 212. But now Lloyd Mangrum had taken a one-shot lead with a 69 for 211, and two other contenders, Cary Middlecoff and Johnny Palmer, were bracketed with Hogan and Harrison at 212. It looked like a stampede finish, but in the afternoon inflation struck the leaders' scores. Middlecoff and Palmer got away poorly and soon eliminated themselves with 79's. George Fazio from Washington, D.C., a former Canadian Open champion, came in early with a 70 for 287. As the afternoon wore on, Fazio's mark became increasingly more impressive. Then Mangrum shot a 76, just enough to tie for the lead. Dutch Harrison also shot a 76, but for him it was one shot too many and he finished at 288.

Hogan reached the 12th hole one over par for the round. If he could manage to play the last seven holes in two over par, the Open would be his. But Ben lost a stroke to par at the 12th when his approach bounced over the green and he missed a five-foot putt coming back. At the 15th green he missed another putt of two-and-a-half feet for his par. Now he must get home in par to win. Ben survived No. 16, the notorious Quarry Hole, a 445-yard par 4 on which the straight route to the green carries over a wide and deep sand quarry. The 17th was a long par 3. Hogan's tee shot reached a trap at the upper left-hand corner of the green. He pitched to within five feet of the cup, only to miss still another short putt. It was his third bogey in six holes. Now if Hogan were going to tie Fazio and Mangrum, a par was required, and par 4 on Merion's 458-yard finishing hole is far from automatic even if the player is not handicapped by exhaustion and by being the center of attraction for 8,000 excited spectators. Hogan hit a long drive on eighteen, then laced a two-iron pin high and 40 feet from the flag. He rolled his first putt about a yard past the hole, then stroked the second one in. Hogan had tied for first place. It was the 18th tie and the sixth triple tie in 50 Open championships.

Before the tournament Lloyd Mangrum had told reporters, "That little man is the only one in golf I've ever been afraid of." In the playoff Hogan confirmed Mangrum's fears. Playing flawless golf, Ben reached the 16th green one stroke up on Mangrum and three strokes better than Fazio. Mangrum, lying 3 about 12 feet from the cup, picked up his ball before he putted and blew off a bug that was crawling on it. Under the rules, lifting the ball to clean it was not permitted on this playoff round, and the U.S.G.A. officials had no choice but to call a two-stroke penalty on Mangrum. That tough break for Mangrum gave Hogan a commanding lead. But on the 17th hole Ben applied his own clincher by sinking a putt from 50 feet for a birdie deuce. That brought Hogan in at 69, four shots better than Mangrum and six ahead of Fazio. The Hawk was back and now there would be no stopping him.

The next challenge to Hogan's progress came not from any human foe but from a most inhuman one. The 1951 Open would be played once more at Oakland Hills outside Detroit. To an earlier generation of players the course had been a terribly hard test of skill. In the 1924 Open at Oakland Hills Cyril Walker had been the only man in the field to break 300, but by 1951 the tournament committee realized that the hazards of the course had grown obsolete. To correct this situation—to give par some meaning again— they hired Robert Trent Jones, the ranking golf architect, to remodel the course. Jones realized that the bunkers which once guarded Oakland Hills' fairways 200 to 220 yards from the tees no longer were much of a threat to the long-hitting pros. He ordered some of the old bunkers removed and built new ones—66 new bunkers in all—farther down the fairways. The fairways themselves were narrowed, particularly in the "landing area," where most of the drives could be expected to fall. Jones made the landing area a target not much broader than the length of a couple of billiard tables. The greens, apparently innocent enough at first glance, were sloped and contoured to have a "wrong side"—one that could cost the player a stroke if he approached from any angle but the correct one. As a finishing touch architect Jones reduced par on the 6,927-yard course from 72 to 70. The anguished howls of the pros when they got their first look at the revamped course could be heard clear to Canada across the river. There was no doubt that Oakland Hills in 1951 was one of the severest tests of a golfer's judgment, courage and skill that had ever been devised. In short, it was murder.

Hogan arrived on the scene early, fresh from winning his first Masters title in April and determined to add a third U.S. Open to his growing collection. Success had failed to take the edge off Ben's competitive urge. In five days of practice Hogan mentally photographed the course. He had become known as "the thinking man's golfer," and he was proud of the monicker. But when the tournament started, Ben made an error in judgment on the very first hole. After hesitating between a two- and three-iron for his second shot, Hogan settled on the two-iron and hit his approach 10 yards over the green. "Bad thinking," he muttered. By sundown Ben had made five more errors and had turned in a dismal 76 that put him in a tie for 41st place. "Stupidest round of golf I ever played," said Ben. But the course had beaten everybody that day. In the field of 162 not a player had matched par 70, and Sam Snead, holding first place with a 71, was only five strokes up on Hogan. Next day for the umpteenth time Snead blew his golden opportunity with a 78. Hogan improved somewhat with a 73, but at the halfway mark he still lagged five shots behind the new leader, Bobby Locke.

Saturday dawned calm and cloudless, a lovely June day. A gallery estimated at 17,500, the largest ever to watch a golf match up to that time, flocked to see if the monster Oakland Hills course could stand up twice more before the onslaught of the pros. In the morning round Hogan began to correct his mistakes. After 13 holes he was three under par. But he let one of those strokes get away on the 14th hole where he took three to get down from the apron. He lost the other two strokes on No. 15, an innocent-looking dogleg to the left, 392 yards long. Hogan pushed his drive into rough on the right, hooked his second weakly into rough on the left, found a bunker with his third shot and after finally pitching on, he holed out for a 6. Hogan finished that round with a 71, not at all bad but frustrating for Ben and his supporters because he had been on the verge of scoring decisively. Instead with 18 holes to go he trailed Locke and Jimmy Demaret, who had come up with a 70, by two strokes.

After a silent lunch Hogan resumed his attack on the course in a mood of sullen belligerence. To avoid trouble on his tee shots he often used a brassie instead of his driver and once he even used a spoon off the tee. He went the first nine holes in even par. On the 10th, a rugged 448-yard par 4, Hogan got off the finest shot of the tournament: a three-iron that soared 200 yards straight for the pin and left him with only a five-foot putt. He made it to go one under par. That birdie merely whet Hogan's appetite. After getting his pars on the 11th and 12th, Ben dropped a 15-footer for a deuce on the short 13th. Two under. A 5 on the 14th hole cost him

A rare sight. Ben Hogan smiles in mid-round after sinking a putt at Winged Foot in 1959. In pursuit of his fifth Open victory at the age of 47, Hogan led at the start but eventually finished eighth behind winner Billy Casper. (*George Silk—Life*)

If any golfer in the world could get safely out of this desperate situation, Arnold Palmer is the man. But even Palmer was confounded by this freak lie atop a rotted tree stump during the playoff for the 1963 championship at Brookline. Arnie took a triple bogey 7 and lost the playoff to Julius Boros. (*Bob Gomel—Life*)

Power, which has become the name of the game, is epitomized in this photograph of young Jack Nicklaus as he pauses at the top of his backswing before exploding his drive during the Open at Oakmont in 1962. (*John Dominis—Life*)

The match of the decade has just ended and Arnold Palmer, who lost, gamely congratulates Jack Nicklaus, who won, after their playoff at Oakmont in 1962. Nicklaus withstood a patented Palmer charge to win his first Open, 71–74. (*John Dominis—Life*)

a stroke. On the 15th, which had been his Waterloo in the morning, Hogan's drive carried the ugly bunker which sat in mid-fairway some 240 yards from the tee. He lofted a six-iron to the green and dropped a four-foot birdie putt. Two under again. Two more pars brought him to the final tee. By now the massive and festive gallery formed a border along every inch of fairway from the tee to the green which was 459 yards, a dozen bunkers and one right-hand dogleg away. Hogan realized that a par 4 would almost surely bring him his third Open victory in his past three tries. Demaret had fallen out of contention with a 78. Locke was playing nine holes behind Hogan and having trouble. Only Haefner was coming close to matching Ben's pace, and Clayt was still a couple of strokes back. With the wind behind him on No. 18 Hogan decided to try to carry with his drive the bunkered ridge that guarded the corner of the dogleg. He succeeded. Now only a straight-on six-iron shot was left. He lofted his approach to the center of the green, 14 feet from the flag. Then with a last decisive stroke Hogan rammed home the putt for a birdie 3. Three under par 67. It was more than enough to win. Haefner finished with the only other sub-par round of the entire tournament, a 69 that left him two strokes behind Hogan at 289. Bobby Locke had a 73 and finished four strokes arrears. Hogan had improved himself with every round: 76, 73, 71, 67. In later years Hogan called his last 18 the best round he ever played. Others called it the greatest round ever played by anyone. As he received his trophy on the lawn outside the clubhouse at Oakland Hills, Hogan spoke with the grim satisfaction of a conqueror. "I'm glad," he said, "that I brought this course, this monster, to its knees." In private he admitted, "If I had to play this golf course every week, I'd go into some other business."

Would Hogan never be beaten? It was the question asked in every locker room in America in the early 1950's, and the answer was that only Hogan could beat Hogan. Ben did beat himself in the 1952 Open at the Northwood Golf Club in Dallas. Again the championship drew a record entry of 1,688, but only 162 players, less than one applicant in 10, survived the sectional qualifying rounds that were held in 28 cities from West Palm Beach to Midland, Texas, to Honolulu.

Hogan opened his title defense with a 69, one under par on the 6,782-yard Northwood course. Another 69 followed on the second round and most of those present were ready to concede to Hogan his fourth Open and his third straight. At 138 he led the field by two strokes. Hogan had made the public forget that only two years before he had been almost a basket case. Now they considered him an unbeatable machine. But Ben was all too human, and when the blistering 94-degree Texas heat got to him on the final day, the Hogan machine slipped a cog. He shot a 74 on the third round. While almost no one was watching, a burly, masculine-looking fellow named Julius Boros slipped in with a 68. That score equaled the best round of the tournament. The crowd did a double take and woke up to the fact that Boros led Hogan by two strokes.

Boros was a 200-pound former prize fighter from Connecticut. He had never won a major tournament and in fact had only turned professional two years earlier as he approached his 30th birthday. Now 32 and attached to the Mid-Pines Club in Southern Pines, North Carolina, Boros was improving steadily. Julius, or Jay as his friends called him, had finished ninth in his first Open in 1950. In 1951 he had tied for fourth.

Boros teed off early for the final round at Dallas and played with a cool nonchalance that amazed the gallery. He chewed on blades of grass, swigged soft drinks and made his shots with a cigaret dangling casually from his lips. More important, he constantly extricated himself from trouble and saved his pars with a hot putter. "He looks cooler than anyone in the gallery," complained one sweating spectator.

Ironically, Boros until this tournament had been considered a strong player from tee to green but not much of a putter. But in fashioning his 68 in the third round at Dallas he used only 11 putts on the back nine. On the final 18 holes Jay took just 29 putts. He scrambled home with a 71 for a 281 and sat back to wait for Hogan. Ben was in his favorite role as pursuer, but the best he could do was another 74 that left him five strokes behind Boros, the new champion. On the last green Porky Oliver, playing with Hogan, holed a 50-foot putt for a birdie to nose out Ben by a stroke for second place.

For the first time since his comeback began, Hogan failed to win a major title in 1952. After losing to Sam Snead in the Masters and to Boros in the Open, Ben took 10 months off from competition. It had been four years since the accident, but Hogan still had to husband his strength with great care. During this layoff Ben celebrated his 40th birthday. When he came out of his temporary retirement in the spring of 1953, it had been almost two years since his last big victory and there were many who thought quite frankly that Hogan's best years were behind him. But these pessimists were soon eating their words, for Hogan was on the threshold of the greatest season any professional golfer has ever enjoyed.

Ben started his campaign at the Masters which he won with a score of 274, five strokes better than the runner-up and five strokes below the old tournament record. His play was so flawless that even Hogan himself had to admit it. "That was the best I have ever played for 72 holes," he said. After Augusta, Hogan won the Pan American Open in Mexico City and the Colonial Open in his home town, Fort Worth, as he warmed up for the main event, the National Open. The Open purse had been increased to $20,500, of which the winner would receive $5,000—as much money as the entire field had received as late as 1937. The site for the

Open was Oakmont, near Pittsburgh, not as terrifying as it had been in 1935 when Sam Parks was the only man in the open field to break 300, but still a mighty test. Sixty of the notorious Oakmont bunkers had been filled in. Nearly 200 bunkers remained, but the current crew of long-hitting pros could knock their drives over most of them. The greens, however, were tricky as always and as slick as window panes.

Hogan arrived in Pittsburgh a week early and went to work to "out-think" the great course. On each hole of his practice rounds he would hit three drives: slice the first, hook the next and belt the third one down the middle. Then he made second shots to the green from each of the experimental drives. Even his putts were used to figure out the rolls and twists of the green. Ben catalogued in his mind every phase of the terrain. He studied the texture of the grass on each green, marking down the fast, the slow and the sliders. He decided which holes to attack and which to play safe. On some holes he reached the conclusion that the wisest way to approach the green was from a lie in the rough. No hole engrossed Hogan more than the 17th, a deceptive par 4 of 292 yards. It was too long for anyone, except possibly Snead, to reach with his tee shot. Traps surrounded the green, and the only opening was a narrow alley in the left-hand corner. Hogan decided to play this hole short into the light rough on the left and chip through the opening to the green.

Hogan's planning paid immediate dividends. His opening round was a smashing 67, five under par and the only score of the day under 70. After a second round of 72 Hogan still led the field by two strokes. His closest pursuer was Sam Snead. Sam was even older than Hogan by a few months, having recently turned 41. But none of the younger generation ever got seriously into the act as the two war horses came slambanging down the stretch. In the morning of the decisive final day Hogan took a 73. Snead had closed the gap to one stroke when he reached the 17th, that odd-sized 292-yard hole. Sam clubbed his drive clear to the green. But then he blew a marvellous chance to pull even by taking three downhill putts from 30 feet. With his 72 Snead still trailed Hogan by a stroke. In the afternoon both men went out in 38. On the 12th hole, a 598-yard prospective birdie, Snead missed another chance to pick up the stroke he lacked. He scuffed his fairway wood, reached the green in three and three-putted for a bogey 6. Hogan lost a stroke to par on the 15th hole when his long approach shot bounded over the green. Then, with three holes to go, Hogan called on his deepest reserves and sprinted for home. The 16th was a par 3, a tough 234-yard shot to a small target. Hogan hit the center of the green with a fine wood shot and two-putted for his par. On No. 17 Ben placed his tee shot in the close rough on the left, according to plan. He chipped through the opening and was left with a safe uphill putt for a birdie 3. He canned it. The 18th was a par 4, 462 yards long. Hogan let fly an impressive drive that brought him within five-iron range. Once more he pinpointed his approach to within birdie range, nine feet from the cup. His putt found the hole for another 3. Hogan's closing sprint of three 3's gave him 38–33–71 for a total of 283. After that it mattered little that Snead never got his game going on the back nine and finished with 76–289, a full six strokes behind Hogan. Sam came in second for the fourth time in his career. For Hogan it was the fourth victory in six years. Ben now climbed the pedestal with Willie Anderson and Bob Jones as the only four-time winners of the Open.

A few weeks later in a cold drizzle at Carnoustie, Scotland, Hogan won the British Open to complete the first "professional grand slam"—Masters, U.S. Open and British Open. It was to be his last major victory.

CHAPTER EIGHT

The Changing Guard

The Open of 1954 was played on the lower course at Baltusrol in New Jersey with its 7,000 yards of dogleg fairways, dipping greens and devilish rough. It was a record-breaker in many ways: the tournament was televised nationally for the first time; player entries (1,928), attendance (40,000) and prize money ($23,280) reached new highs. But one record remained intact: Ben Hogan was frustrated in his attempt to win the championship for an unprecedented fifth time. After strong opening rounds of 71 and 70 Hogan was tied for second place. But a 76 on the third round cost Ben whatever chance he had, and he finished in a tie for sixth place. Ben's putting did not have quite the authority it had during his epic 1953 campaign. As age caught up with Ben, it affected him first in his legs and the early symptoms of infirmity showed up, not on the tee but on the putting green. Ben began occasionally missing the short "unmissable" putts and as his confidence waned, he would hang for endless moments over his ball before he putted it. This hesitation sometimes became so painfully drawn out that even the most sympathetic observers wanted to shout, "C'mon, Ben, hit the ball." For another 10 years and more Hogan re-

134

mained an ageless wonder from tee to green, as good as any younger man and superior to most. But a combination of ill luck and unsteady putting kept him from ever winning another U.S. Open.

Hogan's slip allowed the rest of the starting field of 162 to scramble for the $6,000 first prize—and scramble wildly they did. In the first round Billy Joe Patton, an irrepressible amateur from North Carolina, who in April had come within a stroke of stealing the Masters from Snead and Hogan, shot a one-under-par 69. But the next day Billy Joe, always the very model of inconsistency, fired a 76 and fizzled to a sixth-place finish, tied with Hogan. Replacing Patton in the lead, with 139 for 36 holes, was Gene Littler, a slender blond Californian of 23 who had turned pro only a few months before after winning the 1953 U.S. Amateur. But Gene reacted to the lead as though it were an overheated potato. He shot a third round of 76 which relieved him of the responsibility of holding it any longer. The new leader after 54 holes was Ed Furgol, a tall, gaunt 37-year-old with lines around his eyes that wrinkled wryly when he smiled. Despite an unusual handicap Furgol had run together three consistent rounds of 71–70–71 for a two-stroke lead over Dick Mayer, who moved into second place. As a boy of 11, Furgol had taken a spill in a neighborhood playground and shattered his left elbow. It never mended properly, and Ed grew up with a crooked and withered left arm. To balance his golf swing, Ed learned to keep his right arm bent, too. The result was a quick, cramped swing that incorporated most of the things Furgol taught his students at the Westwood Country Club in St. Louis *not* to do. But Furgol did just fine, thank you, with his constricted swing and he came down the stretch head to head with Mayer, a muscular Nordic blond from Greenwich, Connecticut. A wild sequence of events on the final hole decided the tournament. The 18th on Baltusrol's lower course is a par 5 heavy with hazards. The fairway slants downhill from the tee to a creek at the bottom, well beyond driving range. Either side of the fairway is lined with trees, heavy woods on the right and sparser growth on the left. Beyond the creek the fairway veers to the left demanding an uphill approach to a well-trapped green.

Mayer reached the 18th hole first and sliced his drive deep into the pine trees on the right. His ball landed in an unplayable lie. Mayer drove again, and again the ball disappeared into the right-hand woods. By the time he excavated this ball and holed out, Dick had taken a 7 for a total of 286.

When Furgol came to 18 he did not slice but hooked his drive instead to the left where the trees were more widely spaced. The safeplay for his second shot would have been to chip out laterally into the fairway, but his chances of getting a par that way were slim. Off to the left Furgol saw the fairways of the upper course, which was not being used in the tournament but which had not been ruled out of bounds. The spacing of the trees was such that, although he could not go straight for the green, he could shoot diagonally ahead to the "wrong" fairway. Furgol chose this route. With an eight-iron he pitched out of the trampled rough into the other fairway. From there he had a clear shot through the "back door" to the green 160 yards away. The gallery, which had followed Furgol into the rough, now parted to form a corridor, and Ed lofted a pretty seven-iron shot to the apron. Then Furgol chipped on, four feet above the hole. He paused for a moment to straighten his flat white cap, tucked up the sleeves of his sweater and stroked in the tricky downhill putt. It was a roundabout 5, but every bit as effective as though he had played it down the middle—and for that first national television audience, a lot more exciting. The par gave Furgol 72 and a 284 total, two shots up on Mayer. Only Gene Littler, who was playing even par golf on the final round, still had a chance to catch Furgol and when

Littler missed his birdie putt from eight feet on the last green, the man with the crooked swing was champion.

Ben Hogan wanted desperately to win his fifth U.S. Open, one more than even the immortal Jones and the ancient Willie Anderson had won. In 1955 Hogan, nearing his 43rd birthday, started getting ready for the Open three months in advance. He took time off from his new golf-club manufacturing business in Fort Worth to practice until he had honed every part of his game to a fine edge. In early June he went to San Francisco where the tournament was to be played and spent dozens of lonesome hours getting used to the unusually healthy rough and tricky seaside breezes of the 6,700-yard, par 70 Olympic Country Club course. When opening day arrived, Ben protested that he still wasn't ready. Even though he boosted his diet with vitamin pills and did everything else he could to conserve his strength, he had lost 10 pounds. His stiff left knee—a souvenir of the automobile crash—hurt him badly when he walked, particularly going uphill. Ben soaked the knee in Epsom salts every night and wrapped it in an elastic bandage every morning. "If I'm lucky enough to win here," said Hogan, "I doubt if I will ever play in an important tournament again. It's just too hard. I want to be a weekend golfer."

Three days and 72 holes later Hogan slumped on a bench in the Olympic locker room and accepted a tall Scotch that someone handed him. He was battered and bushed and he limped at almost every step. But apparently the fifth Open championship he coveted was his. His four-round score of 287 was seven strokes over par, but no one else had been able to do much damage to par either.

In the first round less than half the field of 162 players broke 80. Hogan, at 72, was five behind Tommy Bolt's pace-setting 67. Defending champion Ed Furgol shot a 76 and went upward from there until he finished in a tie for 45th place at 312. Sam Snead opened with 79 which was more of

a handicap than even Sam could overcome. He finished tied
for third at 292.

Bolt went up to 77 in the second round but held on to a
share of the lead at 144 with amateur Harvie Ward. Hogan
shot a 73 and trailed them by a stroke. Arnold Palmer, a
muscular young fellow from Latrobe, Pennsylvania, survived the cut with 153. Palmer had recently turned pro after
winning the 1954 U.S. Amateur. He eventually tied for 21st
place at 303 in this Open and earned $226.15.

In the morning of the final day Hogan shot a 72 and
moved into the lead. In the afternoon, while almost all his
challengers staggered into the high 70's, Hogan drove himself to his best golf of the week. For the first time in the
tournament he parred the 17th hole, a 461-yard par 4 that he
hadn't been able to reach in two. This time he chipped on
and one-putted. Another 4 on the last hole gave him a 70,
even par. Now hardly a player on the course had a chance to
catch Hogan. Except one.

Out on the 14th fairway Jack Fleck stepped along with his
long, loose-jointed stride in a state of privacy that was
almost absolute. A marshall patrolling the fairway shouted
the latest news to him: "Hogan's in with 287." At that
moment Fleck told himself, "Now I know I have a chance."
Fleck bogeyed that 14th hole. But on the 15th, a 141-yard
par 3, Fleck dumped his tee shot five feet from the pin and
holed out for a birdie deuce. With three holes to go, Jack
Fleck needed one more birdie to tie the mighty Hogan.
Fleck was 32 years old. In the nine years since he had come
home to Davenport, Iowa, from World War II navy duty
and turned pro, Fleck had taken occasional fliers at the
tournament circuit. But he had never won enough money to
make a go of it. The most notable tournaments he had won
were the Waterloo (Iowa) Open of 1953 and the Rochester
(Minnesota) Open of 1954. The son of an Iowa truck
farmer, Jack got his first look at golf in 1936 by sneaking
onto the Davenport Country Club course to watch Ralph

Guldahl win the Western Open. Later he got a job caddying there and taught himself to play on Mondays when caddies were allowed to use the course. After Jack graduated from high school, he went to work full-time as an assistant in the pro shop. By 1954 he was making his living as the manager and professional at Davenport's two municipal courses. They were located eight miles apart and Jack commuted between them. This year for the first time he had left his wife Lynn to mind the pro shops and was making the full winter-spring tour. And, for the first time, he was consistently finishing in the money. Lanky and loose at 6 feet 1½ inches and 164 pounds, Fleck had a fluid swing and could wallop his wood shots for distance with impressive accuracy. On Olympic's fairways, lined with dark green cedars and pine, he was averaging 260 yards off the tee, long enough to qualify as one of the half-dozen longest hitters of the day. But Fleck was even prouder of a sudden improvement in his putting, accomplished with a new putter manufactured by the Ben Hogan Golf Club Company.

Fleck's first three rounds had been 76–69–75 and he started his final round three shots behind Hogan. Now with three holes to play he was two under par for the round. On the 603-yard 16th hole he pulled his third shot into the rough alongside the green. But his chip shot hopped delicately onto the green and almost rolled into the cup. Fleck tapped in for a par 5. On No. 17, the uphill 461-yard par 5 which had been turned into a par 4 for the Open, Fleck laced into two wood shots and the second one carried to the back of the green. His downhill putt from 40 feet just slid past the cup. Par 4.

In the clubhouse an attendant passed the word: Fleck needs a birdie on 18 to tie Hogan. "Good luck to him," said Ben thinly, and then went off to take his shower. Out on the course the gallery completely encircled the 337-yard finishing hole. Fleck pulled his drive a shade and the ball landed in the rough a scant four inches off the fairway and just over

100 yards from the green. It was not a bad lie—the rough was not heavy at that spot—and Fleck played a three-quarter seven-iron. He hit a fine shot. The ball flew in a low trajectory, barely cleared the bunker that guarded the front entrance to the green and sat down hole-high, seven feet to the right of the cup. The green tilted severely from back to front and its surface was slippery. Throughout the tournament the players had been babying their putts here, hoping to catch a corner of the cup. Not Fleck. He stroked the ball solidly with his Hogan putter, watched it curl slightly downhill and plop into the center of the hole. Birdie 3 for a 67 and a tie with Hogan at 287.

Fleck's finish was all the more fantastic because it was so unexpected. Although Hogan himself had refused to admit he was the winner as long as even the unlikeliest challenger remained on the course, the gallery knew from watching that two pars and two birdies on the final four holes were a nearly impossible requirement. A national television audience was led to believe that Hogan had clinched the title and the network returned to its regular programing. So Fleck, the unknown Iowan whose best previous Open finish was a tie for 52nd place in 1953, was matched with Hogan, the tired but determined Texan who had won it four times before. Of the six sub-par rounds played in the tournament proper, Fleck had recorded two of them. Now, with his putter still blazing hot, Jack found he had one more sub-par round left in him. For the first four holes each man matched par. Hogan lost a stroke on the fifth. He sliced his drive into the rough and, to avoid some low-hanging cypress trees ahead of him, had to play a safety shot to the fairway. Bogey 5, and Ben never again pulled even. Both men parred the seventh. On the short eighth hole Hogan rolled in a downhill 35-footer for a deuce. Fleck, faced with a seven-footer and with the pressure on him, holed his putt to stay a stroke ahead. On the next hole Fleck dropped a 20-foot birdie putt and pulled in front by two.

On the 10th hole Fleck moved three shots ahead. Both were on in two and Hogan's 22-foot putt missed the hole. Fleck had a 13-foot putt across a gentle slope and he canned it for his third straight birdie. Hogan got one stroke back on No. 11 when Fleck drove into the rough and succumbed to his first bogey of the day. But Ben gave the stroke back by three-putting the 12th hole, missing the second putt from one foot. A birdie putt from 20 feet on the 14th hole narrowed Hogan's deficit again to two strokes. They parred the next two. Then on 17 Hogan, for the first time all week, reached the green in two. He almost sank his first putt and did make the second. Fleck's second was short of the green. He pitched over a bunker to within six feet of the pin but missed the putt and took a 5.

As they prepared to hit on the final hole Fleck still led by a stroke, but in the gallery the betting was even money that Hogan would pull it out. But as he drove the ball, Hogan's left foot slipped on a sandy patch on the tee. His shot hooked wildly into the deep rough. When he found the ball barely visible in the foot-high grass, Hogan's face dropped and his lips tightened. Ben hit the ball. It moved one foot. Again he slashed with his wedge. The ball moved three feet. Hogan's fourth stroke reached the fairway, still 100 feet from the green. He was on in five, 30 feet above the cup while Fleck, who was on in two, had only 15 feet to go. The crowd cheered Hogan as he trudged dejectedly onto the green. He acknowledged them with a wave of his white cap. Then, lining up his putt as though the championship were still in the balance, he knocked it in from 30 feet to salvage a 6. Hogan was brokenhearted, but he went down like a champion. Fleck two-putted for a solid par 4. He by no means had backed into the championship. With 69 he was one stroke better than par and three strokes better than Hogan.

There followed an award ceremony in which Hogan posed good-naturedly with Fleck's Hogan-built putter. Then Jack flew home to a hero's welcome in Davenport. For Hogan the search for a fifth Open victory had only begun.

"No one ever *wins* the U.S. Open," Bobby Jones once said. "Everyone else *loses* it." In 1956 everyone lost the Open except Dr. Cary Middlecoff. Cary's victory at the Oak Hill Country Club in Rochester, New York, climaxed a stretch of two seasons during which the fidgety dentist from Memphis was at age 35 probably the best golfer in the world. Every year since 1948 Middlecoff had been among the top 10 money-winners. In 1955 he won six tournaments including the Masters, which he captured by seven strokes, a record margin for that tournament. Early in 1956 Cary won two more tournaments, the Crosby and Phoenix Opens, as he took aim at his second national championship.

From the start the 1956 tournament was known as the "Rhubarb Open" because of the unusual number of arguments it produced. For one thing many of the best players threatened to boycott the tournament because they believed the total purse—$24,000—was too small. Eight lesser tournaments on the P.G.A. circuit were paying more than that. First place was worth $6,000, but the prize money dropped off sharply so that 10th place paid only $416, barely enough to meet caddy fees and hotel and travel expenses. But at the last minute the golf equipment companies who had most of the top players on their payrolls sent the players telegrams urging them to show up at Rochester, and this headed off the boycott. At the tournament itself there were rhubarbs galore: three players lost the caddies they wanted in a hassle over who would caddy for whom; four others lost penalty strokes to various obscure scoring rules; and on the 17th hole of the first round Henry Cotton, the venerable British champion, was accused by the other two men in his threesome, Demaret and Middlecoff, of taking one more stroke than he admitted to. They claimed that he ticked his ball before tapping it into the hole. Cotton denied it and the officials took Henry at his word.

One thing that remained above argument was the Oak Hill course itself. Golf architect Robert Trent Jones had touched up the Oak Hill for the Open, as he had several courses for previous Opens, but this time Jones did not create a monster. Instead the fairways seemed fairly roomy, the rough was not too thickly matted and the greens had no sharp contours. After their practice rounds the roster of starting players agreed unanimously that the course was a fair one. Hogan even called it "easy." Certainly Oak Hill was a pretty course with clusters of red and white oak, maple, linden and evergreens lining the fairways and a rippling brook meandering through. Traps brimming with gleaming silicon sand that had been purchased from a nearby glass mill sparkled in white patches around the greens.

But Oak Hills' dangers were present if not obvious. The last three holes particularly could be damaging to the player who aspired to break par 70. These three were long par 4's—441 yards straightway, 463 yards dogleg right and 449 yards downhill. In four rounds the entire field managed to make only nine birdies on these three holes and they came to be known as Heartbreak Bend.

As the play began Middlecoff and Hogan were cofavorites at 3 to 1 in the betting; but after 18 holes the leader was Bob Rosburg, a portly former college baseball player from Stanford, who shot a 68. Rosburg, however, was the most erratic player of the decade, and he soon surrendered the lead with subsequent rounds of 76, 79 and 81. After 36 holes the new leader was Peter Thomson, a dashing 26-year-old Australian who had won the past two British Opens. At 139 Thomson led Hogan, in second place, by a single stroke. Despite two horrible 7's in his first two rounds Middlecoff was just two strokes off the lead. Another former champion, Ed Furgol, was tied with Middlecoff at 141 and still another, Julius Boros, was locked at 142 with Ted Kroll, a tough tour veteran. Jack Fleck, the defending champion, had 150 and missed qualifying for the final 36 by one stroke.

For the final day Middlecoff was paired with Thomson, and when Peter took a bogey 6 on the long sixth hole, Cary caught him and took the lead. Thomson required 75 strokes to finish the morning round while Middlecoff was in with an even par 70. Gobbling hay fever pills to counteract his allergy to grass, consuming countless cigarets and doing an imitation of St. Vitus before every shot, Middlecoff kept rolling until he reached the final three holes of the tournament. There he faltered, taking a bogey 5 on the 16th hole and another on the 17th. On the final hole it looked like Cary would miss his par again. He hooked his drive into the rough and hit his second short of the green and still in the rough. But from there Middlecoff hit a delicate approach shot with his pitching wedge that ran up to within four feet of the pin. He sank the putt for a par 4. Middlecoff posted his score, another 70 for 281. Then he found himself a seat in the clubhouse to sweat out the challengers. Thomson had finished four strokes back at 285. Another promising young player, Arnold Palmer, had finished with 287, good enough for seventh place. Wesley Ellis, a rangy 24-year-old from San Antonio with very slight credentials, had played three steady rounds of 71–70–71 which had placed him just one shot behind Middlecoff. But on the final round Ellis' bid for an upset ended with his very first swing. His tee shot on the first hole sailed out of bounds and after that Ellis skidded to ninth place.

Three men reached Heartbreak Bend with a solid chance to overtake Middlecoff. How each of them failed, with a national television audience looking on, provided the drama of the 1956 Open. First came Hogan, making another grim effort to win his fifth Open. After a birdie on the 14th hole Ben needed only one more bird to win, or all pars to tie. On the short 15th hole he barely missed his birdie deuce. On 16 he came within inches of holing a 16-footer for his bird. On

17—the 463-yard dogleg—Hogan went over the green with two wood shots, but he chipped out of the rough to about two feet from the flag. Ben set himself to putt. At the last moment he stopped, then set himself again. Finally he tapped the ball. It rolled just over the right-hand corner of the cup and stayed out. Now Hogan needed a 3 to tie on the home hole, 449 yards into a steady headwind. Hogan drove long but into the rough. He dug a tremendous second shot out of the heavy grass and onto the green. Ben putted from 30 feet for his tie and missed. With 70 on the last round for a 282, he still trailed Middlecoff by a stroke.

Next came Boros, munching calmly on a blade of grass but playing spectacular, if erratic, golf. Jay needed one birdie on the last three holes to tie. On the 16th hole his long putt for a birdie lipped the cup. On the 17th he had to scramble just to save his par, getting down in two from a greenside trap. For his last hole Boros hit a good drive, then slashed a low line drive of an iron shot to the right-hand side of the plateau green. His 15-foot putt went right for the cup. But instead of dropping, it hit the corner and spun out. Boros had 69 and a tie for second with Hogan at 282.

Finally came Ted Kroll, a highly respected player but never before a contender in the Open. Kroll actually was ahead of Middlecoff with four holes to play. Pars would bring him in with 280. But Ted lost one stroke to par on the short 16th where his tee shot missed the green. On the next hole bad luck cut him down quite tragically. Kroll pushed his second shot into the rough and the ball came to rest beneath the low branches of a small evergreen. Instead of taking a penalty shot and lifting, which would have killed his chances immediately, Ted tried to push the ball out of its impossible lie with the toe of the blade of his two-iron. He knelt on the ground, wedged himself among the branches and poked at the ball. It moved a few feet. Still on his knees, Kroll poked again and got the ball out from under the tree. Finally he reached the green with his fifth shot and took two putts for a seven. So, the last challenger had lost the Open. In the clubhouse Middlecoff's ordeal was over. "They're all good friends of mine," said the winner of his colleagues, "but I can't say that I'm sorry."

Ben Hogan woke up on the first morning of the 1957 Open at Inverness in Toledo and made the painful discovery that he could not raise his arms above his chest. The day before Ben had practiced for two hours in a puffy wind and had sweated hard without protecting himself sufficiently. Now he felt sharp pains in the muscles of his back and chest. A "cold in the back," he called it. Hogan was due to tee off at 9:36 A.M. U.S.G.A. officials postponed his starting time an hour to allow him a quick trip to a local doctor's office. The doctor tried a diathermy treatment and gave Ben injections of novocain and cortisone. Nothing worked. Hogan couldn't swing a golf club and he knew it. The doctor called it "pleurisy of the chest wall" and said it would go away in a few days. But this was the day the Open began and Hogan had to swallow another bitter disappointment. He located U.S.G.A. president Richard Tufts and told him, "I'm sorry, Dick. I can't make it."

As the word "withdrew" went up behind Hogan's name on the big scoreboard, the rest of the field breathed a collective sigh and went to work in earnest on the 6,919-yard par 70 Inverness course. Before noon everybody had to scatter for cover in the face of black skies and a vicious rainstorm borne on 60-mile-an-hour winds. The storm ripped through the course, upsetting ticket booths and concession stands and threatening to tear away the press tent. But within an hour its violence was spent and within 90 minutes the players went back to work. The Inverness course drained off in short order and the dampening actually helped produce lower scores by slowing down the slick greens and by making some of the championship tees so muddy that the shorter front tees had to be used instead.

Cary Middlecoff opened the defense of his championship by shooting a 71. But no less than 11 players did better than that. The low man was Jimmy Demaret with 68. Jimmy had won three Masters tournaments and a slew of other championships but never the U.S. Open. Now 47 years old and a grandfather, Demaret was putting like a winner—26 putts, in fact, on the first 18 holes.

The rain had slowed down play enough so that darkness prevented five threesomes from finishing their rounds the first day. When they did finish the next morning, Chick Harbert had a 68 to tie Demaret for the lead. But Harbert played a second-round 79 and lost his chance. Even Demaret, with a 73, couldn't hold the lead for long. The new leaders were Billy Joe Patton and Dick Mayer whose twin 138's tied the Open scoring record for the first 36 holes. Patton, the amazing and amusing amateur from Morgantown, North Carolina, had sprayed his drives far and wide all day, but he had one-putted 11 greens. Mayer, always a fine putter, birdied four of the last five holes to earn his share of the lead. Twenty players were bunched between Mayer and Patton and Cary Middlecoff, who was eight strokes off the lead at 146. Without Hogan to worry about, this was truly an "open" Open.

As the third day's play began, the temperature moved into the 90's and the scores of some of the leaders rose almost as high. Mayer slipped to 74 and Billy Joe suffered a 76. Doug Ford, who had been near the top, shot an 80. Middlecoff picked up valuable ground with a 68. Back into the lead, with a 70 for 211, climbed James Newton Demaret. As the final round began, Demaret was the strong sentimental favorite of the gallery. But the heat and humidity appeared to have worn out the old warrior. With four holes to go he had fallen three strokes behind his playing companion, Julius Boros. But at that point Jimmy roused himself for a last charge. On the 69th hole, a demanding, 468-yard par 4, he rifled a long, fading iron to within two feet of the cup and tapped in for a birdie. On the 70th hole he missed the green but scrambled home for his par. On the 71st hole to compensate for his fatigue Demaret used a five-iron for his approach shot although he was only about a seven-iron from the flag. He punched a pretty shot nine feet from the hole and made the putt for another bird. On the finishing hole Demaret played down the middle and had his par all the way. Demaret's courageous finish—birdie, par, birdie, par— brought him home with 72 for 283, one big stroke better than Boros and temporarily in first place. But there were still some challengers on the course and two of them were playing hot golf.

As Demaret was holing out, Dick Mayer was walking to the seventeenth (or 71st) tee followed by a slim and silent gallery. The handsome, 34-year-old blond was one of the most popular players on the tour. The son of Al Mayer, an automobile dealer in Greenwich, Connecticut, and himself a fine amateur player, Dick had practically grown up on the Innis Arden course in Greenwich and later on Winged Foot in Westchester where he had Craig Wood and Claude Harmon for instructors. Dick now had 10 good years of pro competition behind him, but he had won only three tournaments and as one sarcastic fan chided, "All he can win is money." Mayer needed two pars to tie Demaret, one birdie to beat him. He got his par on seventeen. As he teed up at eighteen, Mayer couldn't help but remember his collapse in 1954 on the finishing hole at Baltusrol when a par would have tied for the championship and he took a crushing 7 instead.

The eighteenth at Inverness was a tight little 330-yard par 4. It moved from an elevated tee through a well-trapped valley to a plateau green guarded in front by a steep bunker. Mayer chose a four-wood to stay short of the bunkers and hit a dead-straight tee shot. His second was a wedge that landed near the pin and hopped nine feet above it. His third shot was a putt that broke just a shade and toppled into the cup. 3–282.

Through a clubhouse window Jimmy Demaret watched the putt that eliminated him from the Open, turned gamely to his friends and said, "That was a very good putt the boy made. Very good."

Demaret was out of the running, but Cary Middlecoff wasn't. The good doctor, playing as slowly as ever, needed another 68 (to match his morning round) if he hoped to catch Mayer. Cary got one birdie by canning a long putt at the sixteenth hole and came into eighteen needing one more birdie to tie. Ignoring the traps, he whaled his drive 285 yards down the heart of the fairway. He popped a 40-yard wedge shot just over the front bunker and the ball came to rest nine feet to the right of the pin and slightly above it. The distance was almost identical to the putt Mayer had sunk one hour before. Cary studied his line for a full two minutes, gauging the faint left-to-right break. Then he hit the ball into the hole. Another birdie 3–282.

Middlecoff's matching 68's for the last two rounds equalled Gene Sarazen's record finish (70–66) in 1932 at Fresh Meadow. But the effort drained the last reserves of his energy. The next morning, a Sunday, Cary woke up feeling numb, his mind practically a blank. In 98-degree heat Mayer and Middlecoff squared away for their playoff on the same course where in 1931 Billy Burke and George Von Elm had struggled for an extra 72 holes in their marathon match.

This time the playoff ended a lot quicker. Middlecoff committed two double bogeys and shot a 79. Mayer played steady, conservative golf for a 72 and beat Middlecoff by seven strokes. The championship that Mayer had kicked away in three years before at last was his.

Later in 1957 Mayer won the rich "World" championship at Tam O'Shanter, led the U.S. Ryder Cup team to victory and was named Golfer of the Year. His official earnings were over $65,000. But after that big season Mayer went into a deep and prolonged slump that was compounded by personal problems. By 1960 he was considered a has-been. But in 1965, at age 42, Mayer made a comeback from oblivion by winning the New Orleans Open and its first prize of $20,000.

One golfer who had defeated himself early at Inverness was Tommy Bolt. Fate couldn't seem to resist aiming her wryest tricks at Tommy, perhaps because he was such a responsive victim. On this occasion, the first day of the 1957 Open, the caddy assigned to Bolt failed to show up. Tommy was forced to draft a youngster out of the crowd to tote his bag and when he finally teed off on his delayed first round, he shot a 77. The next morning Tommy started his second round by bogeying the first three holes. That was enough for Bolt. He picked up his ball and left the course.

Twelve months later at Southern Hills Country Club in Tulsa Bolt was one of the 162 golfers who teed off in quest of the 1958 Open championship. They were the remnants of a record 2,132 entries. Prize money had been increased again to $35,000 with a first prize of $8,000. But winning a share of it would be no easy touch. Southern Hills, a tough course to begin with, had been brazenly doctored for the Open. Pin positions for the first round were so mischievously placed that three and four-putt greens became commonplace. Gene Sarazen, who shot an 84, called the course "ridiculous." Temperatures went sizzling into the 90's with humidity to match. On the first round not a single player matched par 70. Ben Hogan, playing with a wrist he had injured in practice, shot a 75 and was never in contention. Sam Snead also had a 75 and when he followed it with an 80, Sam, for the first time in 18 years, failed to qualify for the final 36 holes.

The heat, the souped-up course, the dried-out greens that failed to hold—all of these were ingredients that could have produced a typical Tommy Bolt blowoff. But, surprise! Tommy was one of the coolest men on the course. With a first round of 71 he tied for the lead with two others, former champion Julius Boros and Dick Metz. Metz had been runner-up to Ralph Guldahl in the Open 20 years before, and after several years in semiretirement he was making a comeback at age 50.

Tommy Bolt professed to have brought his notorious public temper under control and was a reformed man. Tommy had reformed periodically before, but this time he seemed to mean it. At the rather advanced golfing age of 39 he had almost a decade of successful touring under his belt, including 10 tournament victories. He was a fine player, but his talent was almost obscured by his reputation as a thrower of tantrums. He had earned the nickname "Terrible Tommy" way back in 1945 for blowing up in a golf tournament in Italy where he was serving as a U.S. Army sergeant. In a reflective moment Bolt could jibe himself about his temper. "I guess I do have a pretty low boiling point," he said, "but I haven't broken nearly as many clubs as people think. Only a dozen or so." Of course, the fans were fascinated by Tommy's tantrums. What duffer hasn't wanted to wrap his club into a corkscrew? But in the year since Inverness, Bolt had, in effect, been deputized. Ed Carter, the P.G.A. tournament director, had Bolt appointed a member of the players' good conduct committee, which was charged with enforcing the P.G.A.'s new $100 fine against club-throwing. To no one's surprise the first man to be fined was committee member Bolt. But over the year he only had to fine himself twice. "Not bad for me," said Tommy.

Bolt was a native Oklahoman from the town of Haworth and the soaking heat seemed to bother him less than it did most of the other players and the 10,000 fans who trudged faithfully in their wake. On the second day the flagsticks were more reasonably placed, the greens were watered periodically through the day and scores came down a bit. Gary Player, 153 pounds of articulate and brilliant young golfer from South Africa, playing in his first Open at age 22, stole the headlines with a 68. It was the only sub-par round of the tournament thus far and gave Player a chance to become the first foreigner since Ted Ray in 1920 to win the U.S. championship. Gary had ripped off five birdies on the back nine which he played in 32 strokes. But Tommy Bolt, with another 71 for 142, managed to hold the lead by one stroke over Player.

A severe test of Bolt's reformation came at the 18th hole of the second round. As he teed off on the uphill 468-yard par 4 hole Tommy had a chance to break par for the day. But it took him three shots to get on and three putts to get in for a double bogey 6. Tired and disgusted with himself, Bolt stalked off and refused to discuss the round with anyone for almost an hour. But after a respite in the air-conditioned clubhouse Tommy got hold of himself again. Perhaps he was inspired by a card he carried in his pocket which read:

"God grant me the serenity to accept the things I cannot change, the courage to change the things I can and the wisdom to know the difference."

Sound advice for any golfer.

More than 15,000 customers turned out the next day to see if Terrible Tommy would go bang. He did not. In the morning round Gene Littler made a rush from five strokes back with a 67, the lowest round of the tournament. But Bolt countered with a 69 of his own. Starting at the ninth hole Tommy put together a torrid streak of 3's, six of them in seven holes, and that all but broke the back of the opposition. As he lunched between rounds on tomato juice and a sandwich, Bolt seemed poised and unruffled by the clubhouse clamor that focused around him. He set his lantern jaw and went out to march through another scorching afternoon. By the 14th hole he knew the championship was as good as his. "I could bogey every hole from here in," he said. By the 18th tee he was able to stand back and admire the gallery that lined his route up to the clubhouse: "Boy, look at that crowd!"

Bolt treated his crowd to a fine drive and a four-wood smack to the green. Two putts and he was home with 72 for a 283. Gary Player, who had closing rounds of 73 and 71, finished in second place four shots back of Bolt. Boros was third at 289 and Littler was fourth with 290. Bolt played his four rounds without going over 72. No other player escaped without at least a 75 on one round.

Said the new champ, "I've always wanted to win this one. And, believe it or not, I had no bad thoughts all the way."

Bolt wore his crown in relative peace, except for one occasion when he told off the director of a tournament in New York. That cost him $500. Two years later, in the 1960 Open at Cherry Hills, Bolt demonstrated he was still Terrible Tommy. After splashing two consecutive balls into a lake on the 18th hole, Bolt hurled his driver into the water after them.

In 1959 the Open returned for the first time in 30 years to Winged Foot in Mamaroneck, New York. Interest and participation in the game had grown marvelously from the relatively modest era when Bob Jones had sunk his famous 12-footer to tie Al Espinosa and then crushed Espinosa in the playoff. To underline this growth the golf fans of New York went all out to make theirs the biggest of all the Opens and their efforts were rewarded with more records and more "firsts" than even the most optimistic among them expected. Prize money was increased by 20 percent and totaled $49,200 for the championship proper plus another $1,300 in qualifying prizes. Entries were received from 2,385 golfers, also a record, and for the first time double qualifying was needed to reduce the field. Nonexempt players had to play their way first through one of 57 district tournaments, then survive one of 13 sectional tournaments to qualify for one of the 150 starting places. Each day of the tournament nearly 15,000 paying customers roamed the West course at Winged Foot watching the play from behind 12 miles of red, white and blue nylon rope that lined the fairways. In three days 43,377 people attended and contributed to a gross tournament revenue of approximately $500,000. Both figures represented healthy jumps over previous record highs. When heavy rains forced postponement of the final round, another 10,000 fans turned out to watch the unscheduled fourth day of play. The champion's share of the purse reached a new high of $12,000 and when the last putt had fallen, the big prize had been won by a refreshingly new kind of champion.

Billy Casper did not fit the mold of slim, grim, young pros who were colorless copies of the great Hogan and who, unlike Hogan, could not be separated one from the other except by program number. Casper's disposition was as sunny as his native California. At 215 pounds and with a waist that measured upward of 38 inches, Billy's trademark was a tummy that shook when he swung like a bowl full of jelly. Ambling from hole to hole on the golf course Billy was unperturbed by the presence and the noise of the gallery. Between shots he would actually smile, chat and even crack jokes about his game. Just about the only thing about golf he didn't like was practice. "I hate it," said Billy, displaying a most un-Hogan-like attitude. Whenever his game went sour, instead of working overtime on the practice tee, Casper was more likely to drop everything and go fishing for a week or two. This sort of therapy invariably did him more good than worry and practice ever did.

Casper's fortunes had climbed steadily since 1954 when he had turned pro while still a seaman in the Navy. In his first tournament, the 1955 Western Open, he won $33.33. In 1958 he had finished first five times, more than anyone else on the tour, and had earned close to $60,000. With his size, Billy could hit a ball as far as almost anyone. But he was respected more for his chipping and putting, a wonderful touch he had developed as a youngster at the San Diego Country Club. Billy made a point of explaining that he learned to chip and putt so well because it was more fun and less work than practicing driving.

Coming into the 1959 Open, Casper at 27 had only recently recovered from a two-month bout with pneumonia. Most of the pretournament attention was concentrated on the two old monarchs, Snead and Hogan. Ben and Sam still held the spotlight at age 47 for the simple reason that none of the younger generation had risen up to take it away from them. (Arnold Palmer had won the 1958 Masters but was still considered a "comer." Jack Nicklaus was a slender teenager still playing with the amateurs.) At Winged Foot both of the old pros made a last gallant bid to win the championship. Hogan started out as though he would steal the tournament with a barrage of birdies. He reached the turn on his first round in 32 strokes and like lightning the word crackled through the gallery: The Hawk is on the move. Ben lost one stroke to par on the 13th hole and on the 18th green he committed the now-familiar Hogan error: he three-putted. But, nevertheless, he was in at 69, one stroke under the harsh par established for the 6,873-yard West course. Hogan was locked in a three-way tie with Dow Finsterwald, the reigning P.G.A. champion, and Dick Knight, a little-known Californian.

Next day Billy Casper played a strong 68 and took the lead by a stroke at 139. Barely a jump behind him at 140 were a fearsome threesome of Hogan, Palmer and Gary Player. At the 13th hole Hogan had roused his gallery by hitting a 50-foot putt across two undulations and in for a deuce. But three putts at the 17th hole kept him from sharing the lead.

Snead had begun the tournament in his usual frustrating manner by taking bogeys at the second and third holes. But Sam contained himself, finished the first round with a decent 73, and added a second-round score of 72. Then, as the weather turned black on the third day, Snead turned hot and climbed into the heart of the race with a brilliant 67. It was his most spectacular Open round since 1940. Three times during the morning thundershowers and flooded greens had forced delays. Once resumed, the play was running almost two hours late and U.S.G.A. officials wisely decided it would be impossible for the 61 finalists in the field to finish their scheduled 36 holes before dark. So, for the first time in 59 Opens they postponed the fourth round until the next day. At 4:30 P.M. the worst storm broke, drenching the course, but by then all except the last seven players had safely finished their third round. Snead's 67 had failed to ruffle Casper who held to his lead with another subpar round of 69. Ironically, Billy was not at the top of his game. As often as not his approach shots found the deep traps that cut so close to the core of almost every green at Winged Foot. But he was recovering with remarkable aplomb and dropping his first putt. On the first nine holes of his third round Casper landed in five bunkers. Each time he came out of the sand and sank the putt for his par.

Coming home Billy one-putted each of the last three holes. His 208 total gave him a lead of three strokes. Closest to him at 211 was Hogan, who by contrast had hit the greens but had three-putted three times on his way to a 71. Snead, Palmer and Bob Rosburg, he of the baseball grip and occasional hot putter, were four shots back at 212. Within range at 213 were Doug Ford, Mike Souchak and Claude Harmon. Harmon, the resident expert at Winged Foot, was trying to become the first home-club pro since Horace Rawlins in 1895 to win the championship. Claude delighted the gallery at the 18th green by sinking a 50-foot putt for a birdie 3 that gave him a 70.

The burden of carrying the lead through an extra night appeared to bother Casper not at all. Play in the fourth round was scheduled to begin Sunday at 2:05 P.M. in deference to a New York law against sporting events before 2:00 P.M. on the Sabbath. While most of the other starters were out warming up, Casper sat in the clubhouse idly reading the Sunday papers and chatting amiably with anyone who happened by. A cold front had moved into the New York area behind the previous day's thunderstorms. The skies were dark, the temperature stayed in the bitter 50's, and a sharp wind blew up to 40 miles an hour in gusts. Casper was among the first to tee off and he went at his business as though he were anxious to get his score up on the board as quickly as possible to put the pressure on his challengers.

At the first hole Billy missed the green but he pitched on and sank a hard four-footer for his par. That set the pattern. On the second hole Casper drove into a trap and was left with an eight-footer for his 4. He made it. On the short third hole his tee shot was far off the green but he chipped to nine feet and holed out again. His approach shot on the fourth found a bunker but he came out pretty as you please to within seven feet and sank the putt. On the long fifth he had an uphill 18-footer for his birdie. Once more, into the cup. By now Casper had one-putted nine consecutive holes, including the last four holes the day before. For sustained excellence it was the most superb stretch of putting that the Open had ever witnessed.

On the sixth hole Casper finally two-putted for the first time all day. He took bogeys at holes seven and eight, but on nine he one-putted again, sinking a seven-footer after being trapped beside the green. He made the turn in 36.

At the 10th hole Casper three-putted for the first and only time in the tournament. At the 12th he took a 6 and at both the 15th and 17th holes he went over par. But in between he dropped a 15-footer for a most important birdie 3 at the 14th hole. When he sales-talked his last putt into the cup on 18 for a 74, four over par, Casper still clutched the lead at 282. He owed much to his putter, which he had used just 114 times in the four rounds. On 31 of the 72 holes Billy had put his first putt into the cup.

Now Casper found himself a comfortable vantage point in the clubhouse near a picture window overlooking the 18th green and sat back to watch the rest of the field struggle to catch him. Ben Hogan was already in—and out. Ben had three-putted the third hole, bogeyed the fourth, and had gone on to finish with a 76, his worst round of the tournament. The extra night's rest didn't help Snead, either. On the short third hole Sam pulled his tee shot far to the left, took a double bogey 5 on the hole and wound up with a 75, five strokes behind Casper.

Claude Harmon made a gallant run and again he sank a long birdie putt that delighted the crowd at the home green. But at 71–284 he was still two strokes shy of the lead. Mike Souchak, one of many successful alumni of Harmon's Winged Foot pro shop, came to the last hole needing a birdie to tie. Mike slapped his approach shot on this 424-yard hole to the back fringe of the green. His chip back was short of the cup. Mike two-putted for a bogey 5 and a tie with Harmon at 284. The last challenger was Bob Rosburg. Bob was running hot. At the 11th hole he holed out from a trap for a birdie 3. At 12 he rolled in a 50-foot putt for another birdie that brought him even with Casper. But Rosburg three-putted the 13th hole and eventually he reached the 18th needing a birdie to tie Casper. After a solid drive Rosburg hit a six-iron that stopped on the front of the green, 30 feet short of the pin. His putt died five feet from the cup and it was all over. Billy Casper, watching from the window, started making plans to go fishing.

CHAPTER NINE

The New Giants

In 1960 Arnold Palmer crowned himself emperor of golf, successor to the line of Hagen, Jones and Hogan. Arnie was 29 and in his sixth season as a professional. The son of a Pennsylvania club pro and a player himself since earliest boyhood, Arnie had turned professional after winning the 1954 U.S. Amateur. A rare combination of a long-ball hitter and confident putter, Palmer had already marked himself as the man to watch by winning a dozen tournaments including the 1958 Masters. In 1959 he led all players with $42,000 in official earnings. Then he began the 1960 campaign with a flourish by winning four winter tournaments, three of them in a row. In April he won his second Masters in spectacular style by birdieing the last two holes.

On the strength of this success Palmer was a clear 4 to 1 favorite when the Open began in June at Cherry Hills, located just south of Denver in the shadow of the snow-topped Rocky Mountains. For the fourth straight year the purse was increased, this time to $60,000. And for the sixth year in succession the starting field of 150 had to be culled from a record number of entries—2,454. Art Wall, qualifying in the Oklahoma sectional, shot a 63–65–128, the lowest

36-hole qualifying score in history. Low scoring was predicted for the Open, too. Cherry Hills measured 7,004 yards, par 71, but golf balls could be hit up to 10 percent farther in the rarefied Colorado atmosphere. At least half the holes at Cherry Hills were considered no more than a drive and a wedge for Palmer and the other big hitters. Although the course played short, tournament officials counted on its deep gullies, plentiful out-of-bounds and nine water holes to keep the pros at bay. And many of the players had trouble getting used to the thin air. Claude Harmon carried an oxygen tube in his bag. Others whiffed oxygen from a supply provided in the locker room. Hogan said he had a difficult time judging distances and Dow Finsterwald disregarded his local caddy's advice so often on which club to use that the frustrated caddy quit in midround.

Another who was slow to acclimatize was Arnold Palmer. On the very first tee shot in the opening round, Arnie drove into a ditch. He took a penalty stroke to drop out, hit his third shot short of the green, the fourth over the green, finally got on in five and sank the putt for a 6. This double bogey by the favorite made it clear it was anybody's tournament to win, and the scramble was on. Palmer finished his first round with a 72. The leader at 68 was Mike Souchak, an alumnus of Duke University who, like Palmer, had played college football and, like Palmer, could sock a golf ball a mile. Mike had gone the first nine in 31 strokes and at 68 for the day he led the field by one shot. Doug Sanders might have tied Souchak except for a freak incident on the last hole. The dominating feature of the 18th at Cherry Hills is a large lake which borders the fairway on the left. Just as Sanders was about to drive, an inconsiderate fish, species unknown, leaped from the lake not 30 feet from the tee. This flabbergasted Sanders to the extent that he skuffed his tee shot into the water and took a 6 on the par 4 hole. He finished with a 70.

On the second day Souchak was even stronger and with a

The battle at Oakmont is done and Jack Nicklaus, having won the national championship at age 22, wraps his wife Barbara in a happy, husbandly hug. (*John Dominis—Life*)

ABOVE. On the brink of collapse from heat exhaustion—but with the 1964 Open championship in his grasp—Ken Venturi walks the final steps at Congressional with the help of U.S.G.A. executive director Joe Dey. BELOW. The Venturis Ken and Conni, manage parched smiles after his stirring comeback victory in the infernal heat at Congressional. After this tournament the Open format was changed to spread the final 36 holes over two days. (*Henry Grossman—Life*)

ABOVE. Turning point of the 1965 Open at Bellerive came on the fifth hole of the playoff when Kel Nagle's drive struck a spectator (*at right*). Nagle played on but his game never recovered. The spectator did. Gary Player defeated Nagle, 71-74. BELOW. Gary the Great. Smaller and a shorter hitter than either Palmer or Nicklaus, the other members of golf's Big Three, Player kept his drives within the slender fairways at Bellerive. A South African, he became the first foreign player since Ted Ray in 1920 to win the U.S. Open. (*Fred Schnell—Life*)

The champion's cup, engraved with the names of past winners, goes to Gary Player following his 1965 victory at Bellerive. In a surprise gesture, Gary gave away the $25,000 first prize that goes with the trophy. (*Fred Schnell—Life*)

67 he opened up a three-stroke lead on the field. His 135 was the lowest score ever shot for the first two rounds of the Open. The cutoff point, low 50 and ties, also was the lowest ever at 147. Arnold Palmer, with an even par 71, avoided the cut with four strokes to spare at 143. But he was languishing in 15th place, a full eight strokes behind Souchak, as the final day began. Standing between Palmer and the lead were no fewer than four former Open champions—Hogan, Boros, Casper and Fleck—not to mention Gary Player, Sam Snead and the current U.S. Amateur champion, a bullnecked 20-year-old junior from Ohio State University named Jack Nicklaus.

For the first 17 holes of the third round Souchak played steady, even-par golf. But the 18th tee again produced freakish trouble. Just as Mike started his backswing, an amateur cameraman hidden in the gallery started his camera whirring. Startled by the sudden sound, Souchak drove out of bounds. He took a 6 on the hole which gave him a 73–208, still two strokes ahead of his nearest pursuers. Palmer gained just one stroke with a 72 that left him seven strokes behind Souchak and still in 15th place as he broke for lunch.

What happened in the afternoon that lovely June Saturday at Cherry Hills was the making of the Arnold Palmer legend. Here is what Palmer did:

On the first hole, a 346-yard par 4, he drove the green and two-putted for a birdie 3. On the second hole, 410 yards, Arnie was just short of the green in 2. He chipped in from 30 feet for a birdie 3. Now Palmer was aroused and charging. "I knew I was on my way," he said later. At the third hole, 348 yards, Arnie put his wedge stiff to the pin and canned his birdie putt of less than a yard. On the fourth, 426 yards, he stuck his wedge 18 feet from the cup and got the putt for still another birdie. He parred the long fifth after driving into the rough, but at the sixth, 174 yards, par 3, he hit the center of the green with a seven-iron and curved a 25-foot sidehill putt into the hole for a deuce. At the seventh, a 411-

yard dogleg, Palmer played a lovely wedge to within six feet and ran in the putt. That made it six birdies in seven holes. The great streak ended at the eighth green where Arnie missed the short putt he needed for par. But at the next hole he got his par and his score for the first nine was an astonishing 30, five strokes below par. It was a total matched only once before in the Open, by Jimmy McHale in 1947.

Now Palmer's name was back on the scoreboard with the leaders and as the field turned into the home stretch the advantage of impetus was all his. Souchak was cracking. He missed a putt from 18 inches at the 10th hole and another of similar length on the finishing hole. He faded to 75 and 283. So much for Mike. But there were a dozen others jamming for the lead. Palmer, certain that the word of his tremendous rally had reached his rivals, coolly switched to a conservative brand of golf and waited for the pressure to have its effect. One by one the others wilted. Jack Fleck proved his 1955 victory was no fluke by going out in 32. But on the home nine he bogeyed two of the last three holes and fell back to a tie with Souchak and four others at 283. For a few minutes young Jack Nicklaus had the lead to himself, five under par for the tournament. But at the 13th (or 67th) hole Jack took three putts from 10 feet and at the next hole he three-putted again. Cancel Jack. For Ben Hogan, playing with Nicklaus, the tournament was two exhausting holes too long. After 70 holes Ben was tied with Palmer at four under. He had hit 34 consecutive greens this day in par or better. But on the next to last hole, a 548-yard par 5, Ben chose to gamble for a birdie on the third shot, a difficult 50-yard pitch over a creek to an island green where the pin was at the front. His soft shot fell just a shade too short. It landed at the edge of the water on the far bank. Hogan took off his right shoe and sock, stood with one foot in the water and splashed the ball to within 18 feet of the pin. He two-putted for a bogey 6. On the 18th hole Hogan hooked his drive into the lake and later missed a short putt that gave him an inglorious 7 and a score of 284. Once again Ben's bid for a fifth championship ended in frustration.

Palmer was playing behind Nicklaus and Hogan and he realized that he needed only to hold onto the gains he had made. Arnold reached the green of the 563-yard 11th hole in two shots and holed out in two putts for his seventh birdie of the round. After that he was content to knock off par after steady par right to the finish. At the 18th, where Hogan had met disaster, Palmer drove with a No. 1 iron and was safe. His four-iron approach was 80 feet to the left of the flag. From there he chipped to within a yard and dropped the putt for his par 4. Arnie's second nine was 35, his round was 65 and his 280 total, four under par, earned him the championship by two strokes.

Palmer's spectacular charge, the unforgettable manner in which he took command of a tournament which he surely had lost, elevated him to the steepletop of world golf. He claimed the throne that Hogan had occupied for so long. But the new emperor had only to glance over his shoulder to see where his next challenge was coming from. Jack Nicklaus, a full 10 years younger than Palmer, had finished second to Arnie by just two strokes. His 282 was the lowest score any amateur had ever made in the Open—including the amateur who won it four times, Bobby Jones.

No champion before him ever got more commercial mileage out of winning the Open than Arnold Palmer. In the year that he held the title Arnie earned more than $200,000. Under the guidance of a young Cleveland attorney, Mark McCormack, Palmer lent his name and often his presence to more business enterprises than any golfer ever had. In doing so he tapped sources of earning power (for himself and for other golfers who followed him) that the oldtimers plain wouldn't believe.

Arnie endorsed lines of golf shirts, socks, slacks, hats, shoes and windbreakers. When he played an exhibition it was booked by his own exhibition company. He staged a series of television exhibitions with Gary Player, another McCormack client who had won the Masters in 1961 and thus joined Arnie as the Big Two. He also signed a syndicated newspaper column and an instruction book, endorsed a cigaret brand and an automobile. A line of golf clubs were sold in his name. There were also Arnold Palmer Pro Shops, golf carts and a variety of golf practicing devices. These ventures succeeded because people *liked* Arnold Palmer—not only because he was such a fine player but also because he had a certain natural quality about him, whether he was making a shot or missing one, that the average citizen found it easy to identify with and admire. As a result people were proud to wear Arnold Palmer shirts and quick to buy anything else that had his name on it.

In 1961 the Open was played for the fourth time at Oakland Hills outside Detroit and Palmer turned up early for two weeks of intensive preparation in the defense of his title. Oakland Hills no longer was the monster it had been 10 years earlier when only Ben Hogan and his runner-up, Clayton Haefner, managed to break par on any round. "The course has matured," said home pro Al Watrous. Architect Trent Jones was called upon to re-examine the course he had practically rebuilt in 1951, but this time Jones recommended only minor changes and even these were on the side of the angels. Seven of the 120 traps were removed, including five from the driving target areas. On the 18th hole, for instance, where in 1951 there had been only 19 steps between the two fairway traps, the left-hand bunker was removed altogether. The rough was lower and not so thick. But the giant undulating greens remained unchanged as Oakland Hills' chief defense. "I can spot a ball on some part of every green," boasted Watrous, "and challenge anyone to get down from there in two putts." One who agreed with that estimate was

Palmer, who predicted: "These roller-coaster greens will kill everyone."

They did kill Palmer. In the first round he three-putted four times and turned in a card of 74. On the other hand, Ben Hogan, who was nearing his 49th birthday, started out as though his historic closing round of 1951 had taken place just yesterday. Spurred by a large and expectant gallery, Ben hit a 50-yard pitch shot into the cup on the second hole for an eagle 3. At the fifth hole he dropped a birdie putt and the crowd was sure it was witnessing another miracle round. But Ben slowed down after that, plopped one shot into the pond in front of the 16th tee and eventually finished with a 71. In first place with a 69, the only sub-par round of the day, was Bobby Brue, a bespectacled young pro who was little known outside the environs of Menominee Falls, Wisconsin.

Brue's secret was simple: he had one-putted 10 greens and used only 26 putts altogether. The following day Brue hung on gamely with a modest 72, but this was not a day for modest golf. Before a record second-day crowd of 14,760, no fewer than 10 players broke 70 in the most bruising attack on par that Oakland Hills had ever experienced. Bob Rosburg and Doug Sanders led the onslaught with 67's and were rewarded with a share of the lead at 139. Hogan, after a 72, was four shots back at 143, sharing a rung with Sam Snead. Palmer had another painful day on the greens and turned in a 75. With 149 for 36 holes Arnie made the cut with not a stroke to spare. But even a fine pair of 70's on the last two rounds could not bring him into contention.

Fine weather on the final day and the prospect of a scrambling finish brought out a gallery of 20,439 who boosted the total attendance to 47,975. Both figures were new records, as were the $68,300 total purse and the $14,000 awaiting the winner. But by noon it began to look as though the day might not produce a winner. Snead faded away toward an eventual 290; Hogan slipped to 289 and finished out of the top 10 places for the first time in any Open he had played in since 1940. After three rounds the only man shooting par golf was Doug Sanders, a lanky Georgian with black curly hair and a quick and choppy swing. Jacky Cupit, a 23-year-old rookie from Longview, Texas, shot the best round of the morning, a 67, to climb into second place at 211, one stroke behind Sanders. Tied with Cupit were Mike Souchak and Bob Goalby, and a dozen other players hovered within range waiting for lightning to strike.

Sanders was playing with an aching backside, the result of a minor accident he had suffered while out in a rowboat earlier in the week. Souchak was coming down with tonsillitis and had been dosing himself with penicillin. Despite their indispositions, Sanders and Souchak appeared to be the pair most likely to make a running fight of it in the afternoon. Souchak teed off 40 minutes ahead of Sanders, birdied three of the first four holes and momentarily took the lead. But Mike came to sudden grief, faded to a 73 and finished with 284. Sanders regained his lead by playing par golf through eight holes but then he, too, came to grief. At the ninth hole Sanders was trapped and took his first bogey 5 for a front nine score of 36. At the 10th hole Doug three-putted and at the 12th, trapped again, he had to swallow a 6. At this point an altogether new name was hoisted to the top of the big scoreboard. Gene Littler had been lying just off the pace all week and now, with barely a shift in gears, his deliberate, marvelously accurate strokes carried him into the lead. Back in 1953 Littler had won the national amateur championship and the next year, his first as a pro, he ran a hard second to Ed Furgol in the U.S. Open at Baltusrol, missing an eight-foot putt for a tie on the last hole.

Gene was a handsome, fair-haired young man with an easy, graceful swing that the purists loved to watch. Gene the Machine they called him, and Bob Jones singled him out as "the coming golfer."

But now Gene Littler was 30, no longer a "comer." For two years, from early 1957 into 1959, he had such a frustrating time of it he considered quitting the tournament tour. "I would have quit," he said, "but my wife wouldn't let me." After taking some lessons from Paul Runyan, the stylist of the '30's, Littler finally started a comeback that earned him five victories in 1959 and two more in 1960. But early in 1961 Gene injured a rib and had to drop off the tour for two months. When he came back, he managed to win just $116 in his first five tournament starts. Just before the Open another sharp-eyed veteran, Ted Kroll, told Littler that he noticed a certain flatness in Gene's swing. So Gene made a last-minute adjustment to a more upright swing. His opening round was a 73. On the second day he was one of the 10 parbusters with a 68. After a third-round 72 he was well up in the pack at 213, three shots behind Sanders. Playing about two holes ahead of Sanders, Littler followed a basic formula for success: stay out of trouble and putt for dough. He was rarely in the rough and had not three-putted all day. Early in the last round Littler's share of the record 20,000 gallery totaled exactly seven people. But with each succeeding birdie his audience grew. He got the first one at the seventh hole, sinking a 15-footer. At the 11th he canned a six-footer for a birdie 3 and followed it up at the 13th with a 15-footer for a deuce. That put Littler out in front, three under par for the round with five holes to go. Now the crowd was king-sized and Gene responded to their applause with four straight pars. At the dogleg 18th, a 456-yard par 4, Gene hit a fair drive but followed it with a badly pulled spoon shot that fell into the deep bunker guarding the left-hand approach to the green. Littler hit out weakly, leaving 30 feet of wavy green between him and the hole. At that moment a shout from the 16th green telegraphed the news that Sanders had birdied the hole. Back on 18 Littler putted and the ball stopped two feet short of the hole. For 35 holes Gene had met the challenge of Oakland Hills' greens and refused to three-putt. Did he have one more putt left in him?

He did. Littler stepped up and punched the two-footer into the hole. It was only a bogey 5, but it meant a 68 and 281.

Now Sanders needed another birdie on one of the last two holes to tie. He tried. At the 17th hole his putt from 16 feet away rolled over the edge of the cup. At the 18th he drove into the rough at the corner of the dogleg. From there he faded a courageous two-iron around some pesky evergreens and almost hit the front of the green. With a last stab he chipped at the cup from 30 feet. The ball broke to the left and missed the cup by three inches. Sanders finished at 282 in a second-place tie with Bob Goalby.

In the press tent nearby, Gene Littler got the word and finally allowed himself a large grin. "Men," he said, "it's been a long wait."

In 1960 at Cherry Hills Jack Nicklaus, at the age of 20, had come within two strokes of winning the U.S. Open. The next summer at Oakland Hills Nicklaus tied for fourth place, three shots behind champion Gene Littler. Put the two Opens together and young Jack had the best two-year record of any man in the tournament. And he was still only a part-time player.

After winning the U.S. Amateur in the fall of 1961, Nicklaus made the decision to turn professional. Early in 1962, as his 22nd birthday approached, Jack joined up with the pro tour—and golf has not been the same since. For several seasons Nicklaus had dominated the amateur game as no one had since Bob Jones. Jack had started playing when he was 10 years old as a partner for his father, who owned a chain of drug stores in Columbus, Ohio. He soon became a pupil of Jack Grout, the pro at Scioto Country Club in Columbus. Under Grout, Jack became one of the first young players to learn that the prime requisite of modern golf is to powder the ball. "Let the horses go," Grout told him. "Control can come later." When he was 13, Jack banged out a 69 from the back tees at Scioto, a 7,095-yard course that had been the site of Bob Jones' victory in the 1926 Open.

At 16 Nicklaus won his first big tournament, the Ohio Open. He surprised a field full of professionals by shooting a 64 in the first round and leading all the way. At 19 Jack had won the U.S. Amateur. The next year, playing in the 1960 World Amateur Team championship at Merion, Nicklaus strung together four brilliant rounds of 66, 67, 68, 68. His 269 was a full 18 strokes better than Hogan's score at Merion when Ben won the 1950 Open. In 1961 Jack won his second U.S. Amateur at Pebble Beach. By now he was a married man and a father, anxious to become financially independent and eager to devote full time to the game.

From the moment Kid Nicklaus turned professional, his course was unalterably set toward an inevitable showdown with the top gun, Arnold Palmer. In his very first professional start, the 1962 Los Angeles Open, Nicklaus was co-favorite with Palmer and Gary Player. But Jack tied for 50th place and took home a purse of $33.33. In 17 succeeding tournaments over the next five months he never missed finishing in the money, but never did he finish first. By early June when he came in second to Gene Littler in the Thunderbird at Clifton, New Jersey, Nicklaus had earned more than $25,000—more than any rookie in history—and was among the top half-dozen money-winners. The absence of a victory nettled him but aside from that Jack was enjoying himself immensely. He liked traveling the circuit; he could now afford to have his family travel with him much of the time, and he could even indulge himself in 10 hours sleep on nights when he didn't have a morning starting time. "I've never had so much fun in all my life," he said. "Best of all I can work on my golf as much as I want."

The pros generally take Mondays off, but after the Thunderbird Nicklaus said, "I'm too charged up to rest." He went directly to Oakmont, where the Open was to begin on Thursday, and went out to play a practice round.

The Oakmont course, which straddles the Pennsylvania Turnpike a few miles northeast of Pittsburgh, was spruced up tougher than ever for its fourth turn as host to the Open. Tommy Armour, who had won there in 1927, called it Hades and Lew Worsham, the resident pro, assured everyone that the old girl had not softened with age. Oakmont has no water at all and with the exception of one hole its trees were not a threat to the pros. The exception was the short 17th where a cluster of young spruce was planted in the elbow of the dogleg to prevent anyone from taking the short cut to the green as Ben Hogan had in 1953. But Oakmont still had sand, acres and acres of sand in 208 traps, including one that covered a quarter of an acre. Even more of a threat were Oakmont's notorious greens with the grass clipped down to a lightning-quick eighth of an inch.

Nicklaus studied the course in his personal, detailed style. On each hole he picked out a landmark—a trap, a tree, a drainpipe—and stepped off the distance from it to the nearest and farthest edge of the green. He wrote down the yardage and other notes to himself on the back of a scorecard. During the tournament he would only need to step off the distance from his ball to the landmark, glance at the scorecard and have a precise idea of the length and difficulty of his approach to the green.

Arnold Palmer did not have to make a special study of Oakmont. Arnie had grown up just 40 miles away in Latrobe, Pennsylvania, and this was practically his home turf. He had played the course before "at least 200 times" including the 1953 Open when, as an amateur, he had failed to make the cut. Palmer in 1962 was in the third year of his reign over tournament golf. He had won 33 titles including his first British Open in 1961 and, in the spring of 1962, his third Masters.

Palmer's name headed the list of money-winners for a third straight season and with $60,000 already in the bank Arnie appeared likely to surpass the one-year record of

$75,000 he had set in 1960. After winning the Masters, Palmer once more was in position to shoot for the professional grand slam. If, of course, he could win the Open. At the Thunderbird Arnie complained of a sinus infection, a summer cold and an upset stomach. He finished in 35th place. Sunday night, after flying home from New Jersey, Arnie cut his finger unpacking luggage from his private plane. The gash affected his handshake but did not seem to bother his golf.

Only Ben Hogan was missing from the roster of fine golfers who teed off at Oakmont. Hogan had not finished in the top 10 the year before and it had been more than five years since his last Open victory, so for the first time since 1940 Ben did not automatically qualify on past performance for a place in the starting field. The U.S.G.A. advised Hogan he would have to try to qualify at one of the sectional tournaments. He sent in his application, but on the day of the qualifying rounds Hogan announced that he was suffering from bursitis in his left shoulder and withdrew from the competition.

But everyone else was there, including bigger crowds than the Open had ever attracted before. Opening day attendance on a Thursday was 17,837; on Friday 19,971; on Saturday 24,492. Each day was a record and the three-day total of 62,300 surpassed the old record by about 15,000.

Most of the massive mob pressed in around Palmer and Nicklaus who were paired together for the first two rounds. They were Arnie's Army all the way, a hometown crowd that cheered Palmer every time he took even a practice swing or dropped a six-inch putt. An occasional voice from the sideline would even exhort Palmer to step on Nicklaus' ball or kick it into a trap. All this failed to ruffle the self-contained young Nicklaus. It was Palmer, in fact, who seemed a bit embarrassed by the display.

The lesson Nicklaus had learned from his practice rounds was that he could charge the dangerous Oakmont course and get away with it. It was an approach exactly opposite the one Sam Parks had used to win there in 1935. But Nicklaus was no Parks. Hitting the ball hard on every shot, Jack birdied the first three holes and took a fast lead. But on the ninth hole the world turned sour for Jack. He drove into a trap, failed to get out with his first explosion, blasted the next one into a ditch and finally two-putted for a 70. Palmer, after going out in even par 36, had some adventures of his own. He bogeyed the 10th, 11th and 12th holes in succession, three-putting the last two. Then, in the patented Palmer method, he strung together five straight 3's. The streak included birdies at the 14th, where he sank a 10-footer, the 15th, where he dropped a five-footer, and the 292-yard 17th, where despite the spruce trees he drove the green and two-putted from 20 feet.

At sundown the lead belonged to Gene Littler, the defending champion, who had shot a 69. Heavy rain the day before the tournament had washed out the last practice round and Littler had only one day in which to get acquainted with the course. But Gene made himself at home with a two-under-par round that featured a spectacular eagle 3 on the ninth hole where he chipped his ball into the cup from 35 yards away.

Bob Rosburg and Bobby Nichols were one swing back at 70. Palmer, who had avoided all 208 of Oakmont's traps, had a 71 and Nicklaus a 72.

The next day Arnold Palmer made his move as fog and overflow crowds slowed down the play. On the first hole Palmer's five-iron was stiff to the pin and he sank the two-footer for a bird. He added another birdie at the seventh and one more at the ninth to reach the turn in 33. On the 10th hole his eight-foot putt for a par hung precariously on the very lip of the cup. Palmer waited, as the rules then allowed, and he waited. After three minutes and 25 seconds he gave up and tapped the ball in. On the 17th he made up for that bogey with his only birdie on the back nine. Arnold was in with a 68 and a 139 that tied for the lead with Bob Rosburg. Rosburg, putting boldly and well, birdied two of the last three holes to cap off a 69. Littler shot a 74 and fell four shots off the pace. Nicklaus broke par with a 70 and now trailed Palmer by three.

Palmer and Nicklaus had new playing companions for Saturday's final two rounds, but each hour brought them closer to the eventual showdown. Each man had his troubles. On the third hole Palmer got caught in the parallel ridges of the notorious Church Pews trap. Later he sank a 35-foot putt for an eagle deuce on his favorite 17th hole. But on the next tee a low-flying airplane disturbed him and he bogeyed the hole. His third round was 73, and Nicklaus with a 72 cut his lead to two strokes.

Nicklaus, playing just ahead of Palmer, went the front nine of the afternoon round in 35. Palmer came into the ninth hole needing a par 5 for a 34. But his second shot caught the rough and when he tried to come out Arnie flubbed a shot that went only about 10 feet. He took a 6. At about the same time Nicklaus ran home a 14-foot putt for a birdie on No. 11. "I figured then we were all square," said Jack. Not quite, but when Palmer bogeyed the short 13th hole, the match was even and both men parred in from there. Nicklaus two-putted the 18th green for his seventh straight par. Palmer came to the same green needing a 12-foot birdie putt to win. The crowd stood 20 deep on tiptoes or peered through cardboard periscopes to watch him go for it. But the ball broke left of the hole and rolled by.

Nicklaus, with a 69, had made up two strokes on Palmer to earn a tie at 283. Now the two giants came face to face at last. Palmer was 32 and, except for an occasional lapse on the greens, was playing the best golf of his life. Nicklaus, at 22, had set a simple goal: "I want to be the best golfer the world has ever seen."

Another mob of 10,000 turned out for the Sunday afternoon playoff and they left no doubt whom they considered the Good Guy in this melodrama. "C'mon, Arnie!" they shouted hoarsely. Nicklaus' best shots were rewarded with silence. Practically the only Nicklaus fans around were his wife and father and a handful of buddies who had made the trip from Columbus.

But Nicklaus reacted to Arnie's Army as though he had cotton in his ears. He slowed down his play to an indolent pace, a tactic that never failed to irritate Palmer. On the first hole Palmer drove into the rough, knocked his six-iron approach over the green, overshot the pin by 15 feet with a chip shot and two-putted for a weak bogey 5. Nicklaus got his par and took a one-stroke lead. On the fourth hole, a 544-yard par 5, Palmer outdrove Nicklaus for the first time. Jack hooked into the six-inch rough, played out safely with a three-iron and was faced with a nearly impossible third shot. A monstrous trap blocked his approach to the pin which was set in the neck of the pear-shaped green 100 yards away. But Nicklaus lofted a wedge that came down at the pin like a diving falcon and stopped six feet away. He made the birdie putt and led Palmer by two. After eight holes Palmer was four strokes down and his cause seemed all but lost. But then Arnie's putter, which had been suffering from a bad case of the "crookeds," suddenly went straight. Palmer hit on birdie putts at the ninth hole, the 11th and the 12th. Now he trailed by a single stroke. It was an old-fashioned Palmer charge and everyone knew it, including his 22-year-old opponent. "Don't be scared," Nicklaus told himself. "Remember, you've played twelve holes and you're one up. That's all that counts. Just play your own game. Nobody here expects you to win anyway."

On the 161-yard 13th hole Palmer underclubbed himself, barely made the front of the green and three-putted from 40 feet. Right there Palmer's charge ended where it had begun —on the putting green. Nicklaus parred the 13th and led by two strokes again. At the 18th hole Palmer bogeyed for a final 74. By then it was academic. Nicklaus never flinched as he finished with a string of pars for a 71.

The youngster from Ohio with a build like a blockhouse had beaten the best, to become the youngest Open champion since 1923 when Bob Jones won for the first time. Where Jones in his prime could drive a ball 240 yards and the modern pros increased the distance to about 260, Nicklaus made 285-yard drives a habit and could go over 300 yards as easy as not. But even more awesome than his power was Jack's unwavering stability under pressure. Over 90 holes of championship play on Oakmont's oceanic greens, the new champion had three-putted only once.

Anyone who has watched Jack Nicklaus take a golf course apart can be forgiven for shaking his head and predicting flatly that the Ohio Bear would never lose another tournament. But no sooner said than Nicklaus does lose his next tournament, and lose it big. Golf is that kind of game. Nicklaus' victory in the 1962 Open was anything but a fluke. Later that season he won two more official tournaments and added a $50,000 windfall by winning the first television "world series" of golf. His first victory in 1963 came at Palm Springs where he demolished Gary Player in their 18-hole playoff. In April at Augusta he won the Masters—the youngest winner ever—with a clutch finish that edged Tony Lema by a stroke. Then he turned his attention to the defense of his national championship.

This was the 50th anniversary of the historic 1913 Open in which Francis Ouimet upset Vardon and Ray, and in recognition of the occasion the Open returned to the Country Club in Brookline, Massachusetts. Ouimet himself was on hand, a gentleman in his early 70's now, and a reminder that all the great moments of American golf had taken place within the span of one man's lifetime. A severe New England winter had damaged the venerable Country Club course. The fairways were skinnier than ever and the greens were not always in the best condition. Scoring was set back almost to the 1913 level, when a 75 was a card to be proud of.

Few scores sailed higher than those of Jack Nicklaus. He shot a 76 the first day, a 77 the second and, just like that, was eliminated from the tournament. Not many of the pros were matching par 71 on the Country Club's wooded pathways. Bob Gadja of Forest Lake Country Club in Bloomfield Hills, Michigan, provided the first day's surprise with a 69. But Gadja never again got below 80. Arnold Palmer, working hard to erase the memory of his 1962 playoff defeat, fired a 69 the second day and moved into a tie for the lead at 142 with Dow Finsterwald and Jacky Cupit. As the final two rounds began, sans Nicklaus, a mean northeaster swept in and made sure there would be no par golf shot this day. In the morning winds Palmer shot a 77, Cupit a 76 and Finsterwald a fatal 79. Tony Lema, who had been three strokes behind the leaders, edged closer with a 74.

The final holes shaped up as a test of nerves between Palmer, Cupit and Lema. Out ahead of them on the course Julius Boros was playing good golf and setting the early pace. It looked as though Jay would finish well up among the leaders, but that was no surprise. In a dozen Opens since 1950 Boros had finished in the top five places seven times, including his victory over Hogan in 1952. Boros birdied the 16th hole and the 17th, too. Par on the last hole gave him a 72 and 293, nine over par for the tournament. Boros sat down with a glass of beer and waited to see who would be first to improve on his score.

The first to fail was Lema. Tony bogeyed both of the last two holes and finished with 295. Next came Palmer, needing a pair of pars to take the lead. Arnie reached the 17th green in two but he three-putted—it was getting to be a habit. That bogey 5 and a par on the 18th gave Palmer a 74–293, and a tie with Boros.

Now the big cup was Jacky Cupit's for the taking if he could play the last two holes in one over par. Athough he was only 25, Cupit was no stranger to pressure spots like this one. As an amateur he had won 39 tournaments in five years and had played on three N.C.A.A. championship teams at the University of Houston. Four of his older brothers had become professional golfers. When Jacky did the same thing in 1961, he won a tournament—the Canadian Open—in his first summer on the tour and was named Rookie of the Year.

Now he had the Country Club's tricky 17th hole to execute. Twin bunkers guarded the corner of the left-hand dogleg. Cupit decided to play short of this hazard and used a spoon for his tee shot. The decision was costly. Instead of falling short, his ball reached the sand and rolled up the face of a bunker. Cupit sacrificed one shot just to get safely out of the trap. He hit his third shot to the back edge of the green. Then, just as Palmer had, Cupit three-putted. Double bogey 6. Cupit's lead was gone but he parred the 18th hole for a 75–293 and a place in a three-man playoff.

Memories of Ouimet, Vardon and Ray were close to the surface next day as the threesome of Cupit, Palmer and Boros teed off. Cupit seemed edgy. Palmer had spent a sleepless night nursing an upset stomach and he looked pale and drawn. Boros was his imperturbable self. Even the discovery that his locker had been broken into and all but three of his golf balls stolen failed to rile him. "Three is more than I'll need anyway," he said. On the fourth hole Boros dropped a birdie putt and took a lead that he never lost. Boros was giving away 10 years to Palmer and 18 years to Cupit. But Palmer suffered an atrocious triple bogey 7 on the 11th hole when his ball landed in a rotten tree stump. He wound up with a painful 76. Cupit did better than that, with a 73, but Boros stayed under par to win by three strokes with a solid 70. It was his first sub-par round of the tournament.

Just three months past his 43rd birthday, Boros was the oldest man to win the national championship with the exception of Ted Ray, who was a month older than Boros

when he won in 1920. For Boros it had been 11 years
between his first Open triumph in 1952 and his second in
1963. No one will be very surprised if he should win it again
in 1974.

Ken Venturi watched through sweat-blurred eyes as his
putt from 10 feet broke perceptively to the left and fell with
a click into the cup. Venturi dropped his putter and threw
back his head in a gesture of exhaustion and relief. "My
God," he said, "I've won the Open."

It had been a long climb. Like most of the best players,
Ken Venturi got an early start in golf. His father ran the pro
shop at Harding Park Municipal golf course in San Francisco, and Ken spent every hour he could there practicing
and learning the game. By the time Ken was 17 he was
playing in national junior tournaments. Then he won the San
Francisco City championship, the youngest player in years
to do so. Eventually Ken came under the influence of Ed
Lowery. Yes, the same Eddie Lowery who in 1913 had
played hookie from grade school to caddy for Francis Ouimet in the Open at Brookline. Lowery had gone west, made
his fortune as a Lincoln-Mercury dealer, and become the
patron of several young San Francisco golfers of promise.
Venturi was one of these. In 1952 Lowery introduced his
protégé to Byron Nelson and the first time they played
together Ken shot a 66. "How was that?" asked the youngster, angling for a compliment. "Meet me on the first tee
tomorrow at nine A.M.," replied Nelson. "There are six or
seven things wrong with your game that need fixing." That
was the beginning of a long tutor-pupil relationship between
the old master and the young man of promise. Before long
Nelson had removed the quirks in Venturi's grip and
straightened out his swing. Ken was hitting long iron shots
that even the Nelson of old would have envied. Moving up
through the amateur ranks, Venturi made the Walker Cup
team in 1953. The next year he was drafted into the Army.

When he came out at the end of 1955, a short refresher course with Nelson got him back on his game. Early in 1956 Venturi was one of 42 amateurs who were invited to play that year in the Masters. From that moment on the name Venturi was marked for fame—and controversy.

No amateur had ever won the Masters and no 24-year-old upstart from California was deemed likely to. But Ken shot a marvelous 66 on the first day and led all the way to the last few holes of the tournament. By informal tradition Byron Nelson was usually paired with the leader on the last day of the Masters. But because of the student-teacher relationship between Nelson and Venturi, Bob Jones and Cliff Roberts, who run the Masters, decided that Nelson should play with someone else. Instead Venturi drew Sam Snead for a playing companion and Sam, who had a chance at first place himself, had little to say to the young amateur. Venturi shot an 80 and lost the tournament by a single stroke.

The press met a sorely disappointed Venturi at San Francisco airport that night and the next day Ken was quoted across the nation complaining that he had not been given a fair shake at the Masters. It was the kind of sour grapes that could be forgiven only on grounds of youth and self-anger.

In the minds of many people Venturi was labeled a sorehead and crybaby—tags that died hard. Things went well for Ken the next few years—almost too well. Late in 1956 he turned professional and in his first four pro seasons he won 10 championships. In 1960 he again came within a breath of winning the Masters, but Arnold Palmer birdied the final two holes to beat him out. Ken did win the Bing Crosby and the Milwaukee Opens in 1960, finished fifth or better in 14 tournaments and headed home to his lovely wife Conni and their two young sons with earnings of $41,230 in his kick. He did not win another tournament for four years.

In 1960 Arnold Palmer was the dominating influence in golf and Venturi was convinced he had to start hitting the ball farther, like Palmer, if he were to stay in the first rank.

So he set out to develop a controlled hook. But in pressing for distance Ken did something disruptive to his swing. Soon he had lost his groove altogether. Then his confidence went. Whenever he was faced with a clutch shot he backed away from it. On the pro tour that's all the margin you need—to lose.

While playing at Palm Springs early in 1962, Venturi suffered a pinched nerve that practically paralyzed his right side. For a time Ken could barely lift his hand high enough to comb his hair and, when he swung, pain flashed through his chest. Doctors tried cortisone and whirlpool baths and deep heat but only slowly did the pain disappear. In 1962 he started in 27 tournaments and earned only $6,951.39. The next year was worse. In 27 starts Venturi never finished higher than 18th. He collected checks in only eight tournaments and they totaled $3,848.33. The golden boy of such recent memory was reduced to begging for invitations to tournaments that once had pleaded for his presence. When he arrived at the players' registration desk for one tournament, he was told bluntly that he had not been invited. It was a humiliating experience. But somewhere in these lean years of disappointment and self-doubt was the forging of the man Venturi. Not many tears were shed for Venturi when he was down. "Let the self-centered so-and-so stew," was the reaction of many. "I never had an Arnie's Army," reflected Ken. "But I'll tell you I've had Venturi's Vultures sitting out there the past three years!"

By the beginning of 1964 Venturi had money and courage remaining for just one more tournament season. Physically he was fine again. His hook was gone and in practice he could practically knock the bottom out of a bucket with his irons at 200 yards. But in January at the Los Angeles Open he missed the cut. Later he missed at the Crosby Open and again at Palm Springs. He went home to practice some more, convinced now that his real trouble was mental. "I was scared," he said. Back on the tour in March, Venturi won

$1,100 at Pensacola, his first four-figure check in two years. Two weeks later at Doral he won $950. Then he waited for his annual invitation to the Masters. It never came. "Somehow," he said in disbelief, "I believed I would *always* be invited to the Masters."

Back in San Francisco Ken listened to a tip from his old friend Ed Lowery who showed him that he was not positioning himself squarely to the ball before he hit it. His hips had pointed one way and his shoulders the other. Early in June Venturi received the last invitation to the $100,000 Thunderbird tournament—only because he telephoned the tournament chairman and begged for it. Ken finished in a tie for third in the Thunderbird and earned $6,250. As soon as he could get to a phone, he called his wife in San Francisco. They both cried.

Two days after the Thunderbird Venturi qualified for the Open by shooting 77–70 in a sectional tournament, passing 45 others who were ahead of him after the morning round. It was the first time in four years he had qualified for the Open.

Jack Nicklaus and Arnold Palmer were cofavorites in the 1964 championship to be played over the big, rambunctious Congressional Country Club outside Washington. The hellish heat of summer had settled on the Potomac Valley and Congressional, at 7,053 yards, was the longest course in Open history.

On the eve of the tournament Venturi received a letter from Father Francis Kevin Murray, a parish priest in San Francisco who had become Ken's friend and counselor. The six-page letter said in part, "Keep your composure. Never let anything great that happens get you too elated, never let anything bad get you down. Ask that the Lord let you play to the best of your ability. You are truly the new Ken Venturi, born out of suffering and turmoil but now wise and mature and battle-toughened."

The first day of the Open was 84 degrees and muggy, and

the new Ken Venturi shot a 72. But the old Arnold Palmer, chipping beautifully and using fewer than 30 putts for the first time all year, shot a 68. Jack Nicklaus also was on the verge of busting par when he ran out of gas and bogeyed each of the last three holes. Nicklaus turned in a card of 72 and was not again in contention. Tony Lema remarked after his round, "This is some course. If we're going to play two rounds here Saturday, they'd better have the oxygen and ambulances ready."

On Friday Venturi shot a 70. Palmer continued to subdue the big course with a 69. But the big news was a 64 produced by 29-year-old Tommy Jacobs. Tommy called Congressional "the toughest course I've ever played." But he had teed off with the "dew sweepers" at 8:30 A.M. when the air was clear and the temperature 75. By midday when the heat reached 92 degrees, Tommy was safely home with his six birdies and twelve pars. His 64 tied the Open record established in 1950 at Merion by Lee Mackey, Jr., and put Jacobs in first place with 136, one stroke ahead of Palmer and six ahead of Venturi. For the second year in a row the defending champion, in this case Julius Boros, failed to qualify for the last 36 holes.

The last day at Congressional was a killer. It was as though 20,000 people were caught inside a steam boiler. The temperature gauge kept rising, to 96 . . . 98 . . . 100 degrees. Perspiration turned shirts and trousers into sopping rags. Palmer and Jacobs were paired together and Arnie had to scramble from the start. His first two shots found the rough and he barely saved his par. At the fifth hole Jacobs laid an approach shot two feet from the pin and got his birdie. Palmer three-putted for a bogey and trailed by three strokes. Arnie never did get a birdie on the morning round. He settled for a 75 that left him six shots off the pace. Jacobs played flawlessly until the eighth: he was trapped there and again at the ninth. Both slips cost him bogeys and he made the turn in 36.

With disturbing frequency on the front nine, Palmer and Jacobs and the thousands who were following them could hear shouts of applause from the gallery two holes ahead that was watching Ken Venturi. On the first hole of the morning Venturi had stuck his approach 10 feet from the pin. His birdie putt stopped on the lip of the cup and sat there. Venturi and his playing companion, Raymond Floyd, waited for a full minute. Finally, the ball fell into the hole. From that point Venturi exploded on a fantastic binge of pinpoint golf. He knocked in a 15-foot birdie on the fourth hole and another on the fifth. Ken was hitting some of the best long shots ever seen in the Open. On the eighth hole he sank his longest putt, from 25 feet, and on the tough ninth hole he rolled in a 10-footer for his fifth birdie. Venturi had shot an incredible 30, equaling the Open record for nine holes and wiping out the six-stroke lead of Tommy Jacobs. But the effort had taken its toll. Venturi walked up the hilly ninth fairway as though he were barely going to make it. He had eaten very little breakfast and had failed to fortify himself with salt pills against the dehydrating heat. Now he was tied for the lead, but he still had 27 holes to play. In the Washington inferno they seemed like a thousand.

On the back nine Venturi treated the sweating multitude to another demonstration of precision golf. He birdied the 180-yard 12th hole to go six under. He parred the rest until he reached 17. As he waited his turn to putt on the 17th green, Venturi sat slumped on the end of his golf bag. Then he stroked his long first putt a foot and a half past the hole. The ball stopped in a footprint and when he tapped it back toward the hole, it jumped to the left and missed. Three putts and his first bogey. "I was shaking so badly," Venturi said later, "that I could barely hold my putter. I know it wasn't nerves because I was shaking all over."

On the 18th hole Venturi pushed his drive into the right-hand rough. But he lofted out with an eight-iron and chipped to within four feet of the flag. Once more he missed his par putt. It was a 66 for Ken but when Jacobs finished a few minutes later with a 70, Venturi was two strokes out of the lead.

At this point Dr. John Everett, a Congressional Club member, entered the picture. Seeing that Venturi was suffering from heat exhaustion and dehydration, he had Ken lie down in the locker room during the hour between his rounds. Instead of letting him eat lunch, Everett kept Ken on a diet of tea and salt tablets—a dozen of them during the afternoon. Almost too soon it was 2:30 and Venturi went back into the suffocating heat for another four-hour ordeal. Everett went, too, carrying a wet towel wrapped around a plastic bag of ice which he passed to Venturi from time to time. Also at Ken's side was Joe Dey, executive director of the U.S.G.A., lending unofficial sanction to the incredibly slow pace Venturi was setting.

Slow it was, and slower it got. Dripping wet from head to shoe, the 33-year-old Venturi trudged from hole to hole, from shot to shot, often stopping altogether, then barely pushing one foot in front of another. But by some miracle his golf was not affected. Venturi parred the first five, three-putted the sixth but got that stroke back at the ninth by holing a downhill 12-footer for his birdie 4. His even-par golf was better than Jacobs could do. Tommy's 206 had set a new Open record for 54 holes but on the final round he went three over par on the first two holes and lost the lead. When Jacobs bogeyed at the ninth hole and again at the 10th, it was Venturi's Open for the taking if only he could finish. On the 13th hole Venturi hit his putt into the cup from 18 feet for a birdie. That was the adrenalin he needed to finish. Now he led by four strokes and he held grimly to that margin to the end. As Venturi tramped down the long hill to the 18th green in the blazing late afternoon sunlight, the gallery lining the slopes on either side set off echoing waves of applause. "Hold your head up, Ken," Joe Dey told him. "You're the champion now."

Venturi straightened up and lifted his familiar flat white cap to the crowd. They cheered anew and Venturi grinned back at them. Ken's approach had caught the bunker beside the green and his recovery shot left him a 10-foot putt. A 4 here would give him an even par 70, a four-stroke victory and, at 278, a total score second only to Hogan's record 276 at Riviera in 1948. It would also end the ordeal.

Venturi stepped up to the ball and putted away.

The site selected for the 65th Open Championship of the United States Golf Association was Bellerive Country Club, a new course fashioned out of rolling green farmland west of St. Louis. As a club Bellerive could trace its roots back almost as far as the origins of golf in the United States. But the club had moved twice in the face of spreading metropolis. Its latest grounds, designed by Architect Robert Trent Jones, had been in use for just five years.

Like many Open courses in recent years, Bellerive was a big sprawling layout with little finesse and only a couple of holes that could be called easy on the eye. It looked like a hitters' course—at 7,191 yards it was longer even than Congressional had been the year before. Even Jack Nicklaus who at 6 to 1 was the favorite to win the championship wrote that Bellerive put *too much* premium on power. But power alone never won an Open and to many an old hand it looked like the secret of Bellerive would be merely to keep the ball in play—and putt like mad!

Bellerive's membership of 400 had been preparing for their Open for more than two years. There were 25 volunteer committees for everything from admissions and apparel to scorekeeping and finance. A small army had been recruited: 400 gallery marshals, 130 Pinkerton guards, 200 scorekeepers, parking attendants, messengers and many more.

For the first time the Open was to be televised in color and N.B.C. arrived with a dozen cameras, tons of equipment and a crew of 75. It was a far cry from the first simple unit used to telecast the 1947 Open, also in St. Louis, when a strictly local audience of some 600 sets watched in suspense as Snead tied Worsham, only to lose in a playoff. Color TV was undoubtedly the most efficient way to watch the tournament. But still the live crowds came, dressed in shorts and polo shirts and visored caps. They trampled through the dry and dusty fields, waited in long lines to buy a refreshing St. Louis beer and pressed down against the fairway ropes to get an occasional glimpse of the golfers at their labors.

And labor they did. "I sure don't enjoy playing this course," said one young pro. "It's too much work."

In a controversial break with tradition, the double round on the final day had been done away with and instead a single round was scheduled for each of the four days. U.S.G.A. officials argued that the double round had become more a test of endurance and less a test of golf. They pointed to Ken Venturi who had been forced to play for eight and a half hours in the Washington heat to win his championship. The new arrangement also enabled television to carry the tournament on two days instead of just a single broadcast on Saturday.

In order to keep the gallery down to manageable size, a limit of 20,000 was put on each day's attendance. But this time no limit was needed, probably because the players whom the crowd wanted most to see were gone from contention almost before the tournament began. Jack Nicklaus had won the recent Masters with a superlative 271, nine strokes ahead of anyone else, and there was serious talk of how he might string this Open, the British Open and the P.G.A. together into a slam. But on the first day Jack drove wildly, missed putts that could have redeemed him and shot a 78. Arnold Palmer looked to be playing well enough, but he just couldn't score, as his 76 testified. On the fifth hole, a 465-yard par 4, Palmer's drive bounced into a masonry drain. By local rule it was considered part of a water hazard and he was penalized a stroke. "This course baffles me," muttered Arnold and the next day, still as baffled as ever, Palmer shot another 76 for 152 and missed the cut. It was the first time in four years that had happened to Palmer in any tournament.

Palmer went home, where Ben Hogan had been all along. For the fourth year in a row Hogan refused to submit to playing in qualifying rounds and did not enter. "It's a shame," said Fred Corcoran, the sage promotor. "Ben is so accurate this might have been his course."

Sam Snead was present, trying for the umpteenth time since 1937 to be a winner. Sam survived the cut and finished in 24th place, pretty good for a gaffer of 53, but he was never in serious contention.

For the third straight year the defending champion missed the cutoff. But Ken Venturi was a special case. After winning the Open, Ken had gone on to an excellent year in 1964. But now he was faced with a new trauma. Since January he had been suffering from a rare circulatory ailment in his hands. The main nerve controlling both sensation and movement in his fingers was being squeezed as it passed through a tunnel in his wrists. His fingers had gone numb and as far as any sense of touch was concerned, he might as well have been swinging a baseball bat instead of a golf club. Venturi had gone to Mayo Clinic for treatment and each night soaked his hand in hot paraffin. But the trouble persisted. If he had not been defending champion, Venturi would not even have tried to play at Bellerive. But try he did and in doing so he grew a foot in stature and earned more admirers than he had ever had before. It was a brave try and the crowd applauded him at every green. But the course was unrelenting and Venturi took 40 putts on his way to an 81. The next day Ken shot a 79. He went out like a champion, rifling home a 35-foot birdie putt on the last hole. From St. Louis Venturi returned to Mayo's where doctors operated on his wrists to relieve the pressure. They predicted Ken would soon be swinging a golf club again with his pet touch.

Almost from the start the tournament belonged to the two best foreign players in the field. One was Kelvin Nagle, a husky 44-year-old from Sydney, Australia. Nagle had never won a tournament in the U.S. on his frequent visits here, but in 1960 he had beaten Arnold Palmer for the British Open crown. Nagle was not a long ball hitter. But he was very straight, his putter was working and the result was a 68 and the first-round lead.

Two strokes back in a tie for third place sat Gary Player of Johannesburg, South Africa. Player was 29 and he had won a bushelful of tournaments including the Masters, the British Open and the P.G.A. More than once he had made a run at the U.S. Open, and with Palmer and Nicklaus he was considered part of golf's Big Three. Up to a point, Gary was a feature writer's dream. There were more instant angles to the Gary Player story than any golfer since Sam Snead. A dark and handsome 150-pounder, Gary had built up his muscles and at the same time the length of his drives by lifting weights every day until he developed the physique of a welterweight champion. As a boy he had broken his neck diving into a shallow pool but recovered. He followed a diet of wheat germ, raisins, bananas, nuts and honey. On even the hottest days he always appeared on the golf course wearing a black shirt and black trousers—black gave him strength, he said. He was generous with compliments for his fellow players, for the course and for all Americans, who had been "so decent" to him. His brown eyes glistened as he talked longingly of earning enough money so he could spend more time with his wife and five small children back home on the ranch in South Africa.

"If he weren't in such dead earnest," said one listener, "I'd swear he was putting me on."

Earnest or not, Gary Player was an excellent golfer and the sight of his name among a raft of lesser-known players at the top of the standings was bad news for those farther back who hoped to make up ground. The others might blow, but

Player was not likely to. By swinging so hard he almost fell down on his follow-through, Gary could drive for respectable distance and on the second day he forged his second par 70 and took the lead. One stroke back after a 73 was Kel Nagle, tied with Mason Rudolph of Tennessee for second place.

Player slipped a stroke over par on the third day but nevertheless, his 71–211 stretched his lead to two strokes. Nagle had a 72 and held on to second place, this time in a tie with Kentuckian Frank Beard. Nagle benefited from an unusual ruling on the 12th hole. He drove into a rutted area 30 yards wide of the fairway, and asked the U.S.G.A. official on the hole if he could lift the ball without penalty because he considered it "ground under repair." The official, one of 27 volunteers assigned to various parts of the course, turned him down. Nagle played his original ball after dropping it out of the unplayable lie and took a bogey 5. But he also played out the hole with a second, provisional ball and got his par 4 with that one. Some fans who had been watching the incident insisted that the day before Raymond Floyd had received a free lift from the same spot. U.S.G.A. director Joe Dey spent the next hour hunting down the official who had been at the 12th hole the day before. He eventually found the man and learned that Floyd had indeed been given relief on grounds that his ball was in a rut made by a burrowing animal. Nagle's case was quickly reviewed, the ruling reversed and a stroke saved.

The next afternoon that stroke grew to look very large. With three holes to play Player was coasting toward certain success with a three-shot lead over Nagle, who was the last remaining contender. Kel had just taken a six at the 15th hole, catching a trap with his fairway wood and then three-putting. "I've blown it!" said Nagle and when Player, in the next twosome, parred the hole, it appeared that he had. But Player, who until now had been the very model of consistency, finally suffered a horror hole of his own. At the 218-

yard 16th, Gary ballooned his tee shot into a trap to the right of the green and the ball nestled two-thirds buried in the sand. It was a tough shot and Gary exploded out 15 feet from the flag. He putted three feet past the hole. Then with a furious glare he curled his next putt around the rim and out. It was a double bogey 5. At almost the same moment Nagle was making good a birdie putt on the 606-yard 17th. Now they were even and when neither man could make another birdie putt on the holes remaining, the tie stood up. Nagle, 69–282. Player 71–282.

For the 23rd time the Open championship came down to a basic golf match, man to man. Either way there would be a new champion, a good one, and the first foreign winner since Ted Ray in 1920. Should Nagle win at 44, he would be the oldest champion ever. The turning point came early and in unfortunate fashion. Player led by a stroke as they teed off on the fifth hole. Nagle pulled his drive into the gallery that lined the rough and his ball struck a gray-haired lady, Miss Alma Pearson of Milwaukee. Miss Pearson sank to the ground, blood spurting from the wound in her forehead. As Nagle approached the cluster of first aid men and nurses around the unconscious woman, he looked shaken. His ball had bounded 20 feet away, still in the rough on a downhill lie. As Nagle prepared for his recovery shot, Player told him, "Don't let it get to you, Kel. It happens to all of us." But instead of reaching the fairway, Nagle again pulled the ball into the crowd and hit a second woman, Mrs. Dorothy Barrea of Plainfield, New Jersey. This time it was a glancing blow on the ankle. The ball bounced into the fairway. It was a dazed Nagle who selected a wood and hit his third shot into a greenside trap. Three strokes later the nightmarish hole was over, but Nagle had taken a double bogey 6. Player had his routine 4 and led by three shots. That was all Gary needed. He was playing meticulous if unspectacular golf and by the time television picked up the match at the 15th hole, it was all over: Player led by five strokes. A couple of conservative bogeys on the last two holes served only to chop the final margin to three. Player, 71, Nagle, 74. Miss Pearson, who had been carted off in a stretcher, returned to the course to show Nagle the eight new stitches in her scalp and assure him she was all right. But she was too late to help.

At the award ceremony Player announced that he was donating $5,000 of his purse to cancer research and another $20,000 to the U.S.G.A. for the betterment of junior golf. He also paid his caddy $2,000. As his purse for winning totaled $26,000, Gary's net income for the week came to a minus $1,000.

But the purse is insignificant when compared to the half-million or so that a United States Open champion can earn on the side, a fact that was not lost on the flock of young professionals who finished close upon the heels of Gary Player. Most of their names have an unfamiliar ring: Geiberger, Wysong, Beard . . . Floyd, Devlin and Graham . . . Oppermann and Huckaby. Most of them will never attract our attention again. But if history is a reliable guide to coming events, then among the losers at Bellerive were a half-dozen future winners of the United States Open.

Appendix

The First Ten Finishers and Ties of the
U.S. OPEN [1895–1965]

1895

Newport Golf Club, Newport, Rhode Island, October 4
11 entries — $355 prize money

Horace Rawlins (Newport)	45	46	41	41	173
Willie Dunn (Shinnecock Hills)	43	46	44	42	175
James Foulis (Chicago)	46	43	44	43	176
*A. W. Smith (Toronto)	47	43	44	42	176
William F. Davis (Newport)	45	49	42	42	178
Willie Campbell (Brookline)	41	48	42	48	179
John Patrick (Tuxedo)	46	48	46	43	183
John Harland (Western)	45	48	43	47	183
Samuel Tucker (St. Andrews)	49	48	45	43	185
John Reid (Philadelphia)	49	51	55	51	206
William Norton (Lakewood)	51	58	withdrew		

1896

Shinnecock Hills Golf Club, Long Island, New York, July 18
28 entries — $355 prize money

James Foulis (Chicago)	78	74	152
Horace Rawlins (Sadaquada)	79	76	155
G. Douglas (Brookline)	79	79	158
*A. W. Smith (Toronto)	78	80	158
John Shippen (Shinnecock Hills)	78	81	159
*Jim Whigham (Onwentsia)	82	77	159
Joe Lloyd (Essex)	78	82	160
Willie Tucker (St. Andrews)	78	82	160
R. B. Wilson (Shinnecock Hills)	82	80	162
A. Ricketts (Albany)	80	83	163

* Denotes Amateur

1897

Chicago Golf Club, Wheaton, Illinois, September 17
  35 entries — $355 prize money

Joe Lloyd (Essex)	83	79	162
Willie Anderson (Watch Hill)	79	84	163
James Foulis (Chicago)	80	88	168
Willie Dunn (New York)	87	81	168
Willie Hoare (Pittsburgh)	82	87	169
A. Ricketts (Albany)	91	81	172
Bernard Nicholls (Lenox)	87	85	172
Horace Rawlins (Sadaquada)	91	82	173
*Jim Whigham (Onwentsia)	87	86	173
Dave Foulis (Chicago)	86	87	173

1898

Myopia Club, Hamilton, Massachusetts, June 17–18
  49 entries — $355 prize money

Fred Herd (Washington Park)	84	85	75	84	328
Alex Smith (Washington Park)	78	86	86	85	335
Willie Anderson (Baltusrol)	81	82	87	86	336
Joe Lloyd (Essex)	87	80	86	86	339
Willie Smith (Shinnecock Hills)	82	91	85	82	340
Willie Hoare (Dayton)	84	84	87	87	342
Willie Dunn (New York)	85	87	87	84	343
*Herbert C. Leeds (Myopia)	81	84	93	89	347
Bernard Nicholls (Lenox)	86	87	88	86	347
R. McAndrews (Cohasset)	85	90	86	86	347
John Jones (Myopia)	83	84	90	90	347

1899

Baltimore Country Club, Baltimore, Maryland, September 14–15
  81 entries — $650 prize money

Willie Smith (Midlothian)	77	82	79	77	315
George Low (Dyker Meadow)	82	79	89	76	326
Val Fitzjohn (Otsego)	85	80	79	82	326
W. H. Way (Detroit)	80	85	80	81	326
Willie Anderson (New York)	77	81	85	84	327
J. Park (Essex)	88	80	75	85	328

Alex Smith (Washington Park)	82	81	82	85	330
Henry Gullane (St. Davids)	81	86	80	84	331
Laurence Auchterlonie					
(Glen View)	86	87	82	78	333
P. Walker (Onwentsia)	84	86	77	86	333

1900

Chicago Golf Club, Wheaton, Illinois, October 4–5
60 entries — $650 prize money

Henry Vardon (Ganton, England)	79	78	76	80	313
John Henry Taylor					
(Richmond, England)	76	82	79	78	315
David Bell (Midlothian)	78	83	83	78	323
Laurence Auchterlonie					
(Glen View)	84	82	80	81	327
Willie Smith (Midlothian)	82	83	79	83	328
George Low (Dyker Meadow)	84	80	85	82	331
Tom Hutchinson					
(Shinnecock Hills)	81	87	81	84	333
Henry Turpie (Edgewater)	84	87	79	84	334
Stewart Gardner (Lenox)		163		84	89	336
Val Fitzjohn (Sadaquada)		167		89	82	338

1901

Myopia Hunt Club, Hamilton, Massachusetts, June 14–15
60 entries — $650 prize money

Willie Anderson (Pittsfield)	84	83	83	81	331
					85
Alex Smith (Washington Park)	82	82	87	80	331
					86
Willie Smith (Midlothian)	84	86	82	81	333
Stewart Gardner (Garden City)	86	82	81	85	334
Laurence Auchterlonie					
(Glen View)	81	85	86	83	335
Bernard Nicholls (Boston)	84	85	83	83	335
David Brown (Crescent Athletic)	86	83	83	84	336
Alex Campbell (Brookline)	86	83	83	84	336
John Park (Essex)		171		170	341
George Low (Dyker Meadow)		171		170	341

1902

The Garden City Golf Club, Garden City, New York, October 10–11

90 entries — $970 prize money

Laurence Auchterlonie (Chicago)	78	78	74	77	307
Stewart Gardner (Garden City)	82	76	77	78	313
*Walter J. Travis (Garden City)	82	82	75	74	313
Willie Smith (Chicago)	82	79	80	75	316
John Shippen (New York)	83	81	75	79	318
Willie Anderson (Montclair)	79	82	76	81	318
Charles Thom (New York)	80	82	80	77	319
Harry Turpie (Chicago)	79	85	78	78	320
Donald Ross (Oakley, Mass.)	80	83	78	81	322
Alex Ross (Pinehurst)	83	77	84	79	323

1903

Baltusrol Golf Club, Springfield, New Jersey, June 26–27

89 entries — $970 prize money

Willie Anderson (Apawamis)	149	76	82	307 82
David Brown (Wollaston)	156	75	76	307 84
Stewart Gardner (Garden City)	154	82	79	315
Alex Smith (Nassau)	154	81	81	316
Donald Ross (Oakley)	158	78	82	318
Jack Campbell (Brookline)	159	83	77	319
Laurence Auchterlonie (Glen View)	154	84	83	321
*Findlay Douglas (Nassau)	156	82	84	322
John Hobens (Yountakah)	157	82	84	323
Willie Smith (Midlothian)	161	83	79	323
Alex Ross (Wilmington, Del.)	165	78	80	323

1904

Glen View Club, Golf, Illinois, July 8–9

71 entries — $970 prize money

Willie Anderson (Apawamis)	75	78	78	72	303
Gilbert Nicholls (St. Louis)	80	76	79	73	308
Fred Mackenzie (Onwentsia)	76	79	74	80	309

Laurence Auchterlonie					
(Glen View)	80	81	75	78	314
Bernard Nicholls (Elyria, Ohio)	80	77	79	78	314
Robert Simpson (Riverside, Ill.)	82	82	76	76	316
Percy Barrett (Lambton, Ont.)	78	79	79	80	316
Stewart Gardner (Garden City)	75	76	80	85	316
James Foulis (Chicago)	83	74	78	82	317
Donald Ross (Oakley)	80	82	78	78	318

1905

Myopia Hunt Club, Hamilton, Massachusetts, September 21–22
83 entries — $970 prize money

Willie Anderson (Apawamis)	81	80	76	77	314
Alex Smith (Nassau)	76	80	80	80	316
Peter Robinson (Oakmont)	79	80	81	77	317
Percy Barrett (Canada)	81	80	77	79	317
Stewart Gardner (Garden City)	78	78	85	77	318
Alex Campbell					
(The Country Club)	82	76	80	81	319
Gilbert Nicholls (Denver)	82	76	84	79	321
John Hobens (Englewood)	85	82	75	81	323
George Cummings (Canada)	85	82	75	81	323
Arthur Smith (Ohio)	81	77	80	86	324

1906

Onwentsia Club, Lake Forest, Illinois, June 28–29
68 entries — $900 prize money

Alex Smith (Nassau)	73	74	73	75	295
William Smith (Mexico)	73	81	74	74	302
Laurence Auchterlonie					
(Glen View)	76	78	75	76	305
James Maiden (Toledo)	80	73	77	75	305
Willie Anderson (Onwentsia)	73	76	74	84	307
Alex Ross (Brae-Burn)	76	79	75	80	310
Stewart Gardner (Garden City)	80	76	77	78	311
*H. Chandler Egan (Exmoor)	79	78	76	80	313
Gilbert Nicholls (Denever)	76	81	77	79	313
John Hobens (Englewood)	75	84	76	79	314

1907

Philadelphia Cricket Club, Philadelphia, Pa., June 20–21
   82 entries — $900 prize money

Alex Ross (Brae-Burn)	76	74	76	76	302
Gilbert Nicholls (Woodland)	80	73	72	79	304
Alex Campbell					
(The Country Club)	78	74	78	75	305
John Hobens (Englewood)	76	75	73	85	309
Peter Robinson (Oakmont)	81	77	78	74	310
George Low (Baltusrol)	78	76	79	77	310
Fred McLeod (Midlothian)	79	77	79	75	310
David Brown (Boston)	75	80	78	78	311
Bernard Nicholls (Nashville)	76	76	81	78	311
Donald Ross (Oakley)	78	80	76	78	312

1908

Myopia Hunt Club, Hamilton, Massachusetts, August 27–28
   88 entries — $900 prize money

Fred McLeod (Midlothian)	82	82	81	77	322
					77
Willie Smith (Mexico)	77	82	85	78	322
					83
Alex Smith (Nassau)	80	83	83	81	327
Willie Anderson (Onwentsia)	85	86	80	79	330
John Jones (Myopia)	81	81	87	82	331
Jack Hobens (Englewood)	86	81	85	81	333
Peter Robinson (Oakmont)	89	84	77	83	333
Percy Barrett (Lambton)	94	80	86	78	338
Jack Hutchinson (St. Andrews)	82	84	87	85	338
Richard Kimball (New Bedford)	84	86	83	86	339
Tom McNamara (Wollaston)		167		172	339

1909

Englewood Golf Club, Englewood, New Jersey, June 24–25
   84 entries — $900 prize money

George Sargent (Hyde Manor)	75	72	72	71	290
Tom McNamara (Wollaston)	73	69	75	77	294
Alex Smith (Wykagyl)	76	73	74	72	295
Isaac Mackie (Fox Hills)	77	75	74	73	299

Willie Anderson (St. Louis)	79	74	76	70	299
Jack Hobens (Englewood)	75	78	72	74	299
*Walter J. Travis (Garden City)	72	78	77	73	300
Andrew Campbell (Spring Haven)	71	75	77	77	300
Tom Anderson, Jr. (Montclair)	78	74	75	73	300
Bob Peebles (St. Joseph Valley)	76	73	73	78	300
H. H. Barker (Garden City)	75	79	73	73	300

1910

Philadelphia Cricket Club, St. Martins, Pa., June 17–18
75 entries — $900 prize money

Alex Smith (Wykagyl)	73	73	79	73	298
					71
John McDermott (Merchantville)	74	74	75	75	298
					75
Macdonald Smith (Claremont)	74	78	75	71	298
					77
Fred McLeod (St. Louis)	78	70	78	73	299
Tom McNamara (Boston)	73	78	73	76	300
Gilbert Nicholls (Wilmington)	73	75	77	75	300
John Hobens (Englewood)	74	77	74	76	301
Tom Anderson, Jr. (Inwood)	72	76	81	73	302
Jack Hutchinson (Pittsburgh)	77	76	75	74	302
H. H. Barker (Garden City)	75	78	77	72	302

1911

Chicago Golf Club, Wheaton, Illinois, June 23–24
79 entries — $900 prize money

John McDermott (Atlantic City)	81	72	75	79	307
					80
M. J. Brady (Wollaston)	76	77	79	75	307
					82
George Simpson (Wheaton)	76	77	79	75	307
					85
Fred McLeod (St. Louis)	77	72	76	83	308
Gilbert Nicholls (Wilmington)	76	78	74	81	309
Jack Hutchinson (Allegheny)	80	77	73	79	309

George Sargent (Chevy Chase)	76	77	84	74	311
H. H. Barker (Rumson)	75	81	77	78	311
Peter Robinson (Oakmont)	79	76	78	79	312
Alex Ross (Brae-Burn)	74	75	81	82	312

1912
Country Club of Buffalo, Buffalo, New York, August 1–2
131 entries — $900 prize money

John McDermott (Atlantic City)	74	75	74	71	294
Tom McNamara (Boston)	74	80	73	69	296
Alex Smith (Wykagyl)	77	70	77	75	299
Mike Brady (Wollaston)	72	75	73	79	299
Alex Campbell (Brookline)	74	77	80	71	302
George Sargent (Chevy Chase)	72	78	76	77	303
John Dowling (Scarsdale)	76	79	76	74	305
Otto Hackbarth (Hinsdale)	77	77	75	76	305
C. R. Murray (Royal Montreal)	75	78	77	76	306
*Walter J. Travis (Garden City)	73	79	78	77	307
Frank Peebles (Stockbridge)	73	76	83	75	307
Tom Anderson, Jr. (Oakmont)	75	76	81	75	307

1913
The Country Club, Brookline, Massachusetts, September 16–19
165 entries — $900 prize money

*Francis Ouimet (Woodland)	77	74	74	79	304
					72
Harry Vardon (England)	75	72	78	79	304
					77
Edward Ray (England)	79	70	76	79	304
					78
Walter Hagen (Rochester)	73	78	76	80	307
Jim Barnes (Tacoma)	74	76	78	79	307
Macdonald Smith (Wykagyl)	71	79	80	77	307
Louis Tellier (France)	76	76	79	76	307
John McDermott (Atlantic City)	74	79	77	78	308
Herbert Strong (Inwood)	75	74	82	79	310
Patrick Doyle (Myopia)	78	80	73	80	311

1914

Midlothian Country Club, Blue Island, Illinois, August 18–21
  130 entries — $900 prize money

Walter Hagen (Rochester)	68	74	75	73	290
*Charles Evans, Jr. (Edgewater)	76	74	71	70	291
George Sargent (Chevy Chase)	74	77	74	72	297
Fred McLeod (Columbia)	78	73	75	71	297
*Francis Ouimet (Woodland)	69	76	75	78	298
Mike Brady (Wollaston)	78	72	74	74	298
James Donaldson (Glen View)	72	79	74	73	298
Louis Tellier (Canoe Brook)	72	75	74	78	299
John McDermott (Atlantic City)	77	74	74	75	300
Arthur Smith (Arlington)	79	73	76	72	300

1915

Baltusrol Golf Club, Baltusrol, New Jersey, June 15–18
  141 entries — $900 prize money

J. D. Travers (Upper Montclair)	148	73	76	297
Tom McNamara (Boston)	149	74	75	298
Robert MacDonald (Buffalo)	149	73	78	300
Jim Barnes (Whitemarsh Valley)	146	76	79	301
Louis Tellier (Canoe Brook)	146	76	79	301
Mike Brady (Wollaston)	147	75	80	302
George Low (Baltusrol)	152	76	75	303
Fred McLeod (Columbia)	150	76	79	305
Jack Hutchinson (Pittsburgh)	153	76	76	305
George Sargent (Chevy Chase)	152	79	75	306
Jack Park (Maidstone)	154	75	77	306
Emmett French (York)	156	75	75	306
Gilbert Nicholls (Wilmington)	159	73	74	306
Tom Kerrigan (Dedham)	153	76	77	306
Alex Campbell (Baltimore)	151	74	81	306
Wilfred Reid (Seaview)	155	75	76	306
Walter Hagen (Rochester)	151	76	79	306

1916

Minikada, Minneapolis, Minnesota, June 27–30
  94 entries — $1200 prize money

*Charles Evans, Jr. (Edgewater)	70	69	74	73	286

Jack Hutchinson (Allegheny)	73	75	72	68	288
Jim Barnes (Whitemarsh Valley)	71	74	71	74	290
Wilfred Reid (Wilmington)	70	72	79	72	293
Gilbert Nicholls (Great Neck)	73	76	71	73	293
George Sargent (Interlarken)	75	71	72	75	293
Walter Hagen (Rochester)	73	76	75	71	295
R. G. MacDonald (Buffalo)	74	72	77	73	296
Mike Brady (Oakridge)	75	73	75	74	297
Tom Vardon (White Bear Yacht)	76	72	75	74	297
J. J. O'Brien (Mansfield)	76	72	73	76	297

1919

Brae-Burn Country Club, West Newton, Massachusetts, June 9–11

142 entries — $1745 prize money

Walter Hagen (Oakland Hills)	78	73	75	75	301
					77
Mike Brady (Oakley)	74	74	73	80	301
					78
Jock Hutchinson (Glen View)	78	76	76	76	306
Tom McNamara (New York)	80	73	79	74	306
George McLean (Great Neck)	81	75	76	76	308
Louis Tellier (Brae Burn)	73	78	82	75	308
John Cowan (Stockbridge)	79	74	75	81	309
Fred McLeod (Columbia)	78	77	79	78	312
*Charles Evans, Jr. (Edgewater)	77	76	82	78	313
George Bowden (Commonwealth)	73	78	76	86	313

1920

Inverness Country Club, Toledo, Ohio, August 10–13

265 entries — $1745 prize money

Edward Ray (England)	74	73	73	75	295
Harry Vardon (England)	74	73	71	78	296
Jack Burke (Town and Country)	75	77	72	72	296
Leo Diegel (Lake Shore)	72	74	73	77	296
Jock Hutchinson (Glen View)	69	76	74	77	296
*Charles Evans, Jr. (Edgewater)	74	76	73	75	298
Jim Barnes (Sunset Hills)	76	70	76	76	298

*Robert T. Jones, Jr. (Atlanta)	78	74	70	77	299
Willie MacFarlane (Pt. Washington)	76	75	74	74	299
Bob MacDonald (Bob O'Link)	73	78 .	71	78	300

1921
Columbia Country Club, Chevy Chase, Maryland, July 19–22
262 entries — $1745 prize money

James Barnes (Pelham)	69	75	73	72	289
Walter Hagen (New York)	79	73	72	74	298
Fred McLeod (Columbia)	74	76	74	74	298
*Charles Evans, Jr. (Edgewater)	73	78	76	75	302
*Robert T. Jones, Jr. (Atlanta)	78	71	77	77	303
Emmett French (Youngstown)	75	77	74	77	303
Alex Smith (Shennecossett)	75	75	79	74	303
George Duncan (England)	72	78	78	77	305
Clarence Hackney (Atlantic City)	74	76	78	77	305
Emil Loeffler (Oakmont)	74	77	74	81	306

1922
Skokie Country Club, Glencoe, Illinois, July 10–15
323 entries — $1745 prize money

Gene Sarazen (Highland)	72	73	75	68	288
John Black (Oakland, Calif.)	71	71	75	72	289
*Robert T. Jones, Jr. (Atlanta)	74	72	70	73	289
William Mehlhorn (Shreveport)	73	71	72	74	290
Walter Hagen (New York)	68	77	74	72	291
George Duncan (England)	76	73	75	72	296
Leo Diegel (New Orleans)	77	76	73	71	297
Mike Brady (Detroit)	73	75	74	76	298
John Golden (Tuxedo)	73	77	77	71	298
Jock Hutchinson (Glen View)	78	74	71	75	298

1923
Inwood Country Club, Inwood, New York, July 9–15
360 entries — $1745 prize money

*Robert T. Jones, Jr. (Atlanta)	71	73	76	76	296
					76

Robert Cruickshank (Shackamaxon)	73	72	78	73	296 78
Jock Hutchinson (Glen View)	70	72	82	78	302
Jack Forrester (Hollywood, N.J.)	75	73	77	78	303
John Farrell (Quaker Ridge)	76	77	75	76	304
Francis Gallett (Port Washington)	76	72	77	79	304
*W. M. Reekie (Upper Montclair)	80	74	75	75	304
William Mehlhorn (St. Louis)	73	79	75	79	306
Leo Diegel (Friendship)	77	77	76	76	306
Al Watrous (Detroit)	74	75	76	81	306

1924
Oakland Hills Country Club, Birmingham, Michigan, June 5–6
319 entries — $1745 prize money

Cyril Walker (Englewood)	74	74	74	75	297
*Robert T. Jones, Jr. (Atlanta)	74	73	75	78	300
William Mehlhorn (Normandy, Mo.)	72	75	76	78	301
Robert Cruickshank (Shackamaxon)	77	72	76	78	303
Walter Hagen (New York)	75	75	76	76	303
Macdonald Smith (San Francisco)	78	72	77	76	303
Abe Espinosa (San Franciso)	80	71	77	77	305
Peter O'Hara (White Beeches)	76	79	74	76	305
Mike Brady (Winged Foot)	75	77	77	77	306
*Charles Evans, Jr. (Edgewater)	77	77	76	77	307
Eddie Loos (Chicago)	73	81	75	78	307
Dave Robertson (Redford, Mich.)	73	76	77	81	307

1925
Worcester Country Club, Worcester, Massachusetts, June 3–5
445 entries — $1745 prize money

Willie MacFarlane (Oak Ridge)	74	67	72	78 75	291 72
*Robert T. Jones, Jr. (Atlanta)	77	70	70	74 75	291 73
Johnny Farrell (Quaker Ridge)	71	74	69	78	292
*Francis Ouimet (Woodland)	70	73	73	76	292

Gene Sarazen (Fresh Meadow)	72	72	75	74	293
Walter Hagen (Pasadena, Fla.)	72	76	71	74	293
Mike Brady (Winged Foot)	74	72	74	74	294
Leo Diegel (Glen Oaks)	73	68	77	78	296
Laurie Ayton (Evanston)	75	71	73	78	297
Al Espinosa (Glen Coe)	72	71	74	80	297

1926
Scioto Country Club, Columbus, Ohio, July 8–10
694 entries — $2145 prize money

*Robert T. Jones, Jr. (Atlanta)	70	79	71	73	293
Joe Turnesa (Fairview)	71	74	72	77	294
William Mehlhorn (Chicago)	68	75	76	78	297
Gene Sarazen (Fresh Meadow)	78	77	72	70	297
Leo Diegel					
(Mountain View Farm)	72	76	75	74	297
Johnny Farrell (Quaker Ridge)	76	79	69	73	297
Walter Hagen (Pasadena, Fla.)	73	77	74	74	298
Willie Hunter (Los Angeles)	75	77	69	79	300
Willie Klein (Wheatley Hills)	76	74	75	76	301
Macdonald Smith (Lakeville)	82	76	68	75	301
Dan Williams (Shackamaxon)	72	74	80	75	301
Tommy Armour (Congressional)	76	76	74	75	301

1927
Oakmont Country Club, Oakmont, Pennsylvania, June 14–16
898 entries — $2145 prize money

Tommy Armour (Congressional)	78	71	76	76	301
					76
Harry Cooper (El Serreno)	74	76	74	77	301
					79
Gene Sarazen (Fresh Meadow)	74	74	80	74	302
Emmett French (Southern Pines)	75	79	77	73	304
William Mehlhorn (New York)	75	77	80	73	305
Walter Hagen (Pasadena, Fla.)	77	73	76	81	307
Archie Compston (England)	79	74	76	79	308
Johnny Farrell (Quaker Ridge)	81	73	78	76	308
John Golden (Paterson)	83	77	75	73	308
Harry Hampton (Atlantic City)	73	78	80	77	308

1928

Olympia Fields Country Club, Mateson, Illinois, June 21–24
   1,064 entries — $2145 prize money

Johnny Farrell (Quaker Ridge)	77	74	71	72	294
			70	73	143
*Robert T. Jones, Jr. (Atlanta)	73	71	73	77	294
			73	71	144
Roland Hancock					
(Wilmington, N.C.)	74	77	72	72	295
Walter Hagen (New York)	75	72	73	76	296
*George Von Elm					
(Tam O'Shanter)	74	72	76	74	296
Joe Turnesa (Elmsford)	74	77	74	74	299
Gene Sarazen (Fresh Meadow)	78	76	73	72	299
Henry Ciuci (Mill River, Ct.)	70	77	72	80	299
Waldo Crowder (Cleveland)	74	74	76	75	299
Bill Leach (Overbrook)	72	74	73	80	299
Macdonald Smith (Lakeville)	75	77	75	72	299
H. Densmore Shute					
(Worthington, O.)	75	73	79	72	299
Ed Dudley (Unattached)	77	79	68	75	299

1929

Winged Foot Golf Club, Mamaroneck, New York, June 27–30
   1,000 entries — $5,000 prize money

*Robert T. Jones, Jr. (Atlanta)	69	75	71	79	294
			72	69	141
Al Espinosa (Glencoe)	70	72	77	75	294
			84	80	164
Gene Sarazen (Fresh Meadow)	71	71	76	78	296
Denny Shute (Worthington)	73	71	76	76	296
Tommy Armour (Tam O'Shanter)	74	71	76	76	297
*George Von Elm					
(Tam O'Shanter)	79	70	74	74	297
Henry Ciuci (Mill River)	78	74	72	75	299
Leo Diegel (Mexico)	74	74	76	77	301
Pat O'Hara (Verona, Pa.)	74	76	73	78	301
Horton Smith (Joplin)	76	77	74	75	302

1930

Interlachen Country Club, Minneapolis, Minnesota, July 10–12
1,177 entries — $5,000 prize money

*Robert T. Jones, Jr. (Atlanta)	71	73	68	75	287
Macdonald Smith (Lakeville)	70	75	74	70	289
Horton Smith (Cragston)	72	70	76	74	292
Harry Cooper (Glen Elyn)	72	72	73	76	293
John Golden (Wee Burn)	74	73	71	76	294
Tommy Armour (Tam O'Shanter)	70	76	75	76	297
Charles Lacey (Pine Valley)	74	70	77	77	298
Johnny Farrell (Quaker Ridge)	74	72	73	80	299
Bill Mehlhorn (Pensacola)	76	74	75	75	300
Craig Wood (Forest Hill)	73	75	72	80	300

1931

Inverness Club, Toledo, Ohio, July 2–6
1,141 entries — $5,000 prize money

Billy Burke (Round Hill)	73	72	74	73	292
	73	76	77	71	297
George Von Elm (Unattached)	75	69	73	75	292
	75	74	76	73	298
Leo Diegel (Mexico)	75	73	74	72	294
Wiffy Cox (Brooklyn)	76	74	74	72	296
Bill Mehlhorn (Pinewald, N.J.)	77	73	75	71	296
Gene Sarazen (Lakeville)	74	78	74	70	296
Mortie Dutra					
(Long Beach, Calif.)	71	77	73	76	297
Walter Hagen (Unattached)	74	74	73	76	297
*T. Philip Perkins					
(Fox Hills, N.Y.)	78	73	76	70	297
Al Espinosa (Northbrook, Ill.)	72	78	75	74	299
Johnny Farrell (Quaker Ridge)	78	70	79	72	299
Macdonald Smith (Unattached)	73	73	75	78	299

1932

Fresh Meadow Country Club, Flushing, New York, June 23–25
1,011 entries — $5,000 prize money

Gene Sarazen (Lakeville)	74	76	70	66	286

Bobby Cruickshank

(Willowbrook, N.Y.)	78	74	69	68	289
T. Philip Perkins (Unattached)	76	69	74	70	289
Leo Diegel (Mexico)	73	74	73	74	294
Wiffy Cox (Brooklyn)	80	73	70	72	295
Jose Jurado (Argentina)	74	71	75	76	296
Billy Burke (Round Hill)	75	77	74	71	297
Harry Cooper (Glen Oak)	77	73	73	74	297
Olin Dutra (Brentwood, Calif.)	69	77	75	76	297
Walter Hagen (Unattached)	75	73	79	71	298

1933

North Shore Golf Club, Glen View, Illinois, June 8–10
915 entries — $5,000 prize money

*Johnny Goodman (Omaha)	75	66	70	76	287
Ralph Guldahl (St. Louis)	76	71	70	71	288
Craig Wood (Hollywood)	73	74	71	72	290
Walter Hagen (Unattached)	73	76	77	66	292
Tommy Armour (Medinah)	68	75	76	73	292
Mortie Dutra (Red Run)	75	73	72	74	294
Olin Dutra (Brentwood)	75	71	75	74	295
*Gus Moreland (Dallas)	76	76	71	72	295
Clarence Clark (Forest Hill)	80	72	72	72	296
Joe Kirkwood (Unattached)	74	70	79	73	296
Willie Goggin (San Mateo)	79	73	73	71	296
Johnny Farrell (Quaker Ridge)	75	77	72	72	296

1934

Merion Cricket Club, Ardmore, Pennsylvania, June 7–9
1,063 entries — $5,000 prize money

Olin Dutra (Brentwood)	76	74	71	72	293
Gene Sarazen (New York City)	73	72	73	76	294
Wiffy Cox (Dyker Beach)	71	75	74	75	295
Bobby Cruickshank (Virginia)	71	71	77	76	295
Harry Cooper (Glen Oak)	76	74	74	71	295
Billy Burke (Cleveland)	76	71	77	72	296
Macdonald Smith (Nashville)	75	73	78	70	296
Ralph Guldahl (Los Angeles)	78	73	70	78	299
Johnny Revolta (Tripoli)	76	73	77	73	299

| Jimmy Hines (Timber Point) | 80 | 70 | 77 | 72 | 299 |
| Tom Creavy (Albany) | 79 | 76 | 78 | 66 | 299 |

1935

Oakmont Country Club, Oakmont, Pennsylvania, June 6–8
1,125 entries — $5,000 prize money

Sam Parks, Jr. (South Hills)	77	73	73	76	299
Jimmy Thomson (Lakewood)	73	73	77	78	301
Walter Hagen (Detroit)	77	76	73	76	302
Denny Shute (Chicago)	78	73	76	76	303
Ray Mangrum (Los Angeles)	76	76	72	79	303
Henry Picard (Hershey)	79	78	70	79	306
Gene Sarazen (Brookfield)	75	74	78	79	306
Alvin Krueger (Beloit)	71	77	78	80	306
Horton Smith (Oak Park)	73	79	79	75	306
Dick Metz (Mill Road Farm)	77	76	76	78	307
Paul Runyan (Metropolis)	76	77	79	75	307

1936

Baltusrol Golf Club, Springfield, New Jersey, June 4–6
1,277 entries — $5,000 prize money

Tony Manero (Sedgefield)	73	69	73	67	282
Harry Cooper (Glen Oak)	71	70	70	73	284
Clarence Clark (Forest Hill)	69	75	71	72	287
Macdonald Smith (Glendale)	73	73	72	70	288
Henry Picard (Hershey)	70	71	74	74	289
Wiffy Cox (Kenwood)	74	74	69	72	289
Ky Laffoon (Northmoor)	71	74	70	74	289
Ralph Guldahl (Beverly Hills)	73	70	73	74	290
Paul Runyan (Metropolis)	69	75	73	73	290
Denny Shute (Brae Burn)	72	69	73	77	291

1937

Oakland Hills Country Club, Birmingham, Michigan, June 10–12
1,402 entries — $5,000 prize money

Ralph Guldahl (Chicago)	71	69	72	69	281
Sam Snead (Greenbrier)	69	73	70	71	283
Bobby Cruickshank (Virginia)	73	73	67	72	285

Harry Cooper (Chicago)	72	70	73	71	286
Ed Dudley (Philadelphia)	70	70	71	76	287
Albert Brosch (Bethpage)	74	73	68	73	288
Clarence Clark (Forest Hill)	72	75	73	69	289
*Johnny Goodman (Omaha)	70	73	72	75	290
*Frank Strafaci (Shore View)	70	72	77	72	291
*Charles Kocsis					
(University of Mich.)	72	73	76	71	292
Henry Picard (Hershey)	71	75	72	74	292
Gene Sarazen (Brookfield)	78	69	71	74	292
Denny Shute (Brae Burn)	68	76	75	72	292

1938

Cherry Hills Club, Denver, Colorado, June 9–11
    1,223 entries — $6,000 prize money

Ralph Guldahl (Braidburn)	74	70	71	69	284
Dick Metz (Mill Road Farm)	73	68	70	79	290
Harry Cooper (Chicopee)	76	69	76	71	292
Toney Penna (Dayton)	78	72	74	68	292
Byron Nelson (Reading)	77	71	74	72	294
Emery Zimmerman					
(Columbia-Edgewater)	72	71	73	78	294
Frank Moore (Quaker Ridge)	79	73	72	71	295
Henry Picard (Hershey)	70	70	77	78	295
Paul Runyan (Metropolis)	78	71	72	74	295
Gene Sarazen (Brookfield)	74	74	75	73	296

1939

Philadelphia Country Club, West Conshohocken, Pa., June 8–12
    1,193 entries — $6,000 prize money

Byron Nelson (Reading)	72	73	71	68	284
				68	70
Craig Wood (Winged Foot)	70	71	71	72	284
				68	73
Denny Shute (Huntington)	70	72	70	72	284
				76	
*Marvin Ward (Spokane)	69	73	71	72	285
Sam Snead (Greenbrier)	68	71	73	74	286
Johnny Bulla (Chicago)	72	71	68	76	287

Ralph Guldahl (Braidburn)	71	73	72	72	288
Dick Metz (Mill Road Farm)	76	72	71	69	288
Ky Laffoon (Northmoor)	76	70	73	70	289
Harold McSpaden (Winchester)	70	73	71	75	289
Paul Runyan (Metropolis)	76	70	71	72	289

1940
Canterbury Golf Club, Warrensville, Ohio, June 6–9
   1,161 entries — $6,000 prize money

Lawson Little (Bretton Woods)	72	69	73	73	287
					70
Gene Sarazen (Brookfield)	71	74	70	72	287
					73
Horton Smith (Oak Park)	69	72	78	69	288
Craig Wood (Winged Foot)	72	73	72	72	289
Ben Hogan (Century)	70	73	74	73	290
Ralph Guldahl (Chicago)	73	71	76	70	290
Lloyd Mangrum (Oak Park)	75	70	71	74	290
Byron Nelson (Inverness)	72	74	70	74	290
Dick Metz (Oak Park)	75	72	72	72	291
Ed Dudley (Philadelphia)	73	75	71	73	292
Frank Walsh (Rumson)	73	69	71	79	292

1941
Colonial Club, Fort Worth, Texas, June 5–7
   1,048 entries — $6,000 prize money

Craig Wood (Winged Foot)	73	71	70	70	284
Denny Shute (Chicago)	69	75	72	71	287
Johnny Bulla (Chicago)	75	71	72	71	289
Ben Hogan (Hershey)	74	77	68	70	289
Herman Barron (Fenway)	75	71	74	71	291
Paul Runyan (Metropolis)	73	72	71	75	291
E. J. Harrison (Chicago)	70	82	71	71	294
Harold McSpaden (Winchester)	71	75	74	74	294
Gene Sarazen (Lakeview)	74	73	72	75	294
Ed Dudley (Broadmoor)	74	74	74	73	295
Lloyd Mangrum (Monterey Park)	73	74	72	76	295
Dick Metz (Oak Park)	71	74	76	74	295

1946

Canterbury Golf Club, Cleveland, Ohio, June 13–16
 1,175 entries — $8,000 prize money

Lloyd Mangrum (Los Angeles)	74	70	68	72	284
				72	72
Byron Nelson (Toledo)	71	71	69	73	284
				72	73
Victor Ghezzi (Knoxville)	71	69	72	72	284
				72	73
Herman Barron (Fenway)	72	72	72	69	285
Ben Hogan (Hershey)	72	68	73	72	285
Jimmy Demaret (Houston)	71	74	73	68	286
Edward Oliver (Wilmington)	71	71	74	70	286
Dick Metz (Arkansas City)	76	70	72	69	287
Melvin Harbert (Meadowbrook)	72	78	67	70	287
Lawson Little (Monterey)	72	69	76	71	288
E. J. Harrison (Chicago)	75	71	72	70	288

1947

St. Louis Country Club, Clayton, Missouri, June 12–15
 1,356 entries — $10,000 prize money

Lew Worsham (Oakmont)	70	70	71	71	282
					69
Sam Snead (Cascades)	72	70	70	70	282
					70
Bobby Locke (South Africa)	68	74	70	73	285
Edward Oliver (Wilmington)	73	70	71	71	285
*Marvin Ward (Spokane)	69	72	73	73	287
Jim Ferrier (Chicago)	71	70	74	74	289
Victor Ghezzi (Victory Hills)	74	73	73	69	289
Leland Gibson (Blue Hills)	69	76	73	71	289
Ben Hogan (Hershey)	70	75	70	74	289
Johnny Palmer (Badin)	72	70	75	72	289
Paul Runyan (Annandale)	71	74	72	72	289

1948

Riviera Country Club, Los Angeles, California, June 10–12
 1,411 entries — $10,000 prize money

Ben Hogan (Hershey)	67	72	68	69	276

Jimmy Demaret (Houston)	71	70	68	69	278
Jim Turnesa (Elmsford)	71	69	70	70	280
Bobby Locke (South Africa)	70	69	73	70	282
Sam Snead (Greenbrier)	69	69	73	72	283
Lew Worsham (Oakmont)	67	74	71	73	285
Herman Barron (Fenway)	73	70	71	72	286
Johnny Bulla (Phoenix)	73	72	75	67	287
Toney Penna (Cincinnati)	70	72	73	72	287
Smiley Quick (Fox Hills)	73	71	69	74	287

1949
Medinah Country Club, Medinah, Illinois, June 9–11
1,348 entries — $10,000 prize money

Cary Middlecoff (Colonial)	75	67	69	75	286
Clayton Haefner (Eastwood)	72	71	71	73	287
Sam Snead (Greenbrier)	73	73	71	70	287
Jim Turnesa (Briar Hall)	78	69	70	72	289
Bobby Locke (South Africa)	74	71	73	71	289
Buck White (Unattached)	74	68	70	78	290
Dave Douglas (Newark, Del.)	74	73	70	73	290
Johnny Palmer (Unattached)	71	75	72	73	291
Claude Harmon (Winged Foot)	71	72	74	74	291
Pete Cooper (Ponte Vedra)	71	73	74	73	291

1950
Merion Golf Club, Ardmore, Pennsylvania, June 8–11
1,379 entries — $14,900 prize money

Ben Hogan (Hershey)	72	69	72	74	287
					69
Lloyd Mangrum (Tam O'Shanter)	72	70	69	76	287
					73
George Fazio (Woodmont)	73	72	72	70	287
					75
E. J. Harrison (St. Andrews)	72	67	73	76	288
Joe Kirkwood (Kirkwood)	71	74	74	70	289
Jim Ferrier (Chicago)	71	69	74	75	289
Henry Ransom (St. Andrews)	72	71	73	73	289
S. William Nary (Los Serranos)	73	70	74	73	290
Julius Boros (Mid Pines)	68	72	77	74	291

| Cary Middlecoff (Memphis) | 71 | 71 | 71 | 79 | 292 |
| John Palmer (Unattached) | 73 | 70 | 70 | 79 | 292 |

1951
Oakland Hills Country Club, Birmingham, Michigan, June 14–16
1,511 entries — $14,800 prize money

Ben Hogan (Hershey)	76	73	71	67	287
Clayton Haefner (Eastwood)	72	75	73	69	289
Bobby Locke (South Africa)	73	71	74	73	291
Lloyd Mangrum (Tam O'Shanter)	75	74	74	70	293
Julius Boros (Mid Pines)	74	74	71	74	293
Albert Besselink (Hillcrest)	72	77	72	73	294
Paul Runyan (Annandale)	73	74	72	75	294
Fred Hawkins (El Paso)	76	72	75	71	294
Dave Douglas (Newark, Del.)	75	70	75	74	294
Skee Riegel (Tulsa)	75	76	71	73	295
Al Brosch (Cherry Valley)	73	74	76	72	295
Smiley Quick (Los Angeles)	73	76	74	72	295
Sam Snead (Greenbrier)	71	78	72	74	295

1952
Northwood Club, Dallas, Texas, June 12–14
1,688 entries — $14,900 prize money

Julius Boros (Mid Pines)	71	71	68	71	281
Edward Oliver (Cog Hill)	71	72	70	72	285
Ben Hogan (Tamarisk)	69	69	74	74	286
Johnny Bulla (Westmoreland)	73	68	73	73	287
George Fazio (Pine Valley)	71	69	75	75	290
Dick Metz (Maple City)	70	74	76	71	291
Tommy Bolt (Par-Way)	72	76	71	73	292
Ted Kroll (New Hartford)	71	75	76	70	292
Lew Worsham (Oakmont)	72	71	74	75	292
Lloyd Mangrum (Tam O'Shanter)	75	74	72	72	293
Sam Snead (Greenbrier)	70	75	76	72	293
Earl Stewart (Dallas)	76	75	70	72	293

1953
Oakmont Country Club, Oakmont, Pennsylvania, June 11–13
1,669 entries — $20,400 prize money

| Ben Hogan (Tamarisk) | 67 | 72 | 73 | 71 | 283 |

Sam Snead (Greenbrier)	72	69	72	76	289
Lloyd Mangrum (Tam O'Shanter)	73	70	74	75	292
Pete Cooper (Century)	78	75	71	70	294
George Fazio (Pine Valley)	70	71	77	76	294
Jimmy Demaret (Concord)	71	76	71	76	294
Ted Kroll (New Hartford)	76	71	74	74	295
Dick Metz (Maple City)	75	70	74	76	295
Jay Hebert (Kahkwa)	72	72	74	78	296
Marty Furgol (Cog Hill)	73	74	76	73	296
*Frank Souchak (Oakmont)	70	76	76	74	296

1954
Baltusrol Golf Club, Springfield, New Jersey, June 17–19
1,928 entries — $23,280 prize money

Ed Furgol (Westwood)	71	70	71	72	284
Gene Littler (Thunderbird)	70	69	76	70	285
Dick Mayer (St. Petersburg)	72	71	70	73	286
Lloyd Mangrum (Tam O'Shanter)	72	71	72	71	286
Bobby Locke (South Africa)	74	70	74	70	288
Tommy Bolt (Memorial Park)	72	72	73	72	289
Ben Hogan (Fort Worth)	71	70	76	72	289
Shelley Mayfield (Seguin, Texas)	73	75	72	69	289
Freddie Haas (New Orleans)	73	73	71	72	289
*Billie Joe Patton (Mimosa)	69	76	71	73	289

1955
Olympic Country Club, San Francisco, California, June 16–19
1,522 entries — $25,480 prize money

Jack Fleck (Davenport Municipal)	76	69	75	67	287
					69
Ben Hogan (Fort Worth)	72	73	72	70	287
					72
Sam Snead (Greenbrier)	79	69	70	74	292
Tommy Bolt (Chattanooga)	67	77	75	73	292
Julius Boros (Mid Pines)	76	69	73	77	295
Bob Rosburg (Unattached)	78	74	67	76	295
Bud Holscher (Apple Valley)	77	75	71	73	296
Doug Ford (Concord International)	74	77	74	71	296

*E. Harvie Ward, Jr.					
(San Francisco)	74	70	76	76	296
Mike Souchak (Grossinger)	73	79	72	73	297
Jack Burke					
(Concord International)	71	77	72	77	297

1956
Oak Hill Country Club, Rochester, New York, June 14–16
1,921 entries — $25,480 prize money

Cary Middlecoff (Riverlake)	71	70	70	70	281
Julius Boros (Mid Pines)	71	71	71	69	282
Ben Hogan (Fort Worth)	72	68	72	70	282
Ed Furgol (Westwood)	71	70	73	71	285
Peter Thomson (Australia)	70	69	75	71	285
Ted Kroll (Fort Lauderdale)	72	70	70	73	285
Arnold Palmer (Latrobe)	72	70	72	73	287
*Ken Venturi (California)	77	71	68	73	289
Doug Ford (Putnam)	71	75	70	74	290
Wesley Ellis (Greenwood)	71	70	71	78	290
Jerry Barber (Wilshire)	72	69	74	75	290

1957
Inverness Club, Toledo, Ohio, June 13–15
1,907 entries — $28,560 prize money

Dick Mayer (St. Petersburg)	70	68	74	70	282
					72
Cary Middlecoff (Riverlake)	71	75	68	68	282
					79
Jimmy Demaret					
(Concord International)	68	73	70	72	283
Julius Boros (Mid Pines)	69	75	70	70	284
Walter Burkemo (Franklin Hills)	74	73	72	65	284
Ken Venturi (California)	69	71	75	71	286
Fred Hawkins (El Paso)	72	72	71	71	286
Sam Snead (Greenbrier)	74	74	69	73	290
Roberto de Vicenzo (Mexico)	72	70	72	76	290
Chick Harbert (Meadowbrook)	68	79	71	72	290
Billy Maxwell (Odessa)	70	76	72	72	290
*Billy Joe Patton (Mimosa)	70	68	76	76	290

1958

Southern Hills Country Club, Tulsa, Oklahoma, June 12–14
  2,132 entries — $35,000 prize money

Tommy Bolt (Paradise)	71	71	69	72	283
Gary Player (South Africa)	75	68	73	71	287
Julius Boros (Mid Pines)	71	75	72	71	289
Gene Littler (Singing Hills)	74	73	67	76	290
Walter Burkemo (Franklin Hills)	75	74	70	72	291
Bob Rosburg (Silverado)	75	74	72	70	291
Jay Hebert (Mayfair Inn)	77	76	71	69	293
Dick Metz (Shady Oaks)	71	78	73	71	293
Don January (Unattached)	79	73	68	73	293
Ben Hogan (Fort Worth)	75	73	75	71	294
Frank Stranahan (Crystal River)	72	72	75	75	294
Tommy Jacobs (Candlewood)	76	75	71	72	294

1959

Winged Foot Golf Club, Mamaroneck, New York, June 11–13
  2,385 entries — $49,200 prize money

Bill Casper (Apple Valley)	71	68	69	74	282
Bob Rosburg (Palo Alto)	75	70	67	71	283
Claude Harmon (Winged Foot)	72	71	70	71	284
Mike Souchak (Grossinger)	71	70	72	71	284
Doug Ford (Paradise)	72	69	72	73	286
Ernie Vossler (Unattached)	72	70	72	72	286
Arnold Palmer (Laurel Valley)	71	69	72	74	286
Ben Hogan (Fort Worth)	69	71	71	76	287
Sam Snead (Greenbrier)	73	72	67	75	287
Dick Knight (Mission Valley)	69	75	73	73	290

1960

Cherry Hills Country Club, Englewood, California, June 16–18
  2,454 entries — $60,720 prize money

Arnold Palmer (Laurel Valley)	72	71	72	65	280
*Jack Nicklaus (Scioto)	71	71	69	71	282
E. J. Harrison (Old Warson)	74	70	70	69	283
Julius Boros (Mid Pines)	73	69	68	73	283
Mike Souchak (Grossinger)	68	67	73	75	283

Ted Kroll (DeSoto Lakes)	72	69	75	67	283
Jack Fleck (El Caballero)	70	70	72	71	283
Dow Finsterwald (Tequesta)	71	69	70	73	283
Ben Hogan (Fort Worth)	75	67	69	73	284
Jerry Barber (Wilshire)	69	71	70	74	284
*Don Cherry (Wichita Falls)	70	71	71	72	284

1961
Oakland Hills Country Club, Birmingham, Michigan, June 15–17
  2,449 entries — $68,300 prize money

Gene Littler (Singing Hills)	73	68	72	68	281
Bob Goalby (Paradise)	70	72	69	71	282
Douglas Sanders (Ojai)	72	67	71	72	282
Mike Souchak (Grossinger)	73	70	68	73	284
*Jack Nicklaus (Scioto)	75	69	70	70	284
Dow Finsterwald (Tequesta)	72	71	71	72	286
Eric Monti (Hillcrest)	74	67	72	73	286
Doug Ford (Tuckahoe)	72	69	71	74	286
Jacky Cupit (Pine Crest)	72	72	67	76	287
Gardner Dickinson (Tequesta)	72	69	71	75	287
Gary Player (South Africa)	75	72	69	71	287

1962
Oakmont Country Club, Oakmont, Pennsylvania, June 14–17
  2,475 entries — $73,800 prize money

Jack Nicklaus (Scioto)	72	70	72	69	283
					71
Arnold Palmer (Laurel Valley)	71	68	73	71	283
					74
Bobby Nichols (Midland)	70	72	70	73	285
Phil Rodgers (La Jolla)	74	70	69	72	285
Gay Brewer (Crystal River)	73	72	73	69	287
Tommy Jacobs (Bermuda Dunes)	74	71	73	70	288
Gary Player (South Africa)	71	71	72	74	288
Billy Maxwell (Las Vegas)	71	70	75	74	290
Gene Littler (Singing Hills)	69	74	72	75	290
Doug Ford (Brookville)	74	75	71	70	290

1963

The Country Club, Brookline, Massachusetts, June 20–23
  2,392 entries — $88,550 prize money

Julius Boros (Mid Pines)	71	74	76	72	293
					70
Jacky Cupit (Mountain View)	70	72	76	75	293
					73
Arnold Palmer (Laurel Valley)	73	69	77	74	293
					76
Paul Harney (Sunset Oaks)	78	70	73	73	294
Billy Maxwell (Tropicana)	73	73	75	74	295
Bruce Crampton (Australia)	74	72	75	74	295
Tony Lema (San Leandro)	71	74	74	76	295
Gary Player (South Africa)	74	75	75	72	296
Walter Burkemo (Franklin Hills)	72	71	76	77	296
Daniel Sikes, Jr. (Selva Marina)	77	73	73	74	297

1964

Congressional Country Club, Bethesda, Maryland, June 18–20
  2,341 entries — $95,400 prize money

Ken Venturi (Paradise)	72	70	66	70	278
Tommy Jacobs (Bermuda Dunes)	72	64	70	76	282
Bob Charles (De Soto Lakes)	72	72	71	68	283
Billy Casper (Mountain View)	71	74	69	71	285
Gay Brewer (Dallas)	76	69	73	68	286
Arnold Palmer (Laurel Valley)	68	69	75	74	286
Bill Collins (Grossinger)	70	71	74	72	287
Dow Finsterwald (Broadmoor)	73	72	71	72	288
Bob Rosburg (Meriwether)	73	73	70	73	289
Johnny Pott (Gulf Hills Ranch)	71	73	73	72	289

1965

Bellerive Country Club, St. Louis, Missouri, June 17–21
  2,305 entries — $123,890 prize money

Gary Player (South Africa)	70	70	71	71	282
					71
Kel Nagle (Australia)	68	73	72	69	282
					74
Frank Beard (Louisville)	74	69	70	71	284

Julius Boros (Mid Pines)	72	75	70	70	287
Al Geiberger (Carlton Oaks)	70	76	70	71	287
Bruce Devlin (Australia)	72	73	72	71	288
Raymond Floyd (St. Andrews)	72	72	76	68	288
Tony Lema (San Leandro)	72	74	73	70	289
Gene Littler (Las Vegas)	73	71	73	72	289
Dudley Wysong (Casper)	72	75	70	72	289

Selected Bibliography

MAGAZINES
  Life
  Time
  Sports Illustrated
  The American Golfer
  P.G.A. Professional Golfer
  Golf Magazine
  Golf Digest
  U.S.G.A. Golf Journal

NEWSPAPERS
  New York Times
  New York Herald Tribune
  New York World Telegram
  New York Mirror
  Washington Post
  Washington Star
  Chicago Tribune

BOOKS
  Herbert Warren Wind: *The Story of American Golf*
  H. B. Martin: *Fifty Years of American Golf*
  Robert T. Jones: *Golf Is My Game*
  Walter Hagen: *The Walter Hagen Story*
  United States Golf Association: *Record Book of USGA Championships*

Index

221